Capital

A Critique of Political Economy

Volume III – Part II

The Process of Capitalist Production as a Whole

KARL MARX

EDITED BY FRIEDRICH ENGELS

COSIMOCLASSICS

NEW YORK

Capital: A Critique of Political Economy
Vol. III - Part II, The Process of Capitalist Production as a Whole
Cover Copyright © 2007 by Cosimo, Inc.

Capital: A Critique of Political Economy, Vol. III - Part II, The Process of Capitalist Production as a Whole was originally published in 1867.

For information, address:
P.O. Box 416, Old Chelsea Station
New York, NY 10011

or visit our website at:
www.cosimobooks.com

Ordering Information:
Cosimo publications are available at online bookstores. They may
also be purchased for educational, business or promotional use:
- *Bulk orders:* special discounts are available on bulk orders for reading
groups, organizations, businesses, and others. For details contact
Cosimo Special Sales at the address above or at info@cosimobooks.com.
- *Custom-label orders:* we can prepare selected books with your cover or
logo of choice. For more information, please contact Cosimo at
info@cosimobooks.com.

Cover Design by www.popshopstudio.com

ISBN 978-1-60520-010-1

PART VI.

TRANSFORMATION OF SURPLUS PROFIT INTO GROUND-RENT.

CHAPTER XXXVII.

PRELIMINARIES.

THE analysis of landed property in its various historical forms belongs outside of the limits of this work. We shall occupy ourselves with it in this place only to the extent that a portion of the surplus-value produced by the industrial capital falls into the hands of the land owner. We assume, then, that agriculture is dominated by the capitalist mode of production, just as manufacture is, in other words, that agriculture is carried on by capitalists, who differ primarily from the other capitalists only through the element, in which their capital and the wage-labor set in motion by this capital are invested. So far as we are concerned, the capitalist farmer produces wheat, etc., in the same way that the manufacturer produces yarn or machines. The assumption that the capitalist mode of production has seized agriculture implies that it rules all spheres of production and bourgeois society, so that its prerequisites, such as free competition among capitals, the possibility of transferring them from one sphere of production to another, a uniform level of the average rate of profit, etc., are fully matured. The form of landed property which we consider here is a specifically historical one, a form *altered* through the influence of capital and of the capitalist mode of production, and evolved either out of feudal land ownership, or out of small peasants' agriculture carried

720

on for a living, in which the *possession* of land constitutes one of the prerequisites of production for the direct producer, and in which his *ownership* of land appears as the most advantageous condition for the prosperity of *his* mode of production. Just as capitalist production is conditioned in a general way on the expropriation of the laborers from their requirements of production, so capitalist agriculture demands the expropriation of the rural laborers from the land and their subordination to a capitalist, who carries on agriculture for the sake of profit. For the results of our analysis the objection, that other forms of landed property and of agriculture have existed or still exist, is quite irrelevant. Such an objection cannot apply to any one else but to those economists, who treat of the capitalist mode of production in agriculture, and of the form of landed property corresponding to it, as though it were not a historical but an eternal category.

For our purposes it is necessary to study the modern form of landed property, because it is our business to consider the typical conditions of production and commerce, which arise from the investment of capital in agriculture. Without this our analysis of capital would not be complete. We therefore confine ourselves exclusively to the investment of capital in agriculture strictly so-called, that is, capital invested in the production of the principal plant crop, on which a certain population lives. We may say wheat, because it is the principal article of food among the modern capitalistically developed nations (or mining instead of agriculture, because the laws of both are the same).

It is one of the great merits of Adam Smith to have shown that the ground rent for capital invested in the production of such crops as flax, dye stuffs, independent cattle raising, etc., is determined by the ground rent obtained from capital invested in the production of the principal article of subsistence. In fact no progress has been made in this since his time. What we might add in the way of exception or supplement belongs in a separate study of landed property, not here. Hence we shall not speak of landed property outside

2T

of the land destined for the production of wheat in the manner of exports, but shall merely refer to it occasionally by way of illustration.

For the sake of completeness we shall remark, that we include also water, etc., in the term land, so far as it has an owner and belongs as an accessory to the soil.

Landed property is conditioned on the monopolisation of certain portions of the globe by private persons, for the purpose of making these portions the exclusive spheres of their private will and keeping all others away from it.[118] With this in mind, the problem is to ascertain the economic value, that is, the employment of this monopoly on the basis of capitalist production. With the legal power of these persons to use or misuse certain portions of the globe nothing is settled. The use of this power depends wholly upon economic condi-

[118] Nothing could be more comical than Hegel's development of private property in land. According to him, man as an individual must give reality to his will as the soul of external nature, and to this end he must take possession of nature and make her his private property. If this were the destiny of "the individual," of man as an individual, it would follow that every human being must be a landowner, in order to materialise as an individual. Free private property in land, a very recent product, is not a definite social relation, according to Hegel, but a relation of man as an individual to "nature, an absolute right of man to appropriate all things." (Hegel, *Philosophy of Law,* Berlin, 1840, p. 79.) So much at least, is evident, that the individual cannot maintain himself as a landowner by his mere "will" against the will of another individual, who likewise wants to materialise himself in the same piece of land. It requires a good many other things besides the good will. Furthermore, it is absolutely beyond any one's ken to decide, where "the individual" should draw the line for the realisation of his will, whether the presence of his will should materialise in one whole country, or whether it should require a whole bunch of countries by whose appropriation I might "manifest the supremacy of my will over the thing." Here Hegel breaks down. "The appropriation is of a very individual kind; I do not take possession of more than I touch with my body, but the second point is at the same time that external things have a greater extension than I can grasp. While I thus have possession of a thing, something else is likewise in touch with it. I exercise my appropriation by my hand, but its scope may be extended." (P. 90.) But this other thing is again in touch with still another, and so the boundary disappears, within which I might pour my will as the soul of the soil. "If I own anything, my reason at once passes on to the idea that not only this property, but also the thing it touches is mine. Here positive right must fix its boundaries, for nothing more can be deduced from the conception." (P. 91.) This is an extraordinarily naive confession of the "conception," and it proves that this conception, which makes at the outset the mistake of regarding a very definite legal conception of landed property belonging to bourgeois society as an absolute one, does not understand anything of the actual articulations of this property. This implies at the same time the confession, that the "positive" law may, and must, alter its decisions in proportion as the requirements of social, i.e. economic development, change.

tions, which are independent of their will. The legal conception itself signifies nothing else but that the land owner may do with the soil what the owner of commodities may do with them. And this conception, this legal conception of free property in land, arises in the ancient world only with the dissolution of the organic order of society, and in the modern world only with the development of capitalist production. Into Asia it has been imported by Europeans in but a few places. In that Part of our work, which deals with primitive accumulation (Volume I, chapter XXVI), we have seen that this mode of production presupposes on the one hand the separation of the direct producers from their position as mere attachments to the soil (in their capacity of bondsmen, serfs, slaves, etc.), on the other hand the expropriation of the mass of the people from the land. To this extent the monopoly of landed property is a historical premise, and remains the basis, of the capitalist mode of production, just as it does of all other modes of production, which rests on the exploitation of the masses in one form or another. But that form of landed property, which the capitalist mode of production meets in its first stages, does not suit its requirements. It creates for itself that form of property in land, which is adapted to its requirements, by subordinating agriculture to the dominion of capital. It transforms feudal landed property, tribal property, small peasants' property in mark communes, whatever may be their legal form, into the economic form corresponding to the requirements of capitalism. It is one of the great outcomes of the capitalist mode of production, that it transforms agriculture from a merely empirical and mechanically perpetuated process of the least developed part of society into a consciously scientific application of agronomics, so far as this is at all feasible under the conditions going with private property;[119] that it detaches property in

[119] Very conservative agricultural chemists, for instance Johnston, admit that a really rational agriculture meets everywhere insurmountable barriers through the existence of private property. So do writers, who are confessedly advocates of the monopoly of private property on the globe, for instance Charles Comte in his work of two volumes, which has for its special aim the defense of private property. "A nation," says he, "cannot attain to the degree of prosperity and power compatible with its nature, unless every portion of the soil nourishing it is assigned

land on the one side from the relations between master and servant, and on the other hand totally separates land as an instrument of production from property in land and land owners, for whom it represents merely a certain tribute of money, which he collects by force of his monopoly from the industrial capitalist, the capitalist farmer. It dissolves all these connections so thoroughly, that the owner of the land may spend his whole life in Constantinople, while his estates are in Scotland. Private property in land thus receives its purely economic form by discarding all its former political and social trappings and implications, in brief all those traditional accessories, which are denounced as a useless and absurd attachment by the industrial capitalists and their theoretical spokesmen in the heat of their struggle with landed property, as we shall see later. The rationalising of agriculture on the one hand and thus rendering it capable of operation on a social scale, and the reduction *ad absurdum* of private property in land on the other hand, these are the great merits of the capitalist mode of production. Like all its other historical advances it bought these also by first completely pauperizing the direct producers.

Before we pass on to the problem itself, we must make a few more preliminary remarks in order to forestall misunderstanding.

The premises for a capitalist production in agriculture are these: The actual tillers of the soil are wage-laborers, em-

to that purpose which agrees best with the general interest. In order to give to its wealth a strong development, one sole and highly enlightened will should, if possible, take it upon himself to assign to each piece of his domain its task and make every piece contribute to the prosperity of all others. But the existence of such a will . . . would be incompatible with the division of the land into private plots . . . and with the ability of each owner to dispose of his property in an almost absolute manner, according to constitutional guarantees."—Johnston, Comte, and others, have in mind only the necessity of tilling the land of a certain country as a whole, when they speak of an antagonism of private property to a rational system of agronomics. But the dependence of the cultivation of particular products of the soil upon the fluctuations of market prices, and the continual changes of this cultivation with these fluctuations of prices, the whole spirit of capitalist production, which is directed toward the immediate gain of money, contradicts agriculture, which has to minister to the entire range of permanent necessities of life required by a network of human generations. A striking illustration of this is furnished by the forests, which are occasionally managed in a way befitting the interests of society as a whole, when they are not private property, but subject to the control of the state.

ployed by a capitalist, the capitalist farmer, who carries on agriculture merely as a special field of exploitation for his capital, an investment of his capital in a special sphere of production. This renting capitalist pays to the land owner, the owner of the soil exploited by him, a sum of money at definite periods fixed by contract, for instance annually (just as the borrower of money-capital pays a fixed interest), for the permission to invest his capital in this particular sphere of production. This sum of money is called *ground-rent,* no matter whether it is paid for agriculture soil, building lots, mines, fishing grounds, forests, etc. It is paid for the entire time, during which the land owner has rented his land to the capitalist by contract. Ground-rent, therefore, is that form, in which property in land realizes itself economically, that is, produces value. Here, then, we have all three classes together, which constitute the frame work of modern society, and they have divergent interests — wage-laborers, industrial capitalists, land owners.

Capital may be fixed in the soil, may be incorporated in it, either in a transient manner, as it is by improvements of a chemical nature, fertilization, etc., or more permanently, as in drainage canals, irrigation works, leveling, farm buildings, etc. In another place I have called the capital thus incorporated in the soil *land-capital.*[120] It belongs in the categories of fixed capital. The interest on the capital thus incorporated in the soil and the improvements thus made in it as an instrument of production may form a part of the rent paid by the capitalist farmer to the land owner,[121] but it does not constitute that ground-rent, strictly speaking, which is paid for the use of the soil as such, whether it be in a natural state or cultivated. In a systematic treatment of private property in land, which is not included in our plan, this part

---

[120] *The Poverty of Philosophy,* p. 148. There I have made a distinction between land-capital and material land. " By merely applying additional capital to land already transformed into means of production land-capital may be augmented without adding anything to the material land, that is to say, to the extent of the land. . . . As capital, land is not more eternal than any other capital. . . . Land-capital is fixed capital, but fixed capital is used up as well as circulating capital."

[121] I say " may," because under certain circumstances this interest is regulated by the law of ground-rent and may disappear, for instance, in the case of competition between lands of great natural fertility.

of the revenue of the land owner would have to be discussed
at length. But a few words about it will suffice here. The
more transient investments of capital which go with the ordinary processes of production in agriculture, are made without exception by the capitalist farmer. These investments,
like cultivation proper, improve the soil,[122] if cultivation is
carried on in a moderately rational manner and does not reduce itself to a brutal spoilation of the soil, such as used to be
in vogue among the former slave holders in the United States,
a thing against which the land owners may provide by contract. In this way material land is transformed into land-
capital. A cultivated field is worth more than an uncultivated one of the same natural quality. Likewise the more
permanent fixed capitals, which are incorporated in the soil
and worn out in longer time, are largely, and in some spheres
often exclusively, invested by the capitalist farmer. But as
soon as the time stipulated by contract has expired —
and this is one of the reasons why the land owners seek
to shorten the time of contract as much as possible when capitalist production develops — the improvements embodied
in the soil become the property of the land owner as
an inseparable part of the land. In the new contract, which
the land owner makes, he adds the interest for the capital incorporated in the soil to the real ground-rent. And he does
this whether he leases the land to the same capitalist who made
these improvements or to some other capitalist farmer. His
rent is thus increased; or, if he wishes to sell his land (we
shall see immediately how its price is determined), its value
has risen. He sells not merely the soil, but the improved
soil, the capital incorporated in the soil for which he did not
pay anything. Quite aside from the movements of real
ground-rent, this is one of the secrets of the increasing en-
richment of the land owners, of the continuous inflation of
their rents, and of the growing money-value of real estate in
proportion as economic development proceeds. Thus they
pocket a result of social development brought about without

[122] See James Anderson and Carey.

their help, *fruges consumere nati,* they are born to consume
the fruits of the earth. But this is at the same time one of
the greatest obstacles to a rational development of agriculture, because the capitalist renter avoids all improvements
and expenses, for which he cannot expect any returns during
the time of his lease. We find this fact denounced as such
an obstacle, not only in the 18th century by James Anderson,
the actual discoverer of the modern theory of rent, who was
also a practical capitalist farmer and an advanced agronomist
for his time, but also in our own days by the opponents
of the present constitution of landed property in England.

A. A. Walton, in his *" History of the Landed Tenures of
Great Britain and Ireland,"* London, 1865, says on this score:
All the efforts of the numerous agricultural institutes in our
country cannot accomplish any very important or really appreciable results in the actual progress of improved cultivation, so long as such improvements increase in a far higher
degree the value of real estate and the size of the rent roll
of the land owner, than they improve the condition of the
tenant or the farm laborer. The tenants in general know
quite as well as the land owner, his rent collector, or even the
president of an agricultural society, that good drainage, am-
ple manuring, and good management, together with an increased application of labor, cleaning the land thoroughly and
working it over, will produce wonderful results, both in the
improvement of the soil and in an increased production. But
all this demands considerable expense, and the tenants also
know very well, that no matter how much they may improve
the soil or raise its value, the land owner will in the long run
get the principal benefit of it in raised rents and increased
land values. . . . They are cunning enough to observe,
what those speakers [land owners and their agents speaking
at agricultural feasts] always forget to tell them, namely that
the lion's share of all improvements made by the tenants must
always pass ultimately into the pockets of the land owners.
. . . No matter how much the former tenant may have
improved his leasehold, his successor will always find, that

the land owner will raise the rent in proportion to the increased land value due to previous improvements. (Pages
96 and 97.)

In agriculture proper this process does not yet appear quite
so plainly as when the land is used for building lots. The
overwhelming part of the land used in England for building
purposes, but not sold as a freehold, is rented by the land
owners for 99 years, or for a shorter time if possible. After
the lapse of this time the buildings fall into the hands of the
land owner together with the land. The tenants are obliged,
says Walton, to deliver the house to the great land owner in
a good inhabitable condition after the expiration of the lease,
after they have paid up to this time an exorbitant ground-
rent. Hardly has the lease expired, when the agent or in-
spector of the landlord comes, inspects your house, takes care
that you get it into good condition, takes possession of it and
annexes it to the domain of his landlord. The fact is that
if this system is permitted to exert its full effects for some
time longer, the entire ownership of houses as well as of
country real estate will be in the hands of the great landed
proprietors. The whole West End of London, north and
south of Temple Bar, belongs almost exclusively to half a
dozen great landlords, is rented at enormous ground-rents,
and if the leases have not quite expired, most of them expire
in rapid succession. The same applies in a greater or smaller
degree to every city in the Kingdom. But even here this
greedy system of exclusiveness and monopoly does not stop.
Nearly all the docking facilities of our port cities are in the
hands of the great land leviathans in consequence of the same
process of usurpation. (L. c., p. 93.) Under these circumstances it is evident that if the census for England and Wales
in 1861 gives the total population as 20,066,224 and the number of house owners as 36,032, the proportion of the owners
to the number of houses and to the population would take on
a very different aspect, if the great house owners were placed
on one side and the small ones on the other.

This illustration of property in buildings is important. In
the first place, it clearly shows the difference between real

ground-rent and interest on fixed capital incorporated in the soil, which may form an addition to the ground-rent. The interest on buildings, like that on capital incorporated in the soil by the tenant, falls into the hands of the industrial capitalist, the building speculator, or the tenant, so long as the lease lasts, and has in itself nothing to do with the ground-rent, which must be paid annually at stated dates for the use of the soil. In the second place it shows, that the capital incorporated in the soil ultimately passes into the hands of the landlord together with the land, and that the interest on it helps to swell his rent.

Some writers, either acting as spokesmen of landlordism against the attacks of bourgeois economists, or endeavoring to transform the capitalist system of production from a system of antagonisms into one of " harmonies," as did Carey, have tried to represent ground-rent, the specific economic expression of private property in land, as identical with interest. For this would obliterate the antagonism between landlords and capitalists. The opposite method was employed in the beginning of capitalist production. In those days landed property was still regarded by popular conception as the primitive and respectable form of private property, while interest on capital was decried as usury. Dudley North, Locke and others, therefore represented interest on capital as a form analogous with ground-rent, just as Turgot deduced the justification of interest from the existence of ground-rent.— Aside from the fact that ground-rent may, and does, exist in its pure form without any addition for interest on capital incorporated in the soil, these more recent writers also forget, that in this way the landlord does not only receive interest on the capital of other people that cost him nothing, but also pockets this capital of others without any compensating return. The justification of private property in land, like that of all other forms of property within a certain mode of production, is that the mode of production is itself a transient historical necessity, and this includes the conditions of production and exchange, which flow from it. It is true, as we shall see later, that property in land differs from the other kinds of property by the fact that it appears superfluous, and even noxious, at a certain stage of development, even from the point of view of capitalist production.

In another form, ground-rent may be confounded with interest and its specific character overlooked. Ground-rent assumes the shape of a certain sum of money, which the landlord draws annually out of the lease of a certain piece of the globe. We have seen that every sum of money may be capitalised, that is, considered as the interest on an imaginary capital. For instance, if the average rate of interest is 5%, then an annual ground-rent of 200 pounds sterling may be regarded as the interest on a capital of 4,000 pounds sterling. Ground-rent so capitalised forms the purchase price or value of the land, a category which is on its face irrational, just as the price of labor is, since the earth is not the product of labor and therefore has no value. But on the other hand a real relation in production is concealed behind this irrational form. If a capitalist buys land yielding a rent of 200 pounds sterling annually and pays 4,000 pounds sterling for it, then he draws the average interest of 5% on his capital of 4,000 pounds sterling, just as though he had invested this capital in interest-bearing papers or loaned it directly at 5% interest. It is the utilisation of a capital of 4,000 pounds sterling at 5%. On this assumption he would recover the purchase price of his estate in twenty years by its revenues. In England, therefore, the purchase price of land is calculated on so many years' purchase, and this is merely a different expression for the capitalisation of the ground-rent. It is in fact the purchase price, not of the land, but of the ground-rent yielded by it, calculated on the ordinary rate of interest. But this capitalisation of rent has for its premise the existence of rent, for rent cannot be explained and derived from its own capitalisation. Its existence, independent of its sale, is rather the condition from which the inquiry must start.

It follows, then, that the price of land may rise or fall inversely as the rate of interest rises or falls, if we assume that ground-rent is a constant magnitude. If the ordinary rate of interest should fall from 5% to 4%, then the annual ground-rent of 200 pounds sterling would represent the annual self-expansion of a capital of 5,000 pounds sterling instead of 4,000 pounds sterling. The price of the same piece of land would thus have risen from 4,000 to 5,000 pounds sterling, or from 20 years' to 25 years' purchase. The reverse would take place in the opposite case. This is a movement of the price of land, which is independent of the movement of ground-rent itself and regulated only by the rate of interest. But as we have seen that the rate of profit has a tendency to fall in the course of social progress, and that the rate of interest has the same tendency, so far as it is regulated by the rate of profit; and since, furthermore, the rate of interest has a tendency to fall in consequence of the growth of loanable capital, aside from the influence of the rate of profit, it follows that the price of land has a tendency to rise, even independently of the movement of ground-rent and the prices of the products of the soil, of which the rent forms a part.

The mistaking ground-rent for the interest form, which it assumes for the buyer of the land — a mistake due to a complete unfamiliarity with the nature of ground-rent — must lead to the most absurd conclusions. Since landed property is considered, in all old countries, as a particularly noble form of property, and its purchase also as an eminently safe investment of capital, the rate of interest at which ground-rent is bought is generally lower than that of other investments of capital for a long time, so that a buyer of real estate draws, for instance, only 4% on his purchase price, whereas he would draw 5% for the same capital in other investments. In other words, he pays more capital for the ground-rent than he would for the same amount of income in other investments. This leads Mr. Thiers to conclude in his utterly valueless work on *La Propriété* (a reprint of a speech of his made in 1849 against Proudhon in the French National Assembly) that ground-rent is low, while it proves merely that its purchase price is high.

The fact that capitalised ground-rent represents itself as the price or value of land, so that the earth is bought and sold like any other commodity, serves to some apologists as a justification of private property in land, seeing that the buyer pays an equivalent for it the same as he does for other commodities, and that the major portion of property in land has changed hands in this way. The same reason would, in that case, serve also to justify slavery, since the returns from the labor of the slave, whom the slave holder has bought, represent merely the interest on the capital invested in this purchase. To derive from the sale and purchase of ground-rent a justification for its existence signifies to justify its existence by its existence.

It is very important for a scientific analysis of ground-rent, that is of the independent and specifically economic form of property in land on the basis of capitalist production, to study it in its pure form and free from all falsifying and obliterating by-work. And it is no less important for an understanding of the practical effects of property in land, even for a theoretical comprehension of a multitude of facts, which run counter to the conception and nature of ground-rent and yet appear as modes of existence of ground-rent, to know the elements which give rise to such obscurities in theory.

In practice everything appears naturally as ground-rent that is paid in the form of lease money by the tenant to the landlord for the permission of cultivating the soil. Whatever may be the composition of this tribute, whatever may be its sources, it has this in common with real ground-rent that the monopoly of the so-called owner of a piece of the globe enables him to levy such a tribute and impose such a tax. This tribute furthermore shares with the real ground-rent the fact that it determines the price of land, which, as we have indicated above, is nothing but the capitalised income from the lease of the land.

We have already seen, that the interest for the capital incorporated in the soil may form one of those foreign ingredients in ground-rent, an element which must become a continually growing addition to the total rent of a certain country in proportion as economic development proceeds. But aside from this interest it is possible that the lease money may conceal a deduction from the average profit or from the normal wages, or both, being made up of them either in part or wholly, so that in some cases it may not represent any real ground-rent at all and the soil may be valueless. This portion of the profit, or of wages, appears then as ground-rent, because instead of falling normally into the hands of the industrial capitalist or the wage worker, it is paid to the landlord in the form of lease money. Economically speaking neither the one nor the other of these portions constitutes any ground-rent; but in practice they constitute some of the revenue of the landlord, an economic utilisation of his monopoly, just as real ground-rent does, and they have a determining influence on land prices just as ground-rent has.

We are not now speaking of conditions, in which ground-rent, the form of landed property adapted to the capitalist mode of production, formally exists without the capitalist mode of production itself, so that the tenant is not an industrial capitalist, nor the mode of his management a capitalist one. Such is the case in Ireland. The tenant is here generally a small farmer. What he pays to the landlord in the shape of rent absorbs frequently not merely a part of his profit, that is, of his own surplus-labor, to which he is entitled as the possessor of his own instruments of production, but also a part of his normal wages, which he would receive under different conditions for the same amount of labor. Besides, the landlord, who does not do anything for the improvement of the soil, also expropriates him from his small capital, which he incorporates for the greater part in the soil by his own labor, just as a usurer would do under similar circumstances. Only the usurer would at least risk his own capital in the operation. This continual robbery is the center of the disputes over the Irish Land Bill, which has for its principal aim to compel the landlord, when giving notice to his tenant to vacate, should pay him an indemnity for the improvements made by him in the soil, or for the capital incorporated by him in the land.   Palmerston used to meet this demand with the cynical answer: " The House of Commons is a house of landlords."

Nor do we speak of exceptional circumstances, in which the landlord may enforce a high rent even in countries with a capitalist production, although this rent may not be in any way connected with the product of the soil.   Of such a nature is the renting of small patches of ground to laborers in English factory districts, either for small gardens or for amateur agriculture in spare hours.   (Reports of Inspectors of Factories.)

We are speaking of ground-rent in countries with a developed capitalist production.   Among English tenants, for instance, there is a number of small capitalists, who are destined and compelled by education, training, tradition, competition, and other circumstances, to invest their capital as tenants in agriculture.   They are compelled to be satisfied with less than the average profit, and to yield up a part of it to the landlords for rent.   This is the only condition on which they are permitted to invest their capital in the soil, in agriculture.   Since the landlords exert everywhere a considerable, in England even an overwhelming, influence on legislation, they are in a position to exploit this for the purpose of grinding down the entire class of tenants.   The corn laws of 1815, for instance, a bread tax confessedly imposed upon the country for the purpose of securing for the idle landlords a continuation of their abnormally increased rentals during the anti-Jacobin wars, had indeed the effect, with the exception of a few extraordinarily rich years, of keeping the prices of agricultural products above the level which they could have held in free competition.   But they did not have the effect of keeping prices at that level, which had been ordered by the law-making landlords to serve as standard prices in such a way as to form the legal limit for the importation of foreign corn.   But the leases were made out under the impression created by these normal prices.   As soon as the illusion passed away, a new law was made, with new normal prices, which were as much an impotent expression of the greedy landlord's phantasy as the old ones. In this way the tenants were cheated from 1815 to the thirties. Hence we have during all this period the standing subject of agricultural distress. And with it we have during this period the expropriation and the ruin of a whole generation of tenants, and the appropriation of their places by a new class of capitalists.[123]

A much more general and important fact, however, is the depression of the wages of the actual farm laborers below their normal average, so that a portion of the wages is deducted in order to become a part of the lease money and thus flowing into the pockets of the landlord instead of the laborer under the disguise of ground-rent. This is the case quite generally in England and Scotland, with the exception of a few favorably situated counties. The inquiries of the Parliamentarian Committees into the scale of wages made before the , passing of the corn laws in England — so far the most valuable and almost unexploited contributions to a history of wages in the 19th century, and at the same time a monument of disgrace erected for themselves by the English aristocracy and bourgeoisie — proved convincingly and beyond a doubt that the high rates of rent and the corresponding raise in the land prices during the anti-Jacobin wars, were due in part to no other cause but the deductions from wages and the depression of wages even below the physical minimum. In other words, a part of the wages had been paid over to the landlords. Various circumstances such as the depreciation of money, the handling of the poor laws in the agricultural districts, etc., had made these operations possible, at a time when the incomes of the tenants were rising enormously and the landlords amassed fabulous riches. Yes, one of the main arguments for the introduction of the corn laws, used by both tenants and landlords, was that it was physically impossible to depress the wages of the farm laborers still more. This condition of

---

[123] See the anti-corn law prize essays. However, the corn laws always kept prices at an artificially higher level. For the better situated tenants this was favorable. They profited by the stationary condition, in which the protective duties kept the great mass of tenants, who relied with or without reason on the exceptional average price.

things has not been materially altered, and in England as
well as in all European countries a portion of the normal
wages is absorbed by the ground-rent the same as ever. When
Count Shaftsbury, then Lord Ashley, one of the philanthropic
aristocrats, was so extraordinarily moved by the condition of
the English factory laborers and acted as their spokesman
in Parliament during the agitation for a ten hour day, the
spokesmen of the industrials got their revenge by publishing statistics on the wages of the agricultural laborers in the
villages belonging to him (see Volume I, chapter XXV, 5e,
The British Agricultural Proletariat), which showed clearly,
that a portion of the ground-rent of this philanthropist con-
sisted of the loot, which his agents filched for him out of the
wages of the agricultural laborers. This publication is also
interesting for the reason, that the facts exposed by it may
rank in the same class with the worst exposures made by the
Committees in 1814 and 1815. As soon as circumstances
permit of a temporary raise in the wages of the agricultural
laborers, a cry goes up from the capitalist tenants to the effect
that a raising of the wages to their normal level, as customary in other lines of industry, would be impossible and would
ruin them, unless ground-rent were reduced at the same time.
This is a confession, that the tenants deduct a portion from
the wages of the laborers under the name of ground-rent and
pay it over to the landlords. For instance, from 1849 to
1859 the wages of the agricultural laborers rose in England
through a combination of overwhelming circumstances, such
as the exodus from Ireland, which cut off the supply of agricultural laborers coming from that country; an extraordinary
absorption of the agricultural population by the factories; a
demand for soldiers to go to war; an exceptional emigration
to Australia and the United States (California), and other
causes which need not be mentioned here. At the same time
the average prices of grain fell by more than 16% during
this period, with the exception of the poor agricultural years
from 1854 to 1856. The tenant capitalists shouted for a reduction of their rents. They succeeded in single cases. But
on the whole they failed to get what they wanted. They

sought refuge in a reduction of the cost of production, among other things by introducing steam engines and new machinery in abundance, which partly replaced horses and crowded them out of the business, but partly also created an artificial overpopulation by throwing agricultural laborers out of work and thereby causing a fall in wages. And this took place in spite of the general relative decrease of the agricultural population during that decade, compared to the growth of the total population, and in spite of the absolute decrease of the agricultural population in some purely agricultural districts.[124] In the same way Fawcett, then professor of political economy at Cambridge, who died in 1884 as Postmaster General, said at the Social Science Congress, October 12, 1865: "The agricultural laborers began to emigrate and the tenants began to complain, that they would not be able to pay such high rents as they had been accustomed to pay, because labor became dearer in consequence of emigration." Here, then, the high ground-rent is directly identified with low wages. And so far as the level of the prices of land is determined by this circumstance increasing the rent, a rise in the value of the land is identical with a depreciation of labor, a high price of land with a low price of labor.

The same is true of France. "The price of rent rises, because the prices of bread, wine, meat, vegetables and fruit rise on the one side, while on the other the price of labor remains unchanged. If the older people compare the bills of their fathers, taking us back about 100 years, they will find that the price of one day's labor was then the same in rural France as it is now. The price of meat has trebled since them. . . . Who is the victim of this revolution? Is it the rich, who is the proprietor of the estate, or the poor who works it? . . . The raising of the prices of rent is the proof of a national disaster." (*Du Mécanisme de la Société en France et en Angleterre.* Par M. Rubichon, Second edition, Paris, 1837, p. 101.)

We now give some illustrations of rent representing deduc-

[124] John C. Morton, *The Forces Used in Agriculture.* Lecture in the London Society of Arts, 1860, based upon authentic documents, collected by about 100 tenants from 12 Scotch and 35 English counties.

738   *Capitalist Production.*

tions either from the average profit or from the average wages.

The above quoted Morton, real estate agent and agricultural engineer, says that the observation has been made in many localities that the rent for large estates is smaller than for small ones, because " competition for the latter is generally greater than for the former, and because small tenants, who are rarely able to take up any other business but farming, are frequently willing to pay a rent, which they themselves know to be too high, pressed by the want of finding some other business." (John C. Morton, *The Resources of Estates.* London, 1858, p. 116.)

However, he is of the opinion that this difference is gradually disappearing in England, and he attributes this largely to the emigration of the class of small tenants. The same Morton gives an illustration, in which evidently the wages of the tenant himself, and still more surely of the laborers, suffer a deduction for ground-rent. This takes place in the case of estates of 70 to 80 acres, who cannot keep a two-horse plow. " Unless the tenant works as diligently with his own hands as any laborer, he cannot make out on his lease. If he leaves the execution of the work to his men and confines himself to superintending them, he will most likely find very quickly that he is unable to pay his rent." (L. c., p. 118.) Morton concludes, therefore, that unless the tenants of a certain locality are very poor, the leaseholds should not be smaller than 70 acres, so that the tenants may keep two or three horses.

Extraordinary wisdom of Monsieur Léonce de Lavergne, *Membre de l'Institut et de la Société Centrale d'Agriculture.* In his *Economie Rurale de l'Angleterre* (quoted from the English translation, London, 1855), he makes the following comparison of the annual advantages from cattle, that work in France but not in England, where they are replaced by horses (p. 42):

FRANCE		ENGLAND	
Milk	4 million p.st.	Milk	16 million p.st.
Meat	16 million p.st.	Meat	20 million p.st.
Labor	8 million p.st.	Labor	——
	28 million p.st.		36 million p.st.

But the higher amount for England is obtained here, according to his own statement, because m**k** is twice as dear in England than in France, while he counts the same prices for meat in both countries (p. 35); therefore the English milk product reduces itself to 8 million pounds sterling, and the total product to 28 million pounds sterling, the same as in France. It is indeed a strong dose, that Mr. Lavergne lumps the quantities and price differences together in his calculation, when England produces certain articles more expensively than France, so that this appears as an advantage of English agriculture, whereas it signifies at best only a higher profit for tenants and landlords.

That Mr. Lavergne is not only familiar with the advantages of English agriculture, but also believes in the prejudices of the English tenants and landlords, is proved by him on page 48: "One great disadvantage is generally connected with grain plants . . . they exhaust the soil that bears them." Mr. Lavergne believes not only that other plants do not do so, but he also believes that leguminous crops and root crops enrich the soil: "Leguminous plants draw the principal elements of their growth out of the air, while they give back to the soil more than they take from it; therefore they help both directly and indirectly through their return in the shape of animal manure to make good in a double way the damage caused by grain crops and other exhausting crops; hence it is a matter of principle that they should at least alternate with such crops; in this consists the Norfolk rotation." (Pages 50 and 51.)

No wonder that Mr. Lavergne, who believes these fairy tales of the English rural mind, also believes that the wages of the English farm laborers have lost their abnormality since the repeal of the corn tax. See what we have said on this point in another place, Volume I, chapter XXV, 5c, pages 739 to 766. But let us also listen to Mr. John Bright's speech in Birmingham, December 14, 1865. After mentioning the 5 million families that are not represented in Parliament, he continues: "Among these are one million, or rather more than one million in the United Kingdom, who are put down on the luckless list of paupers. Then there is still another million, who are holding themselves just above pauperism, but who are continually in danger of likewise becoming paupers. Their condition and prospects are not any better. Now take a look at the ignorant lower strata of this portion of society. Consider their outcast condition, their poverty, their complete hopelessness. Even in the United States, even in the southern states during the reign of slavery, every negro looked forward to some jubilee year. But these people, this mass of the lowest strata of our country, I am here to express it, have neither the faith in any improvement nor even a longing for it. Did you read the other day that item about John Cross, a farm laborer of Dorsetshire? He worked six days in the week, had an excellent character from his employer, for whom he had worked 24 years for a weekly wage of 8 sh. John Cross had to keep a family of seven children in his hut out of this wage. In order to warm his sickly wife and her suckling babe, he took, or legally speaking he stole, a wooden hurdle worth six pence. For this crime he was sentenced to 14 or 20 days' imprisonment by the justices of the peace. I can tell you that many thousands of cases like that of John Cross may be found in the whole country, and particularly in the South, and that their condition is such, that so far the most sincere investigator has not been able to solve the secret, how they keep body and soul together. And now throw your glances over the whole country and look at those 5 million families and the desperate condition of this stratum of them. Can we not say truly that the mass of the nation excluded from the suffrage toils and toils again and knows almost no rest? Compare them with the ruling class — but if I do that I shall be accused of communism . . . but compare this great toiling and suffrageless nation with that part which may be regarded as the ruling class. Look at their wealth, their showiness, their luxury. Look at their weariness — for there is a weariness also among them, but it is the weariness of satiety — and see how they hasten from place to place, as though it were only a question of discovering new pleasures." (*Morning Star,* December 15, 1865.)

We will show hereafter, in what manner surplus-labor, and consequently surplus-products, are confounded with ground-rent, which is, at least under the capitalist mode of production, qualitatively and quantitatively a specifically determined part of the surplus-product. The natural basis of surplus-labor in general, that is a natural condition without which such labor cannot be performed, is that nature must supply, either in animal or vegetable products of the soil or in fisheries, etc., the necessary means of subsistence by an expenditure of labor which does not consume the entire working day. This natural productivity of agricultural labor (which implies here the labor of gathering, hunting, fishing, cattle raising) is the basis of all surplus-labor; so is all labor primarily and originally directed toward the appropriation and production of food. (The animal supplies at the same time skins for warmth in colder climates; also cave dwellers, etc.)

The same confusion between surplus-product and ground-rent, differently expressed, is shown by Mr. Dove. Originally agricultural and industrial labor are not separated. The second joins into the first. The surplus-labor and the surplus-product of the farming tribe, the house commune or family, comprise both agricultural and industrial labor. Both go hand in hand. Hunting, fishing, agriculture are impossible without suitable tools. Weaving, spinning, etc., were first carried on as side occupations to farming.

We have shown previously, that in the same way in which the labor of the individual workman may be separated into necessary and surplus-labor, the aggregate labor of the working class may be divided so that that portion, which produces the total means of subsistence for the working class (including the means of production required for this purpose) performs the necessary labor for the whole society. The labor performed by all the remainder of the working class may then be regarded as surplus-labor. But the necessary includes by no means only agricultural labor, but also that labor which produces all other products that necessarily pass into the average consumption of the laborer. Socially speaking, some perform only necessary, others only surplus-labor, and vice versa. It is but a division of labor between them. It is the same with the division of labor between agricultural and industrial laborers in general. The purely industrial character of labor on the one side is offset by the purely agricultural one on the other. This purely agricultural labor is by no means natural, but is rather a product, and a very modern one at that, which has not yet been acquired everywhere, of social development, and it corresponds to a very definite stage of development. Just as a portion of the agricultural labor is materialised in products, which either minister only to luxury or serve as raw materials in industry, but do not serve as food, particularly not as food for the masses, so a portion of the industrial labor is materialised in products, which serve as necessary means of consumption of both the agricultural and industrial laborers. It is a mistake to consider this industrial labor, from a social point of view, as surplus-labor. It is in part as much necessary labor as the necessary portion of the agricultural labor. It is likewise but a separated form of a part of industrial labor which was formerly naturally connected with agricultural labor, it is a necessary and mutual supplement to the purely agricultural labor, which is now separated from it. (From a purely material point of view 500 mechanical weavers may produce surplus-fabrics to a far greater degree, that is, more than is required for their own clothing.)

It should finally be remembered in the study of the various forms which appear as ground-rent, that is, of the lease money paid under the name of ground-rent to the landlord for the use of the land for the purposes of production or consumption, that the price of things, which have in themselves no value, not being the products of labor, such as the land, or which at least cannot be reproduced by labor, such as antiquities, works of art of certain masters, etc., may be determined by many accidental combinations. In order to sell a thing, nothing more is required than that it can be monopolised and alienated.

There are three great errors, which should be avoided in the study of ground-rent, and which obscure its analysis.

1) Confusion of the various forms of rent, which correspond to different stages of development of the process of social production.

Whatever may be the specific form of rent, all types of it have this in common that the appropriation of rent is that economic form, in which property in land realises itself, and that ground-rent on its part is conditioned on the existence of private property in land, the ownership of certain portions of the globe by certain individuals. The owner may be the individual representing the community, as in Asia, Egypt, etc., or this private ownership in land may be merely accessory to the ownership of the persons of the direct producers by some individuals, as under the slave or serf system, or it may be a purely private ownership of nature by nonproducers, a mere title to land, or finally it may be a relation to the soil which, as in the case of colonists and small peasants owning land, seems included under a system of isolated and unsocial labor in the appropriation and production of the products of certain pieces of land by the direct producers.

This common element in the various forms of rent, namely that of being the economic realisation of property in land, a legal fiction by grace of which certain individuals have an exclusive right to certain pieces of the globe, misleads into overlooking the differences.

2) All ground-rent is surplus-value, the product of surpluslabor. In its undeveloped form, as natural rent (rent in kind), it is as yet directly the surplus-product itself. This gives rise to the mistaken idea that the rent corresponding to the capitalist mode of production is explained by merely explaining the general prerequisites of surplus-value and profit, whereas this ground-rent is always a surplus over and

above profit. It is a peculiar and specific portion of surplus-value, over and above that portion of the value of commodities, which is known as profit and consists itself of surplus-value (surplus-labor). The general conditions for the existence of surplus-value and profit are: The direct producers must work beyond the time necessary for the reproduction of their own labor-power. They must perform surplus labor in general. This is the subjective condition. The objective condition is that they must be able to perform surplus-labor. The natural conditions must be such that a part of their available labor time suffices for their reproduction and selfmaintenance as producers, that the production of their necessary means of subsistence shall not consume their whole labor-power. The fertility of nature forms a limit here, a starting point, a basis. The development of the social productivity of their labor forms the other limit. Still more strictly speaking, since the production of means of subsistence is the very first condition of their existence and of all production, the labor used in this production, that is the agricultural labor in the widest economic meaning, must be productive enough, so that it will not absorb the entire available labor time in the production of means of subsistence for the direct producers. Agricultural surplus-labor and an agricultural surplus-product must be possible. More widely applied, it means that the total agricultural labor, both necessary and surplus-labor, of a part of society suffices to produce the necessary subsistence for the whole society, including the laborers who are not agricultural. It means that this great division of labor between farmers and industrials must be possible, also that between farmers producing subsistence and farmers producing raw materials. Although the labor of the producers of subsistence consists of necessary and surplus-labor, so far as their own point of view goes, it represents from the social standpoint. only the labor necessary to produce the social subsistence. The same takes place in the case of division of labor within society as a whole, as distinguished from division of labor in the individual workshop. It is the labor necessary for the production of particular articles, for the satisfaction of some particular need of society. If this division is proportional, then the products of the various groups are sold at their values (at a later stage of development at their prices of production), or at prices which are modifications of their values or prices of production due to general laws. It is indeed the law of value enforcing itself, not with reference to individual commodities or articles, but to the total products of the particular social spheres of production made independent by division of labor. Every commodity must contain the necessary quantity of labor, and at the same time only the proportional quantity of the total social labor time must have been spent on the various groups. For the use-value of things remains a prerequisite. The use-value of the individual commodities depends on the particular need which each satisfies. But the use-value of the social mass of products depends on the extent to which it satisfies in quantity a definite social need for every particular kind of product in an adequate manner, so that the labor is proportionately distributed among the different spheres in keeping with these social needs, which are definite in quantity. (This point is to be noted in the distribution of capital to the various spheres of production.) The social need, that is the use-value on a social scale, appears here as a determining factor for the amount of social labor which is to be supplied by the various particular spheres. But it is only the same law, which showed itself in the individual commodity, namely that its use-value is the basis of its exchange-value and thus of its surplus-value. This point has any bearing upon the proportion between necessary and surplus-labor only in so far as a violation of this proportion makes it impossible to realise the value of the commodities and the surplus-value contained in it. For instance, take it that proportionally too much cotton goods have been produced, although only the labor-time necessary for this total product under the prevailing conditions is realised in it. But too much social labor has been expended in this particular line, in other words, a portion of this product is useless. The whole of it is therefore sold only as though it had been produced in the necessary proportion. This quantitative

limit of the quota of social labor available for the various
particular spheres is but a wider expression of the law of
value, although the necessary labor time assumes a different
meaning here.   Only just so much of it is required for the
satisfaction of the social needs.   The limitation is here due
to the use-value.   Society can use only so much of its total
labor for this particular kind of products under the prevailing conditions of production.   But the subjective and objective conditions of surplus-labor and surplus-value in general
have nothing to do with the peculiar form of either the profit
or the rent.   These conditions apply to surplus-value as such,
no matter what special form it may assume.   Hence they
do not explain ground-rent.

3) It is precisely the self-expansion of private property,
the development of ground-rent, which reveals the characteristic peculiarity, that its amount is by no means determined by
the actions of its recipient, but by the independent development of social labor, in which he does not take part.   It may
easily happen, therefore, that something is regarded as a peculiarity of rent (and of the products of agriculture in general), which is really a common feature of all lines of
production and all their products on the basis of the production of commodities, or, more strictly speaking, of capitalist
production.

The amount of ground-rent (and with it the value of the
soil) develops with the progress of social advance as a result
of the total labor of society.   On the one hand this leads to a
growth of the market and of the demand for products of the
soil, on the other it stimulates the demand for the land itself,
which is a prerequisite of competitive production in all lines
of business, even in those which are not agricultural.   Speaking strictly of real-ground rent, this rent, and with it the value
of the soil, develops with the market for the products of
the soil, and thus with the increase of the other than
agricultural population, with its needs and demand for either
means of subsistence or raw materials.   It is the nature of
capitalist production to reduce the agricultural population
continually as compared to the non-agricultural, because in

industry (strictly speaking) the increase of the constant capital compared to the variable capital goes hand in hand with an absolute increase, though relative decrease, of the variable capital; whereas in agriculture the variable capital required for the exploitation of a certain piece of land decreases absolutely and cannot increase, unless new land is taken into cultivation, which implies a still greater previous growth of the non-agricultural population.

In fact we are not dealing here with a characteristic peculiarity of agriculture and its products. On the contrary, the same applies to all other lines of production and products on the basis of a prodution of commodities and of its absolute form, capitalist production.

These products are commodities, use-values, which have an exchange-value which can be realised, converted into money, only to the extent that other commodities form an equivalent for them, that other products face them as commodities and values. They have an exchange-value to the extent that they are not produced as immediate means of subsistence for the producers themselves, but as commodities, as products which become use-values only by their conversion into exchange-values (money), by being gotten rid of. The market for these commodities develops through the social division of labor; the separation of the productive labor into various departments transforms their respective products mutually into commodities, into mutual equivalents, makes them serve mutually as markets. This is in no way peculiar to agricultural products.

Rent can develop as money-rent only on the basis of a production of commodities, more strictly of capitalist production, and it so develops in proportion as the agricultural production becomes a production of commodities. This is the same proportion in which other than agricultural lines of production develop independently of agriculture, for to that extent does the agricultural product become a commodity, an exchange-value, a value. To the same extent that the production of commodities develops as a capitalist production, and as a production of value, does the production of surplus-value and surplus-products proceed. But to the same extent that this continues does property in land acquire the faculty of capturing an ever increasing portion of this surplus-value by means of its land monopoly. Thereby it raises its rent and the price of the land itself. The capitalist performs at least an active function himself in the development of surplus-value and surplus-products. But the land owner has but to capture his growing share in the surplus-product and the surplus-value created without his assistance. It is this which is the characteristic peculiarity of his position, and not the fact that the value of the products of the soil and thus of the land increases in proportion as the market for them expands, the demand grows and with it the world of commodities which are not agricultural products, the mass of producers and products outside of agriculture. But as this is done without the assistance of the landowner, it appears as something specifically his own, that measures of value, measures of surplus-value, and the conversion of a portion of surplus-value into ground-rent should depend upon the process of social production, on the development of the production of the commodities in general. For this reason a man like Dove wants to develop rent out of this element. He says that rent does not depend upon the mass of agricultural products, but upon their value; but this depends upon the mass and productivity of the non-agricultural population. But it is also true of all other products that they cannot develop the character of commodities, unless the mass, the variety and the succession of other commodities form equivalents for them. We have shown this previously in the discussion of the general nature of value. On the one hand the exchangeability of a certain product depends altogether on the multiplicity of commodities existing outside of it. On the other hand this circumstance determines in particular to what extent this product shall be put out as a commodity.

No producer, whether an industrial or farmer, considered by himself alone, produces value or commodities. His product becomes a commodity only in definite social interrelations. It becomes a commodity, in the first place, to the extent that it represents social labor, so that the individual producer's labor counts as a part of the general social labor. And in the second place this social character of his labor appears impressed upon his product through its pecuniary character and through its general exchangeability determined by its price.

Instead of explaining rent, such vagaries confine themselves to explaining merely surplus-value in general, or, still more absurdly, surplus-products in general, and on the other hand they make the mistake of ascribing a character, which belongs to all products in their capacity as commodities, to agricultural products exclusively. This is still more vulgarised by those who pass from a general analysis of value over to the realisation of a certain commodity's value. Every commodity can realise its value only in the process of circulation, and whether it realises its value, and to what extent it does so, depends on the prevailing market conditions.

It is not a peculiarity of ground-rent, then, that the products of agriculture develop into values and as values, that they face other commodities as commodities, and that products not agricultural face them as commodities, or that they develop as specific expressions of social labor. The peculiarity of ground-rent is rather that in proportion as the conditions develop, in which agricultural products develop as commodities (values), and in which they can realise their values, so does also property in land develop the power to appropriate an increasing portion of these values, which were created without its assistance, and so does an increasing portion of the surplus-value assume the form of ground-rent.

CHAPTER XXXVIII.

DIFFERENTIAL RENT. GENERAL REMARKS.

In the analysis of ground-rent we shall start from the assumption, that products paying such a rent, that is, products a portion of whose surplus-value and general price resolves itself into ground-rent, are sold at their prices of production, like all other commodities. It suffices for our purposes to confine ourselves to products of agriculture and mining. In other words, their selling prices are made up of the elements of their cost (the value of the consumed constant and variable capital) plus a profit, which is determined by the average rate of profit and calculated on the total capital advanced, whether consumed or not consumed. We assume, then, that the average selling prices of these products are equal to their prices of production. The question is now, how can a ground-rent develop under these conditions, how can a portion of the profit become converted into ground-rent, so that a portion of the prices of the commodities falls into the hands of the landlord.

In order to show the general character of this form of ground-rent, we assume that most of the factories of a certain country are driven by steam engines, while a certain smaller number of them are driven by natural waterfalls. Let us further assume that the price of production in those industries amounts to 115 for a quantity of commodities which have consumed a capital of 100. The 15% of profit are calculated, not merely on the consumed capital of 100, but on the total capital invested in the production of this value in the commodities. We have previously shown that this price of production is not determined by the individual cost-price of every single producing industrial, but by the cost-price required on an average for the commodity under the average conditions of capital in the entire sphere of production. It is, in fact, the market price of production, as distinguished from its oscillations. For it is in the form of the market price, and in a wider sense of the regulating market price, or market price of production, that the nature of value asserts itself in commodities. It becomes evident, in this way, that it is not determined by the labor time necessary in the case of any individual producer for the production of a certain quantity of commodities, or of some individual commodity, but by the socially necessary labor time. This is that quantity of labor time, which is necessary for

the production of the socially required total quantity of commodities of any kind on the market under the existing average
conditions of social production.

As definite figures are immaterial in this case, we shall
furthermore assume that the cost price in the factories driven
by water power is only 90 instead of 100. Since the regulating market price of production of this quantity of commodities is 115, with a profit of 15%, the factories driven
by water power will also sell their commodities at 115, the
average price regulating the market price. Their profit
would then be 25 instead of 15; the regulating market price
of production would allow them a surplus-profit of 10%, not
because they sell their commodities above the price of production, but because they sell them at the price of production,
because their commodities are produced, or their capital expanded, under exceptionally favorable conditions, under conditions, which are above the average prevailing in this sphere.

Two things become evident at once.

1) The surplus-profit of the producers, who use the natural
waterfall as motive power, is in the same class with all
surplus-profit (and we have already analysed this category
when discussing the prices of production), which is not the
result of mere transactions in the sphere of circulation, of
mere fluctuations of market prices. This surplus-profit, then,
is likewise equal to the difference between the individual
price of production of these favored producers and the general
social price of production regulating the market in this entire
sphere. This difference is equal to the excess of the general
price of production of the commodities over their individual
price of production. The two regulating limits of this excess
are on the one hand the individual cost price, and thus the
individual price of production, on the other hand the general
price of production. The value of the commodities produced
with water power is smaller, because a smaller quantity of
labor is required for their production, namely less labor
materialised in the constant capital. The labor here employed is more productive, its individual power of production is greater than that employed in the majority of the

factories of the same kind. Its greater productive power is shown in the fact that it requires a smaller quantity of constant capital, a smaller quantity of materialised labor, than the others. It also requires less living labor, because the water wheel need not be heated. This greater individual power of production of the employed labor reduces the value, and at the same time the cost price and price of production of the commodity. For the individual industrial capitalist this expresses itself in a lower cost price of his commodities. He has to pay for less materialised labor, and less wages for less labor-power employed. Since the cost price of his commodities is smaller, his individual price of production is also smaller. His cost price is 90 instead of 100. His individual price of production would therefore be only $103\frac{1}{2}$ instead of 115 (100: 115 = 90: $103\frac{1}{2}$). The difference between his individual price of production and the general one is limited by the difference between his individual cost price and the general one. This is one of the magnitudes which form the limits of his surplus-product. The other is the magnitude of the general price of production, into which the average rate of profit enters as a regulating factor. If coal should become cheaper, the difference between his individual cost-price and the general cost-price would decrease, and with it his surplus-profit. If he should be compelled to sell his commodities at their individual value, or at the price of production determined by its individual value, then the difference would disappear. It is on the one side a result of the fact that the commodities are sold at their general market-price, the price brought about by the equalisation of individual prices through competition, on the other side a result of the fact that the greater individual productivity of the laborers employed by him does not benefit the laborers, but their employer, as does all productivity of labor. This productivity represents itself as a faculty of capital.

Since the level of the general price of production is one of the limits of the surplus-product, the level of the average rate of profit being one of its factors, it can have no other source but the difference between the general and the individual price of production, and consequently the difference between the general and the individual rate of profit. An excess of this difference would imply the sale of products above the price of production regulated by the market, not at this price.

2) So far as the surplus profit of the manufacturer using natural water power instead of steam for motive power does not differ in any way from any other surplus profit. All normal surplus profit, that is all surplus profit not due through accidental sales or fluctuations of the market price, is determined by the difference between the individual price of production of the commodities of these particular capitals and the general price of production, which regulates in a general way the market prices of the commodities produced by the capitals of this sphere of production, or the market prices of the commodities of the total capital invested in this sphere of production.

But now we come to the difference.

To what circumstance does the industrial capitalist in the present case owe his surplus-profit, the surplus resulting for him personally from the price of production regulated by the average rate of profit?

He owes it in the last resort to a natural power, the motive power of water, which is found ready at hand in nature and which is not itself a product of labor like coal, which transforms water into steam. The water has no value, it need not be paid by an equivalent, it costs nothing. It is a natural agency of production, which is not produced by labor.

But this is not all. The manufacturer who works with a steam engine also employs natural powers, which cost him nothing and yet make his labor more productive and, to the extent that they cheapen the manufacture of the means of subsistence required for the laborers, increase the surplus-value and with it the profit. These natural powers are quite as much monopolised by capital as the natural powers of social labor arising from co-operation, division, etc. The manufacturer pays for the coal, but not for the faculty of

2V

the water to alter its aggregate state, of passing over into steam, not for the elasticity of the steam, etc. The monopolisation of natural powers, that is of the increased productivity of labor due to them, is common to all capital working with steam engines. It may increase that portion of the product of labor which represents surplus-value as against that portion which is converted into wages. To the extent that it does this, it raises the general rate of profit, but it does not make any surplus-profit, for this consists of the excess of the individual profit over the average profit. The fact that the application of a natural power, of a waterfall, creates a surplus-profit in this case, cannot therefore be due solely to the circumstance that the increased productivity of labor is here due to a natural force. There must be still other modifying circumstances.

Look at the reverse side. The mere application of natural powers to industry may influence the level of the general rate of profit, because it affects the quantity of labor necessary to produce the means of subsistence. But in itself it does not create any deviations from the general rate of profit, and this is the point in which we are interested here. Furthermore, the surplus-profit, which some individual capital may ordinarily realise in its particular sphere of production — for the deviations of the rates of profits in the various spheres of production are continually balanced by competition into an average rate — are due, aside from accidental deviations, to a reduction of the cost-price, of the cost of production. This reduction arises either from the fact that a capital is used in greater than ordinary quantities, so that the dead expenses of the production are reduced, while the general causes increasing the productivity of labor, such as co-operation, division, etc., can exert themselves with a higher degree of intensity, their field of expression being larger. Or it may arise from the fact that, aside from the greater volume of the invested capital, better methods of labor, new inventions, improved machinery, chemical secrets in manufacture, etc., in short new and improved means of production and methods are used, which are above the average. The reduction of the cost price and the surplus profit arising from it arise here from the manner, in which the self-expanding capital is invested. They arise either from the circumstance that it is concentrated in one hand in extraordinarily large masses (a circumstance which is neutralised when capitals of the same size become the average), or from the circumstance that a capital of a certain size expands itself under exceptionally favorable circumstances (a circumstance which is neutralised as soon as the exceptional method of production becomes general or is superseded by a still more developed one).

The cause of the surplus profit, then, arises here from the capital itself (which includes the labor set in motion by it); it is either due to the greater size of the capital employed, or to its more improved application; and there is no particular reason why all the capital in the same sphere of production should not be invested in the same way. In fact, the competition between the capitals tends to neutralise their differences more and more. The determination of value by the socially necessary labor time asserts itself by the cheapening of commodities and the necessity of making commodities under the same favorable conditions. But it is different with the surplus profit of the industrial capitalist who uses water power. The increased productive power of his labor is not due either to his capital or his labor, nor to the mere application of some natural force separate from capital and labor, but incorporated in the capital. It arises from the greater natural power of production of labor in conjunction with some other natural power, which natural power is not at the command of all capitals in this sphere, whereas such a thing as the elasticity of steam is. The application of this other natural power does not follow as a selfunderstood matter, whenever capital is invested in this sphere. It is a monopolised natural power, which, like a water fall, is only at the command of those who can avail themselves of particular pieces of the globe and its opportunities. It is not within the power of capital to call to life this natural premise for a greater productivity of labor, whereas any capital may transform water into steam. Water power is found only locally in nature, and wherever it does not exist, it cannot be created by any investment of capital. It is not dependent upon products which labor can secure, such as machines, coal, etc. It is dependent upon definite natural conditions of definite portions of the globe. That section of industrial capitalists who own waterfalls excludes the other section who do not own any from the application of this power, because the land, and particularly land supplied with water power, is limited. Of course this does not prevent the quantity of water power available for industrial purposes from being increased, even if the number of natural waterfalls in a certain country is limited. Water power may be artificially diverted, in order to exploit its motive force fully. Under certain conditions a water wheel may be inproved so as to use the highest possible amount of water power; in places where the ordinary wheel is not suitable for supplying water, turbines may be used, etc. The possession of this natural power forms a monopoly in the hand of its owner, it is a premise for the increase of the productivity of the invested capital, which cannot be created by the process of production of the capital itself.[125] This natural power, which can be monopolised in this way, is always attached to the soil. Such a natural power does not belong to the general conditions of that particular sphere of production, and not to those conditions, which may be made general.

Now let us assume that the waterfalls with the land on which they are found are held in the hands of persons, who are considered the owners of these portions of the globe, who are land owners. These owners may exclude others and prevent them from investing capital in the waterfalls or using waterfalls by means of capital. They can permit such a use or forbid it. The capital cannot create a waterfall out of itself. Therefore the surplus profit, which arises from this employment of waterfall, is not due to capital, but to the harnessing of a natural power, which can be monopolised and has been monopolised, by capital. Under these circum-

---

[125] As to the extra profit, see the " Inquiry " (against Malthus).

stances the surplus-profit is transformed into ground-rent, that is, it falls into the hands of the owner of the waterfall. If the industrial capitalist pays to the owner of the waterfall 10 pounds sterling annually, then his profit is 15 pounds sterling, that is 15% on the 100 which then make up his cost of production; and he is just as well off, or possibly better, as all other capitalists of his sphere of production, who work with steam. It would not matter, if this capitalist should be the owner of the waterfall. He would in that case pocket the surplus profit of 10 pounds in his capacity as a landowner, not in his capacity as an industrial capitalist, just because this surplus is not due to his capital as such, but to a limited natural power separate from his capital, over which he has command, because he has a monopoly of it. And so it is converted into ground-rent.

1) It is evident that this is always a differential rent, for it does not enter as a determining factor into the average price of production of commodities, but rather is based on it. It always arises from the difference between the individual price of production of the individual capital having command over monopoly of natural power and the general price of production of the total capital invested in that particular sphere of production.

2) This ground-rent does not arise from the absolute increase of the productivity of the employed capital, or of the labor appropriated by it, since this can only reduce the value of commodities; it is due to the greater relative fertility of definite individual capitals invested in a certain sphere of production, as compared with investments of capital, which are excluded from these exceptional and natural conditions favoring the productivity. For instance, if the use of steam should offer overwhelming advantages not attached to the use of water power, or tending to neutralise the benefits to be derived from water power, then, water power would not be used and could not produce any surplus profit, or ground-rent, even though coal has a value and water power has not.

3) The natural power is not the source of the surplus profit, but only its natural basis, because this natural basis

permits an increase in the productive power of labor. In the same way the use-value is the general bearer of the exchange-value, but not its cause. If the same use-value could be created without labor, it would have no exchange-value, yet it would have the same useful effect as ever. On the other hand, nothing can have an exchange-value unless it has a use-value, unless it has this useful bearer of labor. Were it not for the fact that the different values are neutralised into prices of production, and the different individual prices of production into one average price of production regulating the market, the mere increase in the productivity of labor by the use of a waterfall would merely lower the price of the commodities produced with the waterfall, without adding anything to the share of profit contained in those commodities. On the other hand, this increased productivity of labor would not be converted into surplus-value, were it not for the fact that capital appropriates the natural and social productivity of labor as though it were its own.

4) The private ownership of the waterfall has nothing to do with the creation of that portion of the surplus-value (profit), and of the price of a commodity in general, which is produced by the help of the waterfall. This surplus profit would also exist, if private property did not prevail, for instance, if the land supplied with the waterfall were appropriated by the industrial capitalist as masterless booty. Hence private property in land does not create that portion of value, which is transformed into surplus profit, but it merely enables the landowner, who has possession of the waterfall, to coax this surplus profit out of the pocket of the industrial capitalist into his own. It is the cause, not of the creation of this surplus profit, but of its transformation into ground-rent, of the appropriation of this portion of the profit, or of the price of commodities, by the owner of the land or of the waterfall.

5) It is evident that the price of the waterfall, that is the price which the owner of it would receive if he were to sell it to some other man, perhaps to the industrial capitalist, would not enter directly into the general price of production

of the commodities, although it would enter into the individual cost-price of the industrial capitalist. For the rent arises here from the price of production of the commodities produced by steam machinery, and this price is regulated independently of the waterfall. Furthermore, this price of the waterfall is an irrational expression, behind which a real economic relation is concerned. The waterfall, like the earth in general, and like any natural force, has no value, because it does not represent any materialised labor, and therefore it really has no price, which is normally but the expression of value in money. Where there is no value, it is obvious that it cannot be expressed in money. This price is merely capitalised rent. The ownership of land enables the landowner to catch the difference between the individual profit and the average profit. The profit thus acquired, which is renewed every year, may be capitalised, and then it appears as the price of a natural power itself. If the surplus profit realised by the use of the waterfall amounts to 10 pounds sterling per year, and the average interest is 5%, then these 10 pounds sterling annually represent the interest on a capital of 200 pounds sterling; and this capitalisation of the annual 10 pounds sterling, which the waterfall enables its owner to catch, appears then as the capital-value of the waterfall itself. That it is not the waterfall itself, which has a value, but that its price is a mere reflex of the appropriated surplus profit, which the use of the waterfall yields to the industrial capitalist, capitalistically calculated, becomes at once evident in the fact that the price of 200 pounds sterling represents merely the product of a surplus profit of 10 pounds sterling for 20 years, whereas the same waterfall will enable its owner to catch these 10 pounds sterling every year for 30 years, or 100 years, or an indefinite number of years, so long as circumstances remain the same. On the other hand, if some new method of production, which is not suitable for water power, should reduce the cost price of the commodities produced by steam machinery from 100 to 90 pounds sterling, the surplus profit, and with it the rent, and with it the price of the waterfall, would disappear.

Now that we have explained our general conception of differential rent, we will pass on to its consideration in agriculture, strictly so-called. What applies to it will also apply on the whole to mines.

CHAPTER XXXIX.

THE FIRST FORM OF DIFFERENTIAL RENT.

(*Differential Rent I.*)

RICARDO is quite right when he writes the following sentences:

"Rent is always the difference between the produce obtained by the employment of two equal quantities of capital and labor" (*Principles,* p. 59). [He means differential rent, for he assumes that no other rent but differential rent exists.] He should have added "On the same quantities of land," so far as ground-rent and not surplus profit in general is concerned.

In other words, surplus profit, if normal and not due to accidental transactions in the process of circulation, is always produced as a difference between the products of two equal quantities of capital and labor. This surplus profit is transformed into ground rent, when two equal quantities of capital and labor are employed on equal quantities of land with unequal results. However, it is by no means absolutely necessary that this surplus profit should arise from unequal results of equal quantities of invested capital. The various investments may also employ unequal quantities of capital. Indeed, this is generally the case. But equal aliquot parts, for instance 100 pounds sterling of each, give unequal results; that is, their rates of profit are different. This is the general prerequisite for the existence of surplus profit in any sphere, where capital is invested. The second prerequisite is the transformation of this surplus profit into ground-rent (and of rent in general as distinguished from profit); it should always be analysed, when, how, under what conditions this transformation takes place.

Ricardo is also right in the following sentence, provided it is limited to differential rent: "Whatever diminishes the inequality in the produce obtained on the same or on new land, tends to lower rent; and whatever increases that inequality, necessarily produces an opposite effect and tends to raise it." (P. 74.)

However, among these causes are not merely the general ones (fertility and location), but also 1) the distribution of taxes, according to whether it works uniformly or not; it always has the latter effect, for instance in England, when it is not centralised and when the tax is levied on the land, not on the rent; 2) the inequalities arising from the different development of agriculture in different parts of the country, since this line of industry, on account of its traditional character, is more difficult to level than manufacture; 3) the inequality in the distribution of capital among the capitalist tenants. Since the capture of agriculture by the capitalist mode of production, the transformation of independently producing farmers into wage workers, is in fact the last conquest of this mode of production, these inequalities are greater here than in any other line of industry.

After these preliminary remarks I will give a brief summary of the peculiarities of my own analysis as distinguished from that of Ricardo, etc.

We consider first the unequal results of equal quantities of capital, applied to different lands of equal area; or on lands with unequal areas, but calculated on the same aliquot parts of it.

The two general causes of these unequal results independent of capital, are 1) Fertility. (With reference to this first point the analysis should state, what is included in the natural fertility of lands, and what elements enter into it.) 2) The location of the lands. This is a deciding factor in colonies, and in general determines the succession in which lands shall be taken under cultivation. Furthermore it is evident that these two different causes of differential rent, fertility and location, may work in opposite directions. A certain soil may be very favorably located and yet be very poor in fertility, and vice versa. This circumstance is important, for it explains how it is that the work of opening the soil of a certain country to cultivation may equally well proceed from the worse to the better soil, instead of vice versa. Finally it is clear that the progress of social production has on the one hand the general effect of leveling the differences arising from location as a cause of ground-rent, by creating local markets and improving locations by means of facilities for communication and transportation; and that, on the other hand, it increases the differences of the individual locations in a certain district by separating agriculture from manufacture and forming great centers of production on the one hand while relatively isolating the agricultural districts on the other hand.

For the present, however, we leave this point, location, out of consideration and confine ourselves to natural fertility. Aside from climatic factors, etc., the difference in natural fertility is one of the chemical compositions of the top soil, that is of its different contents in plant nourishment. However, assuming the chemical composition and natural fertility in this respect to be the same for two areas, the actual fertility will be different according to whether these elements of plant nourishment have a form, in which they may be more or less easily assimilated and immediately utilised for nourishing plants. Hence it will depend partly upon the chemical, partly upon the mechanical development of agriculture, to what extent the same natural fertility may be made available in fields of the same natural fertility. Fertility, although an objective quality of the soil, always implies economic relations, a relation to the existing chemical and mechanical development in agriculture, of course it changes with such a development. By dint of chemical applications (such as the use of certain liquid manures to stiff clay loam, or burning of heavy clay soils) or of mechanical appliances (such as special plows for heavy soils) the obstacles may be removed, which made a soil of the same fertility as some other actually less fertile (drainage also belongs under this head). Or even the succession of soils in cultivation may be changed thereby, as was the case, for instance, with light sandy soil and heavy clay soil in a certain period of development of English agriculture. This shows once more that historically, in the succession of soils under cultivation, one may pass just as well from very fertile soils to less fertile ones as vice versa. The same may come to pass by any artificially created improvement in the composition of the soil, or by a mere change in the methods of agriculture. Finally the same result may be brought about by a change in the succession of the predominant kinds of soil, owing to different conditions of the subsoil, as soon as it is likewise taken into cultivation and turned over into top layers. This is caused either by the employment of new methods of agriculture (such as planting of stock feed), or any mechanical appliances, which either turn the subsoil into top layers, or mix it with the top soil, or cultivate the subsoil without throwing it up.

All these influences upon the differential fertility of different lands amount to the practical result that for the economic fertility the state of the productivity of labor, in this case the faculty of agriculture of making the natural fertility of the soil immediately available, a faculty which varies in different periods of development, is as much an element in the so-called natural fertility of the soil as its chemical composition and its other natural qualities.

We assume, then, the existence of a certain stage of development of agriculture. We assume furthermore, that the predominant succession of soils is calculated with reference to this stage of development, a thing which is, of course, always the case with simultaneous investments of capital on the different soils. Under such circumstances differential rent may form either in an ascending or a descending succession, for although the succession is an established fact for the totality of the actually cultivated lands, a movement of succession leading to this formation always preceded it.

Let us assume the existence of four kinds of soil, A, B, C, D. Let us furthermore assume that the price of one-quarter of wheat is three pounds sterling, or 60 shillings. Since rent is here merely a differential rent, this price of 60 shillings per quarter for the worst soil is equal to the cost of production, that is equal to the capital plus the average profit.

Let A be this worst soil and yield for each 50 shillings of expenditure one-quarter of wheat worth 60 shillings, so that the profit is 10 shillings, or 20%.

Let B yield for the same expenditure 2 quarters of wheat, or 120 shillings. This would be 70 shillings of profit, or a surplus profit of 60 shillings.

Let C yield for the same expenditure 3 quarters, or 180 shillings; total profit 130 shillings, surplus profit 120 shillings.

Let D yield 4 quarters, 240 shillings, 190 shillings of profit, 180 shillings of surplus profit.

Then we shall have the following succession:

Table I.

Class of Soil	Product		Capital Advanced	Profit		Rent	
	Quarters	Shillings		Quarters	Shillings	Quarters	Shillings
A	1	60	50	$\frac{1}{6}$	10	–	--
B	2	120	50	$1\frac{1}{6}$	70	1	60
C	3	180	50	$2\frac{1}{6}$	130	2	120
D	4	240	50	$3\frac{1}{6}$	190	3	180
Totals	10	600				6	360

The respective rents are: D = 190 sh. — 10 sh., or the difference between D and A; C = 130 — 10 sh., or the difference between C and A; B = 70 — 10 sh., or the difference between B and A; and the total rent for B, C, D equals 6 quarters, or 360 shillings, equal to the sum of the differences between D and A, C and A, B and A.

This succession representing a certain product in a certain condition may, abstractly considered, descend from D to A, from very fertile to less and less fertile soil, or rise from A to D, from relatively poor to more and more fertile soil, or may fluctuate in a now rising, now descending curve, for instance from D to C, from C to A, from A to B (and we have already mentioned the reasons why this might take place in reality).

The process leading to the descending succession took place in the following manner: The price of one-quarter of wheat rose gradually from, say, 15 shillings to 60 shillings. As soon as the 4 quarters produced by D (assume them to have been so many million quarters) did not suffice any more, the price of wheat rose to a point where the missing supply could be raised by C. That is to say, the price of wheat must have risen to 20 shillings per quarter. When it had risen to 30 shillings per quarter, B could be taken under cultivation, and when it reached 60 shillings per quarter, A could be taken in, and the capital invested in it did not have to be content with a lower rate of profit than 20%. In this way a rent was formed for D, first of 5 shillings per quarter, or 20 shillings for the 4 quarters produced by it; then of 15 shillings per quarter, or 60 shillings, then of 45 shillings per quarter, or a total of 180 shillings for 4 quarters.

If the rate of profit of D originally was likewise 20%, then its total profit on 4 quarters of wheat was also but 10 shillings, but this stood for more grain when the price was 15 shillings than it does when the price is 60 shillings. But since the grain enters into the reproduction of labor-power, and a portion of each quarter has to make good some wages and another some constant capital, the surplus-value under this condition was higher, and to that extent, other things being the same, the rate of profit. (The matter of the rate of profit will have to be analysed separately and in detail.)

On the other hand, if the succession went the opposite way, that is, if the movement started from A, then the price of wheat at first rose above 60 shillings, when new land had to be taken under cultivation. But when the necessary supply was raised by B, a supply of 2 quarters, the price fell once more to 60 shillings. B raised wheat at a cost of 30 shillings per quarter, but sold it at 60 shillings, because its supply sufficed just to cover the demand. In this way a rent was formed, first of 60 shillings for B, and in the same way for

C and D; always assuming that the market price remained at
60 shillings, although C and D relatively raised wheat having a value of 20 and 15 shillings respectively, because the
supply of the one-quarter raised by A was as much needed as
ever to satisfy the total demand. In this case the rising of
the demand above the supply first raised by A, then by A
and B, would not have made it possible to cultivate successively B, C and D, but would merely have caused a general
extension of the sphere of cultivation, by which the more
fertile lands came under its control later.

In the first succession, an increase in the price would
raise the rent and lower the rate of profit. The lowering of
the rate of profit might be entirely or partially checked by
opposing circumstances. This point will have to be treated
later. It should not be forgotten, that the general rate of
profit is not determined uniformly in *all* spheres of production by the surplus-value. It is not the agricultural profit,
which determines the industrial profit, but vice versa. But
of this more anon.

In the second succession the rate of profit on the invested
capital would remain the same. The mass of profit would
present itself in less grain; but the relative price of grain,
compared with that of other commodities, would have risen.
Only, whatever increase there might be in the profit, would
separate itself from the actual profit in the form of rent, instead of flowing into the pockets of the capitalist tenant and
appearing as a growing profit. The price of grain, however, would remain unchanged under the conditions assumed
here.

The development and growth of differential rent would
remain the same, both with unaltered and with increasing
prices, and with a continued progress from worse to better
land as well as with a continued regression from better to
worse land.

So far we have assumed 1) that the price rises in the one
succession and remains stationary in the other; 2) that there
is a continual progression from better to worse soil, or from
worse to better soil.

But now let us assume that the demand for grain rises from its original figure of 10 to 17 quarters; furthermore, that the worst soil A is displaced by another soil A′, which raises 1⅓ quarters at a price of production of 60 shillings (50 sh. cost plus 10 sh. for 20% profit), so that its price of production for one-quarter is 45 shillings; or, perhaps, the old soil A may have become improved through a continued rational cultivation, or may be cultivated more productively at the same cost, for instance, by the introduction of clover, etc., so that its product with the same investment of capital rises to 1⅓ quarters. Let us also assume that the classes B, C and D of soil supply the same product as ever, but that new classes of soil have been introduced, for instance, A′ of a fertility between A and B, furthermore B′ and B″ of a fertility between B and C. In that case we should witness the following phenomena:

1) The price of production of one-quarter of wheat, or its regulating market price, would have fallen from 60 shillings to 45 shillings, or by 25%.

2) The cultivation would have proceeded simultaneously from more fertile to less fertile soil, and from less fertile to more fertile soil. The soil A′ is more fertile than A, but less fertile than the hitherto cultivated soils B, C and D. And B′ and B″ are more fertile than A, A′ and B, but less fertile than C and D. The succession would thus have proceeded in crisscross fashion. Cultivation would not have proceeded to soil absolutely less fertile than A, etc., but it would have proceeded to relatively less fertile than the soils C and D; on the other hand, cultivation would not have taken up soil absolutely more fertile, but at least relatively more fertile compared to the hitherto least fertile soils A or A and B.

3) The rent on B would have fallen; likewise the rent on C and D; but the total rental would have risen from 6 quarters to 7⅔; the mass of the cultivated and rent paying lands would have increased, and the mass of the product would have risen from 10 quarters to 17. The profit, if remaining the same for A, expressed in grain, would have risen; but the

rate of profit itself might have risen, because the relative surplus-value did. In this case the wages, and with them the investment of variable capital, and with it the total investment, would have been reduced on account of the cheapening of the means of subsistence. The total rental would have fallen from 360 shillings to 345 shillings.

Let us draw up the new succession.

Table II.

Class of Soil	Product		Capital Invested	Profit		Rent		Price of Production per Quarter
	Qrs.	Sh.		Qrs.	Sh.	Qrs.	Sh.	
A	1 1/3	60	50	2/9	10			45 sh
A'	1 2/3	75	50	5/9	25	1/3	15	36 sh
B	2	90	50	8/9	40	2/3	30	30 sh
B'	2 1/3	105	50	1 2/9	55	1	45	25 2/7 sh
B˙	2 2/3	120	50	1 5/9	70	1 1/3	60	22 1/2 sh
C	3	135	50	1 8/9	85	1 2/3	75	20 sh
D	4	180	50	2 8/9	130	2 2/3	120	15 sh
Total	17					7 2/3	345	

Finally, if only the classes of soil A, B, C and D were cultivated, but their productivity raised in such a way that A would produce 2 quarters instead of 1, B, 4 quarters instead of 2, C, 7 quarters instead of 3, and D, 10 quarters instead of 4, so that the same causes would have acted differently upon the various classes of soil, the total production would have increased from 10 quarters to 23. Assuming that the demand would absorb these 23 quarters by an increase of the population and the falling of prices, we should get the following table:

Table III.

Class of Soil	Product		Capital Invested	Price of Production per Quarter	Profit		Rent	
	Qrs	Sh			Qrs.	Sh.	Qrs.	Sh.
A	2	60	50	30	1/3	10		
B	4	120	50	15	2 1/3	70	2	60
C	7	210	50	8 4/7	5 1/3	160	5	150
D	10	300	50	6	8 1 3	250	8	240
Total	23						15	450

The numbers in this and in other tables are arbitrarily chosen, but the assumptions are quite rational.

The first and principal assumption is that the improvement in agriculture acts differently upon different soils, and in this case more so upon the best classes of soil, C and D, than upon the A and B classes. Experience has shown that this is indeed the case, although the opposite may also take place. If the improvement should affect the lesser soils more than the better ones, the rent on these last ones would have fallen instead of rising.

But in our table we have assumed that the absolute growth of the fertility of all classes of soil is simultaneously accompanied by an increase of the higher relative fertility of the better classes of soil, C and D, which implies an increasing difference between the various products with the same investment of capital, and thus an increase of the differential rent.

The second assumption is that the total demand must keep step with the increase of the total product. In the first place, one need not imagine such an improvement to come abruptly, but gradually, until the succession in table III is reached. In the second place, it is a mistake to say that the consumption of necessities of life does not grow with their cheapening. The abolition of the corn laws in England proved the reverse (see Newman), and the contrary view is derived merely from the fact that great and sudden differences in the harvests, caused by the weather, bring about at one time an extraordinary fall, at another an extraordinary rise in the prices of cereals. While in such a case the sudden and short cheapness does not get time to exert its full effect upon the extension of consumption, the opposite takes place when the cheapening process arises out of the lowering of the regulating price of production itself and has permanency. In the third place, a portion of the grain may be consumed in the shape of whiskey or beer. And the rising consumption of these articles is by no means confined within narrow limits. In the fourth place, this matter depends partly upon the increase of the population, and for the other part the country may be a grain exporting one, as England was far beyond the middle of the 18th century, so that the demand is not regulated by the boundaries of a mere national consumption. Finally the increase and cheapening of the wheat production may have the result of making wheat instead of rye or oats the principal article of consumption for the masses, so that

2W

the demand for it may grow for this reason alone, just as the opposite may take place when the product decreases and prices rise.— Under these assumptions, and with the figures previously chosen, succession No. III would show a fall in the price per quarter from 60 shillings to 30, that is 50%, that production compared to succession No. I would increase from 10 quarters to 23, in other words, by 130%; that the rent would remain stationary upon the soil B, be doubled upon C, and more than doubled upon D, and that the total rental would increase from 18 pounds sterling to 22, a growth of $22\frac{1}{9}\%$.

A comparison of these three tables (taking table I twice, one rising from A to D, and one descending from D to A), which may be considered either as existing gradations under some definite stage of society, for instance, as existing side by side in three different countries, or as succeeding one another in different periods of development in the same country, would show:

1) That the succession, when complete, whatever may have been the course of its formative process, always has the appearance of being in a descending line; for in studying the rent, the point of departure will always be the soil producing the maximum of rent, and the closing point will be the soil yielding no rent.

2) That the price of production of the worst soil, which yields no rent, is always the regulating market price, although this market price in .table I, if its succession was formed in an ascending line, could not remain stationary, unless better and better soil were cultivated. In that case the price of the grain produced on the best soil is a regulating one to the extent that it depends upon the quantity produced on such soil in what measure the soil of class A shall remain the regulator. For instance, if B, C, D should produce more that the demand calls for, then A would cease to be the regulator. This is what Storch has in mind, when he adopts the best class of soil as the regulating one. In this manner the American price of cereals regulates the English price.

3) Differential rent arises from the differences in the nat-

ural fertility of the soil which depends upon the prevailing degree of development of cultivation (leaving aside for the present the question of location), in other words, from the limited area of the best lands, and from the circumstance that equal capitals must be invested in unequal soils, which yield unequal products with the same capital.

4) The existence of differential rent and of a graduated succession of differential rents may be due quite as much to a descending succession, which leads from the better to the worse soils, as to an ascending one, which takes the opposite direction. Or it may be brought about by alternating forward and backward movements. (Succession No. II may form by a process from D to A, or from A to D; succession No. II comprises both movements.)

5) According to its mode of formation, differential rent may develop with a stationary, rising or falling price of the products of the soil. With a falling price the total production and the total rental may rise, and rent may form on hitherto rentless lands, even though the worst soil A may have been displaced by a better one, or may itself have become improved, and although the rent may decrease on other better, or even the best, lands (table II); this process may also be accompanied by a fall of the total rent (in money). Finally, when prices are falling on account of a general improvement of cultivation, so that the product and the price of the product of the worst soils decrease, the rent may remain the same or may fall on a part of the better soils, but rise on the best soils. It is true that the differential rent of every soil, compared with the worst soil, depends upon the price, say, of the quarter of wheat, when the difference of the quantity of products is given. But when the price is given, differential rent depends upon the magnitude of the differences of the quantity of products, and if, with an increasing absolute fertility of all soils that of the better soil grows relatively more than that of the worse soil, the magnitude of this difference grows to that extent. In this way (see Table I), when the price is 60 shillings, the rent of D is determined by its differential product as compared to A, in other words,

by its surplus of 3 quarters. The rent is therefore three times sixty, or 180 shillings. But in Table III, in which the price is 30 shillings, the rent is determined by the quantity of the surplus product of D as compared to A, that is 8 quarters, and therefore it is eight times thirty, or 240 shillings.

This does away with the primitive misconception of differential rent still found among men like West, Malthus, Ricardo, to the effect that it necessarily requires a progress toward worse and worse soil, or an ever decreasing productivity of agriculture. It rather may exist, as we have seen, with a progress to a better and better soil; it may exist when a better soil takes the lowest position formerly occupied by the worst soil; it may be accompanied with a progressive improvement of agriculture. Its premise is merely the inequality of the different kinds of soil. So far as the development of productivity is concerned, it implies that the increase of absolute fertility of the total area does not do away with this inequality, but either increases it, or leaves it unchanged, or merely reduces it somewhat.

From the beginning to the middle of the 18th century England's cereal prices fell continually in spite of the falling prices of gold and silver, while at the same time (viewing this entire period) there was an increase of rent, of the rental, of the area of the cultivated lands, of agricultural production, and of the population. This corresponds to Table I combined with Table II in an ascending line, but in such a way that the worst land A is either improved or eliminated from the grain area; this does not imply that it was not used for other agricultural or industrial purposes.

From the beginning of the 19th century (the date should be given more precisely) until 1815 there is a continual rise in the cereal prices, accompanied by a steady growth of the rent, of the rental, of the volume of the cultivated lands, of agricultural production, and of the population. This corresponds to Table I in a descending line. (Quote here some passages on the cultivation of inferior lands in those times.)

In Petty's and Davenant's time, the farmers and land owners complain about the improvements and the breaking of new ground; the rent on the superior soils falls, the total rental increases through the extension of the soils yielding rent.

(These three points should be illustrated later on by quotations; likewise the difference in the fertility of the different cultivated portions of the soil in a certain country.)

The general rule in differential rent is that the market-value always stands above the total price of production of the mass of products. For instance, take Table I. The ten quarters of the total product are sold at 600 shillings, because the market price is determined by the price of production of A, which amounts to 60 shillings per quarter. But the actual price of production is:

A	1 qr. = 60 sh.	1 qr. = 60 sh.
B	2 qrs. = 60 sh.	1 qr. = 30 sh.
C	3 qrs. = 60 sh.	1 qr. = 20 sh.
D	4 qrs. = 60 sh.	1 qr. = 15 sh.
	10 qrs. = 240 sh.	Average 1 qr. = 24 sh.

The actual price of production of these 10 quarters is 240 shillings. But they are sold at 600 shillings, 250% too dear. The actual average price for 1 quarter is 24 shillings; the market price is 60 shillings, also 250% too dear.

This is a determination by the market-value, which is enforced on the basis of capitalist production by means of competition; it creates a false social value. This arises from the law of the market-value, to which the products of the soil are subject. The determination of the market-value of the products, including the products of the soil, is a social act, although performed by society unconsciously and unintentionally. It rests necessarily upon the exchange-value of the product, not upon the soil and its differences in fertility.

If we imagine that the capitalistic form of society is abolished and society is organized as a conscious and systematic association, then those 10 quarters represent a quantity of independent labor, which is equal to that contained in 240 shillings. In that case society would not buy this product of the soil at two and a half times the labor time contained in it. The basis of a class of land owners would thus be destroyed. This would have the same effect as a cheapening of the product to the same amount by foreign imports. While it is correct to say that, by retaining the present mode of production but paying the differential rent to the state, the prices of the products of the soil would remain the same, other circumstances remaining unchanged, it is wrong to say that the value of the products would remain the same, if capitalist production were superseded by association. The sameness of the market prices for commodities of the same kind is the way in which the social character of value asserts itself on the basis of capitalist production, as it does of any production resting on the exchange of commodities between individuals. What society in its capacity as a consumer pays too much for the products of the soil, what constitutes a minus for the realisation of its labor time in agricultural production, is now a plus for a portion of society, for the landlords.

A second circumstance, important for the analysis to be given under II in the next chapter, is the following:

It is not merely a question of the rent per acre, or per hectare, nor in general of a difference between the price of production and the market price, nor between the individual and general price of production per acre, but it is also a question of how many acres of each class of soil are under cultivation. The point of importance is here primarily the magnitude of the rental, that is, of the total rent of the entire cultivated area; but it serves us at the same time as a transition to the development of a rise in the rate of the rent, although there is neither a rise in the prices, nor an increase in the differences of the relative fertility of the various kinds of soil when prices are falling.

We had above:

Table I.

Class of Soil	Acres	Cost of Production	Product	Rent in Grain	Rent in Money
A	1	3 p. st.	1 qr.	0	0
B	1	3 p. st.	2 qrs.	1 qr.	3 p. st.
C	1	3 p. st.	3 qrs.	2 qrs.	6 p. st.
D	1	3 p. st.	4 qrs.	3 qrs.	9 p. st.
Totals	4		10 qrs.	6 qrs.	18 p. st.

Now let us assume that the number of cultivated acres is doubled in every class. Then we have:

Table I a.

Class of Soil	Acres	Cost of Production	Product	Rent in Grain	Rent in Money
A	2	6 p. st.	2 qrs.	0	0
B	2	6 p. st.	4 qrs.	2 qrs.	6 p. st.
C	2	6 p. st.	6 qrs.	4 qrs.	12 p. st.
D	2	6 p. st.	8 qrs.	6 qrs.	18 p. st.
Totals	8		20 qrs.	12 qrs.	36 p. st.

Let us assume two other cases, and let the first be one, in which production expands on the two inferior classes of soil, in the following manner:

Table I b.

Class of Soil	Acres	Cost of Product Per Acre	Cost of Product Total	Product	Rent in Grain	Rent in Money
A	4	3 p/st.	12 p/st.	4 qrs.	0	0
B	4	3 p/st.	12 p/st.	8 qrs.	4 qrs.	12 p/st.
C	2	3 p/st.	6 p/st.	6 qrs.	4 qrs.	12 p/st.
D	2	3 p/st.	6 p/st.	8 qrs.	6 qrs.	18 p/st.
Totals	12		36 p/st.	26 qrs.	14 qrs.	42 p/st.

Finally let us assume an unequal expansion of production and of the cultivated area on all four classes, in the following manner:

Table I c.

Class of Soil	Acres	Cost of Product Per Acre	Cost of Product Total	Product	Rent in Grain	Rent in Money
A	1	3 p/st.	3 p/st.	1 qr.	0	0
B	2	3 p/st.	6 p/st.	4 qrs.	2 qrs.	6 p/st.
C	5	3 p/st.	15 p/st.	15 qrs.	10 qrs.	30 p/st.
D	4	3 p/st.	12 p/st.	16 qrs.	12 qrs.	36 p/st.
Totals	12		36 p/st.	36 qrs.	24 qrs.	72 p/st.

In the first place, the rent per acre remains the same in all these four cases I, I a, I b and I c. For in fact the result of the same investment of capital per acre of the same class of soil has remained unchanged. Nothing more has been assumed than a fact which may be observed in any country at any given moment, namely that the various classes of soil participate in certain definite proportions in the entire cultivated area. And furthermore, a fact which may be observed in any two countries that are compared, or in the same country at different periods of time, namely that the proportion varies in which the cultivated area is distributed among these classes.

If we compare Ia with I, then we see, if the cultivation of the soils of all four classes grows in the same proportion, that a doubling of the cultivated acres doubles the total production, and at the same time doubles the rent in grain and money.

If we compare Ib and Ic successively with I, we see that in both cases a triplication of the area subject to cultivation takes place. It rises in both cases from 4 acres to 12, but in Ib it is the classes A and B which get the greatest share of the increase, although A pays no rent, and B yields the smallest differential rent. But of 8 newly cultivated acres A and B get 3 each, or 6 between the two of them, whereas C and D get only 1 acre each, or together 2 acres. In other words, three-quarters of the increase go to A and B, and only one-quarter to C and D. According to this assumption and comparing Ib with I, the trebled area of cultivation does not result in a trebled product, for the product does not increase from 10 to 30, but only to 26. On the other hand, seeing that a considerable portion of the increase takes place on A, which does not yield any rent, and since the principal portion of the remaining increase takes place on B, the rent in grain rises only from 6 quarters to 14, and the rent in money from 18 pounds sterling to 42.

But if we compare Ic with I, where the soil yielding no rent does not increase in area, and the soil yielding a minimum rent increases but slightly, while the principal portion of the increase takes place on C and D, we find that the trebled area results in an increase of production from 10 quarters to 36, more than three times the quantity. The rent in grain has risen from 6 quarters to 24, or quadrupled; and so has the money rent from 18 pounds sterling to 72.

In all these cases the price of the agricultural product naturally remains stationary. The total rental increases in all cases with the extension of cultivation, unless it takes place exclusively on the worst soil, which does not pay any rent. But the growth is unequal. In proportion as the extension of cultivation takes place upon the superior classes of soil and consequently the quantity of the products grows not merely at the ratio of expansion of the area, but even faster, the rent in grain and money increases. In proportion as the worst soil and the class next above it share principally in the expansion of the area (provided that the worst soil represents a constant class), the total rental does not rise in proportion to the extension of cultivation. If there are two countries, in which the class A, that yields no rent, is of the same nature, the rental stands in the reverse ratio to the aliquot part represented by the worst soil and the lesser classes next above it in the total area of the cultivated soil, and therefore in the reverse ratio to the quantity of the products of equal investments of capital on the same total areas of land. The proportion between the quantity of the worst cultivated soil and that of the better soil, within the total cultivated area of a certain country, thus has the opposite effect upon the total rental than the proportion between the quality of the worst cultivated soil and that of the better soil has upon the rent per acre and, other circumstances remaining the same, upon the total rental. The confounding these two things has given rise to many mistaken objections to differential rent.

The total rental, then, increases by the mere extension of the cultivation, and by the consequent greater investment of capital and labor in the soil.

But the most important point is this: Although it is our assumption that the proportion of the rents upon the various classes of soil remains the same, calculated per acre, and therefore also the rate of rent considered with reference to the capital invested in each acre, yet we must observe the following: If we compare Ia with I, the case in which the number of cultivated acres and the capital invested in them have been proportionately increased, we find that just as the total production has increased proportionately to the expanded agricultural area, that is just as both of them have been doubled, so has the rental. It has risen from 18 pounds sterling to 36, just as the number of acres has risen from 4 to 8.

If we take the total area of 4 acres, we find that the total rental amounted to 18 pounds sterling, or the average rent, including the soil which does not pay any rent, 4½ pounds sterling. This calculation might be made, say, by a landlord owning all 4 acres. And in this way the average rent is statistically calculated upon a whole country. The total rental of 18 pounds sterling is secured by the investment of a capital of 10 pounds sterling. We call the ratio of these two figures the rate of rent; in the present case it is 180%.

The same rate of rent follows in Ia, where 8 instead of 4 acres are cultivated, but all classes of land have shared in the same proportion in the increase. The total rental of 36 pounds sterling gives for 8 acres and an invested capital of 20 pounds sterling an average rent of 4½ pounds sterling per acre and a rate of rent of 180%.

But if we consider Ib, in which the increase has taken place mainly upon the two inferior classes of soil, we find there a rent of 42 pounds sterling upon 12 acres, or an average rent of 3½ pounds sterling per acre. The invested total capital is 30 pounds sterling, and the rate of rent 140%. The average rent per acre has decreased by one pound sterling, and the rate of rent has fallen from 180 to 140%. Here then we have an increase of the total rental from 18 pounds sterling to 42, and yet a fall of the average rent, calculated both per acre and per capital, while production grows also, but not proportionately. This takes place, although the rent upon all classes of soil, both per acre and per capital, remains the same. It does so, because three-quarters of the increase go to the class A, which does not pay any rent, and upon class B, which pays only the minimum rent.

If the total extension in the case Ib had taken place only upon the soil A, then we should have 9 acres upon A, 1 acre upon B, 1 acre upon C and 1 acre upon D. The total rental would be 18 pounds sterling, the same as before, the average rent upon the 12 acres would be 1½ p. st. per acre; and a rent of 18 pounds sterling on an invested capital of 30 pounds sterling would give a rate of rent of 60%. The average rent, both per acre and per invested capital, would have decreased, and the total rental would not have increased.

Finally, let us compare Ic with I and Ib. Compared to I, the area has been trebled, also the invested capital. The total rental is 72 pounds sterling upon 12 acres, or 6 pounds sterling per acre against 4½ pounds sterling in case I. The rate of rent upon the invested capital (72: 30 pounds sterling) is 240% instead of 180%. The total product has risen from 10 quarters to 36.

Compared to Ib, where the total area of the cultivated acres, the invested capital, and the difference between the cultivated classes are the same, but the distribution different, the product is 36 quarters instead of 26, the average rent per acre is 6 pounds sterling instead of 3½, and the rate of rent with reference to the same invested total capital is 240% instead of 140%.

No matter whether we regard the various conditions in Tables Ia, Ib and Ic as existing side by side in different countries, or as existing successively in the same country, we come to the following conclusions: so long as we have the conditions mentioned hereafter, that is, so long as the price of cereals remains unchanged, because the worst rentless soil has the same product; so long as the differences in the productivity of the different cultivated soils remain the same; so long as the respective products of the same invested capitals are the same for aliquot parts (acres) of the areas cultivated in every class of soil; so long as the ratio between the rents per acre of each class of soils and with the same rate of rent upon the capital invested in each portion of the same kind of soil is constant: 1) the rental always increases with the extension of the cultivated area and with the consequent increased investment of capital, with the exception of the case in which the entire increase falls on the rentless soil. 2) Both the average rent per acre (total rental divided by the total number of acres) and the average rate of rent (total rental divided by the invested total capital) may vary very considerably; both of them in the same direction, but in different proportions compared to one another. If we leave out of consideration the case, in which the increase takes place upon the rentless soil, we find that the average rent per acre and the average rate of rent upon the capital invested in agriculture depend upon the proportional shares, which the various classes of soil claim in the cultivated area; or, what amounts to the same, upon the distribution of the employed total capital among the classes of soil of different fertility. Whether much or little land is cultivated, and whether the total rental is therefore larger or smaller (with the exception of the case, in which the increase is confined to A) the average rent per acre, or the average rent per invested capital, remains the same so long as the proportions of the participation of the various classes of soil in the total cultivated area remain unchanged. In spite of the rise, even of a very considerable one, in the total rental with the extension of cultivation and the expansion of the invested capital, the average rent per acre and the average rent per capital fall whenever the extension of the rentless lands, or of the lands of inferior fertility, increases more than that of the superior rent paying ones. On the other hand the average rent per acre and the average rent per capital increase in proportion as the better lands constitute a greater part of the total area and employ a relatively greater share of the invested capital.

Hence, if we consider the average rent per acre, or hectare, of the total cultivated soil, in the way that is generally done in statistical works, by comparing either different countries at different epochs, or different epochs in the same country, we find that the average level of the rent per acre, and consequently the total rental, corresponds in certain proportions (although by no means equal ones, but rather more rapidly moving ones) to the absolute, not to the relative, productivity of agriculture in a certain country, that is, to the mass of products brought forth by it on an average upon the same area. For the larger the share taken by the superior soils in the total cultivated area, the greater is the mass of products brought forth by equal investments of capital upon equally large areas of land. And the higher is the average rent per acre. In the opposite case the reverse takes place. In this way the rent does not seem to be determined by the ratios of differential fertility, but of absolute fertility, and the law of differential rent seems thereby abolished. For this rea-son certain phenomena are disputed, or perhaps they are explained by non-existing differences in the average prices of cereals and in the differential fertility of the cultivated lands, whereas such phenomena are merely due to the fact that the ratio of the total rental, either to the total area of the cultivated soil, or to the total capital invested in this soil, so long as the fertility of the rentless soil remains the same and with it the price of production, and so long as the differences of the various classes of soil remain unchanged, is determined not merely by the rent per acre or the rate of rent per capital, but quite as much by the proportional number of acres of each class of soil in the total number of cultivated acres; or, what amounts to the same, by the distribution of the invested total capital among the various classes of land. Curiously enough this fact has been completely overlooked so far. At any rate we see (and this is important for the progress of our analysis), that the relative level of the average rent per acre, and the average rate of rent (or the ratio of the total rental to the total capital invested in the soil), may rise or fall, through the mere extensive expansion of cultivation, while prices remain the same, the differential fertilities of the various soils remain unaltered, and the rent per acre is constant, or while the rate of rent for the capital invested per acre in every actual rent paying class of soil, or for every rent paying capital, remains unchanged.

We have to make the following additional remarks with reference to the form I of the differential rent, which also apply partly to form II:

1) We have seen that the average rent per acre, or the average rate of rent per capital, may rise with an extension of cultivation, with stationary prices, and unaltered differ-

ential fertilities of the cultivated lands. As soon as all the land in a certain country has been appropriated, while the investment of capital in land, the cultivation of the soil, and the population, have reached a certain level — all of which conditions are matters of fact as soon as the capitalist mode of production becomes the prevailing one and invades also agriculture — the price of the uncultivated soil of various classes (assuming differential rent to exist) is determined by the price of the cultivated lands of the same quality and equivalent location. The price is the same — after deducting the cost of breaking the ground — although this soil does not carry any rent. The price of the land is, indeed, nothing but the capitalised rent. But even in the case of cultivated lands their price pays only future rents, as for instance, when the regulating rate of interest is 5% and the rent for twenty years is paid in advance at one time. When land is sold, it is sold as a rent paying land, and the prospective character of the rent (which is here considered as a fruit of the soil, which it is only seemingly) does not distinguish the uncultivated from the cultivated soil. The price of the uncultivated lands, like their rent, which it represents as though it were its contracted formula, is quite illusory, so long as the land is not actually used. But it is thus determined beforehand and realised as soon as a purchaser is found. Hence, while the actual average rent of a certain land is determined by its real average rental per year and by its proportion to the entire cultivated area, the price of the uncultivated portions of land is determined by that of the cultivated land, and is therefore but a reflex of the capital invested in cultivated land and of the results obtained by such investments. Since all lands with the exception of the worst carry rent (and this rent, as we shall see under the head of differential rent II, rises with the mass of the capital and the corresponding intensity of cultivation), the nominal price of the uncultivated portions of the soil is thus formed, and thus they become commodities, a source of wealth for their owners. This explains at the same time, why the price of land increases in the whole region, even in the uncultivated part (Opdyke). The speculation in land, for instance in the United States, rests merely upon this reflex, which capital and labor throw on the uncultivated land.

2) The advance in the extension of the cultivated soil in general takes place either toward inferior soil, or upon the various existing soils in different proportions according to the way in which they present themselves. The step toward inferior soil naturally is never made voluntarily, but cannot be due to anything but to rising prices (assuming the capitalist mode of production to be a fact), and under any mode of production it will be a result of necessity. However, this is not absolutely so. An inferior soil is preferred to a relatively better soil on account of its location, which decides the point during all extension of cultivation in new countries; furthermore for the reason that, while the formation of the soil in a certain region may belong to the superior ones, the better will nevertheless be relieved here and there by inferior soil, so that the inferior soil must be cultivated along with the superior on account of its location. If inferior soil is surrounded by superior soil, then the better soil gives to the poorer soil the advantage of location as against other and more fertile soil, which is not connected with the already cultivated soil, or with soil about to be cultivated.

In this way the state of Michigan was one of the first to export corn. Yet its soil is on the whole poor. But its vicinity to the state of New York and its water routes by lakes and by the Erie Canal gave to it the advantage before the naturally more fertile states which were farther west. The example of this state, as compared to the state of New York, shows us also the transition from superior to inferior soil. The soil of the state of New York, particularly the western portion of it, is far more fertile, particularly in the raising of wheat. This fertile soil was made sterile by robbing it, and now the soil of Michigan appeared as the more fertile.

"In 1836 wheat flour was shipped from Buffalo to the West, principally from the wheat belt of New York and Canada. At present, only 12 years later, enormous supplies

of wheat and flour are brought from the West, by way of
Lake Erie, and shipped East upon the Erie Canal, in Buffalo
and the neighboring port of Blackrock.   The export of wheat
and flour was particularly stimulated by the European fam-
ine in 1847.   The wheat in western New York thus became
cheaper, and the raising of wheat less profitable; this caused
the New York farmers to throw themselves more upon cattle
raising and dairying, fruit growing, etc., lines in which the
Northwest, in their opinion, will be unable to compete with
them directly."   (J. W. Johnston, *Notes on North America*,
London, 1851, I, p. 222.)

3) It is a mistaken assumption that the land in colonies,
and in new countries generally, which can export cereals at
cheaper prices, must for that reason be necessarily of a greater
natural fertility.   The cereals are not only sold below their
value in such cases, but below their price of production,
namely below the price of production determined by the rate
of profit in the older countries.

The fact that we, as Johnston says (p. 223) " are accustomed to connect with these new states, which ship annually
such large supplies of wheat to Buffalo, the idea of great
natural fertility and endless stretches of rich soil," depends
primarily upon economic conditions.   The entire population
of such a country, for instance of Michigan, is at first almost
exclusively engaged in agriculture, and particularly in producing agricultural goods in large masses, which they can alone
exchange for products of industry and tropical goods.   The
whole surplus product of this population appears, therefore,
in the shape of cereals.   This distinguishes from the outset
the colonial states founded on the basis of the modern world
market from those of former, particularly of antique, times.
They receive from the world market finished products, which
they would have to make themselves under different circumstances, such as clothing, tools, etc.   Only on such a basis
were the southern states of the Union enabled to make of cotton their staple product.   The division of labor upon the
world market permitted this.   Hence, if they seem to produce a large surplus product in spite of their youth and small

relative population, it is not due to the fertility of their soil, nor to the productivity of their labor, but to the onesided form of their labor, and therefore of the surplus product, in which this labor is incorporated.

Furthermore, a relatively inferior soil, which is newly cultivated and was never touched by civilisation before, has accumulated much easily soluble plant food, at least in its upper layers, provided the climatic conditions are not extremely hard, so that it will yield crops without any manure for a long time, even with very superficial cultivation. The western prairies have the additional advantage of requiring hardly any expenses for clearing, since nature has cleared them herself.[126] In less fertile districts of this kind a surplus is produced, not through the great fertility of the soil or the yield per acre, but through the large number of acres, which may be superficially cultivated, because this soil costs the cultivator little or nothing compared with older countries. For instance, where share farming exists, as it does in certain parts of New York, Michigan, Canada, etc., there this condition is found. A family cultivates superficially, say, 100 acres, and although the product per acre is not large, the product of 100 acres yields a considerable surplus for sale. In addition to this cattle may be kept on natural pastures for almost nothing, without any artificial grass meadows. It is the quantity, not the quality of the soil, which decides the point here. The possibility of this superficial cultivation is naturally more or less rapidly exhausted, in a reverse ratio to the fertility of the new soil, and in a direct ratio to the export of its products. " And yet such a country will yield excellent harvests, even of wheat; whoever skims the first cream off the soil, will be able to ship an

---

[126] [It is precisely the rapidly growing cultivation of such prairie or steppe districts which of late turns the renowned statement of Malthus, that the population " presses upon the means of subsistence," into ridicule, and has created the reverse of it in the complaints of the agrarians, who wail that agriculture and with it Germany will be ruined, unless the means of subsistence which are pressing upon the population are kept out by force. The cultivation of these steppes, prairies, pampas, llanos, etc., is only in its beginnings; its revolutionising effect on European agriculture will, therefore, make itself felt later on even more than hitherto. — F. E.]

abundant surplus of wheat to the market" (L. c., p. 224). In countries of older civilisation the property relations, the determination of the price of the uncultivated soil by that of the cultivated, etc., make such an extensive economy impossible.

That this soil does not have to be very rich, as Ricardo imagines, nor soils of equal fertility have to be cultivated, may be seen from the following: In the state of Michigan 465,900 acres were planted in 1848 with wheat and produced 4,739,300 bushels, or an average of $10\frac{1}{5}$ bushels per acre; deducting the seed grain this leaves less than 9 bushels per acre. Of the 29 counties of this state 2 produced an average of 7 bushels, 3 an average of 8 bushels, 2 one of 9, 7 one of 10, 6 one of 11, 3 one of 12, 4 one of 13 bushels, and only one county produced an average of 16 bushels, and another of 18 bushels per acre (L. c., p. 226).

In practical agriculture a higher fertility of the soil coincides with a greater immediate utilisation of this fertility. This may be greater in a naturally poor soil than in a naturally rich one; but it is the kind of soil which a colonist will take up first, and must take up from lack of capital.

4) The extension of cultivation to greater areas — aside from the case just mentioned, in which recourse must be had to inferior soil than that hitherto cultivated — upon the various classes of soil from A to D, for instance, the cultivation of larger tracts of B and C, does not presuppose by any means a previous rise of the prices of cereals, any more than the annually increasing expansion, for instance of cotton spinning, presupposes a continual rise in the price of yarn. Although a considerable rise or fall of market prices affects the volume of production, nevertheless, aside from this, that relative overproduction which is in itself identical with accumulation always takes place even with average prices, whose stand has neither a paralysing nor an exceptionally stimulating effect upon production. This takes place in agriculture as well as in all other capitalistically managed lines of production. Under different modes of production, this relative overproduction is effected directly

by the increase of population, and in colonies by continual immigration. The demand increases constantly, and in anticipation of this new capital is continually invested in new land, although the products of this land will vary according to circumstances. It is the formation of new capitals, which in itself brings this about. But so far as the individual capitalist is concerned, he measures the volume of his production by that of his available capital, to the extent that he himself can still superintend it. What he aims at is to occupy as much room as possible on the market. If there is any overproduction, he does not blame himself, but his competitors. The individual capitalist may expand his production by appropriating a larger aliquot share of the existing market, or by expanding the market itself.

CHAPTER XL.

THE SECOND FORM OF DIFFERENTIAL RENT.

(*Differential Rent II.*)

So far we have considered differential rent only as the result of the different productivity of different investments of capital upon equal areas of land with different fertilities, so that the differential rent was determined by the difference between the yield of the capital invested in the worst, rentless, soil and that of the capital invested in the superior soils, Here we had the invested capitals side by side upon different areas of land, so that every new investment of capital signified a more extensive cultivation of the soil, an expansion of the cultivated area. But in the last analysis the differential rent was by its nature merely the result of the different productivity of equal capitals invested in land.

But could it make any difference, perhaps, whether masses of capital of different productivities are invested successively on the same piece of land, or side by side on different pieces of land, provided that the results are the same?

In the first place, it cannot be denied that it is immaterial, so far as the formation of surplus profit is concerned, whether 3 pounds sterling of cost of production are invested in one acre of A and yield one-quarter of wheat, so that 3 pounds sterling are the price of production and regulating market price of 1 quarter, while 3 pounds sterling of cost of production applied to one acre of B give 2 quarters, and with them a surplus profit of 3 pounds sterling, while in the same way 3 pounds sterling of cost of production applied to one acre of C give 3 quarters and 6 pounds sterling of surplus profit, and finally 3 pounds sterling of cost of production applied to one acre of D give 4 quarters and 9 pounds sterling of surplus profit; or whether the same result is accomplished by applying these 12 pounds sterling of cost of production, or 10 pounds sterling of capital, with the same results and in the same succession upon one and the same acre. It is in either case a capital of 10 pounds sterling, a part of whose successively invested shares of a value of $2\frac{1}{2}$ pounds sterling each, whether invested in four acres of different fertility side by side, or successively upon one and the same acre, does not yield any surplus profit on account of their different products, whereas the other parts yield a surplus profit in proportion to the difference of their yield from that of the rentless investment.

The surplus profits and the various rates of surplus profit for different parts of the value of capital are formed in the same way in either case. And the rent is nothing but a form of this surplus profit, which constitutes its substance. But at any rate, there are some difficulties in this second method in the way of the transformation of surplus profit into rent, of this change of form, which implies the transfer of the surplus profit from the capitalist tenant to the owner of the land. This accounts for the obstinate resistance of the English tenants to an official statistics of agriculture. It accounts for the struggle between them and the landlords over the ascertainment of the actual results of an investment of capital (Morton). For the rent is fixed when the lease for the land is made out, and after that the surplus profits arising from excessive investments of capital flow into the pockets of the tenant so long as the lease lasts. Therefore the tenants fought for long leases, and on the other hand the landlords enforced by their superior numbers an increase of the tenancies at will, which could be cancelled annually.

It is evident from the outset that even though it is immaterial for the law forming the surplus profit, whether equal capitals are invested with unequal results side by side upon equal areas of land, or whether they are invested successively on the same land, it does make a considerable difference for the conversion of surplus profit into ground-rent. The latter method confines this conversion within boundaries, which are narrower on one side and less definite on the other. For this reason the business of the tax assessor, as Morton shows in his "*Resources of Estates,*" becomes a very important, complicated and difficult profession in countries with an intensive cultivation (and economically we mean by intensive cultivation nothing else but the concentration of capital upon the same piece of land, instead of its distribution over adjoining pieces of land). If the improvements of the soil are of the more permanent kind, the artificially raised differential fertility of the soil coincides with its natural fertility as soon as the lease expires, and this leads to the assessment of the rent by the basis of that which is due to the mere differences of fertility in different soils generally. On the other hand, so far as the formation of surplus profit is determined by the magnitude of the working capital, the amount of the rent paid by a certain amount of capital is added to the average rent of the country and care is taken that the new tenant commands sufficient capital to continue cultivation in the same intensive manner.

In the study of differential rent II, the following points must be noted:

1) Its basis and point of departure, not merely historically, but even as concerns its movements at any given period, is differential rent I, that is the simultaneous cultivation side

by side of soils of different fertility and location; in other
words the simultaneous application, side by side, of different
portions of the total agricultural capital upon soil areas of
different quality.

Historically this is a matter of course. In colonies the
colonists have but little capital to invest. The principal
agents of production are labor and land. Every individual
head of a family seeks to acquire for himself and his, an independent field of employment, apart from that of his fellow
colonists. This must be generally the case even under precapitalist modes of production in agriculture proper. In the
case of sheep pastures, and generally of cattle raising as an
independent line of production, the exploitation of the soil
is more or less collective, and it is extensive from the outset.
The capitalist mode of production starts out from former
modes of production, in which the means of production are
actually or legally the property of the tiller himself, in which
agriculture is carried on by professionals. Naturally this
mode of agriculture gives way but gradually to the concentration of means of production and their transformation into
capital with a simultaneous change of direct producers into
wage workers. So far as the capitalist mode of production
asserts itself here in a typical manner, it does so at first
mainly in sheep pastures and cattle raising; after that it
does not assert itself by a concentration of capital upon a relatively small area of land, but in production on a larger
scale, so that the expense of keeping horses and other costs
of production may be saved; but in fact not by investing
more capital in the same land. It is furthermore in the nature of field tillage that capital, which implies at this stage
also the means of production already produced, should become the dominating element of agriculture, when cultivation
has reached a certain hight and the soil has become correspondingly exhausted. So long as the tilled land constitutes
a small area compared to the untilled, and so long as the
strength of the soil has not been exhausted (and this is the
case so long as cattle raising prevails with meat as the staple
food, before agriculture proper and plant food have become

dominant), the beginnings of the new mode of production show their opposition to peasants' economy mainly by large tracts of land which are tilled for the account of some capitalist, in other words, the new mode of production itself starts out with an extensive application of capital to larger areas of land. It should therefore be remembered from the outset, that differential rent No. I is the historical basis from which a start is made. On the other hand, the movement of differential rent No. II puts in its appearance at any given moment only upon a territory, which is itself but the variegated basis of differential rent No. I.

2) In differential rent No. II, the differences in the distribution of capital (and of the ability to get credit) among tenants are added to the differences in fertility. In manufacture proper, each line of business rapidly develops its own minimum volume of business and a corresponding minimum of capital, below which no individual business can be carried on successfully. In the same way each line of business develops, above this minimum, a normal size of capital, which the mass of producers must be able to command and do command. Whatever exceeds this, can form extra profits; whatever is below this, does not get the average profit. The capitalist mode of production invades agriculture but slowly and unevenly, as may be seen in England, the classic land of the capitalist mode of production in agriculture. To the extent that no free importation of cereals exists, or that its effect is but limited, because its volume is small, the producers working upon inferior soil and thus with worse than average conditions of production determine the market price. A large portion of the total mass of capital invested in husbandry and available for it is in their hands.

It is true that the farmer spends much labor on his small plot of land. But it is labor isolated from the objective social and material conditions of productivity, labor robbed and stripped of these conditions.

This circumstance makes it possible for the real capitalist tenants to appropriate a portion of the surplus profit; this would not be so, at least so far as this point is concerned, if

the capitalist mode of production were as uniformly developed in agriculture as in manufacture.

Let us first consider the formation of surplus profit in
differential rent No. II, without taking notice for the present
of the conditions under which the conversion of this surplus
profit into ground rent may take place.

It is evident, in that case, that differential rent No. II is
but a different expression of differential rent No. I, but that
it coincides with it in substance. The different fertility of
the various kinds of soil exerts its influence in the case of
differential rent No. I only to the extent that it brings about
unequal results of the capitals invested in the soil, so that
the products of equal capitals, or of equal aliquot parts of
unequal capitals, are unequal. Whether this inequality takes
place for different capitals invested successively in the same
land, or for capitals invested in various tracts of different
classes of soil, cannot alter anything in the differences of
fertility, or in the differences of their products, nor in the
formation of the differential rent for the more productively
invested parts of capital. It is still the soil which shows
different fertilities with the same investment of capitals, only
that in this case the same soil does for a capital successively
invested in different portions what different kinds of soil do
in the case of differential rent No. I for various equally large
portions of social capital invested in them.

If the same capital of 10 pounds sterling, which is shown
by Table I to be invested in the shape of separate capitals
of 2½ pounds sterling by different tenants in one acre of each
of the soils A, B, C and D, were invested successively in one
and the same acre D, so that its first investment yielded 4
quarters, the second 3 quarters, the third 2 quarters and the
fourth 1 quarter (or vice versa), then the price of the 1 quarter, which is furnished by the least productive capital, namely
the price of 3 pounds sterling, would not pay any differential
rent, but would determine the price of production, so long as
the supply of wheat with a price of production of 3 pounds
sterling would be needed. And since our assumption is that the
capitalist mode of production prevails, so that the price of 3

pounds sterling includes the average profit made by a capital of
2½ pounds sterling generally, the other three portions of capital
of 2½ pounds sterling each will make surplus profits according to the difference of their product, since this product is not
sold at their own price of production, but at the price of production of the least productive investment of 2½ pounds sterling, which does not pay any rent and whose price of production is determined by the general law of prices of production.
The formation of the surplus profits would be the same as in
Table I.

We see here once more that differential rent No. II is conditioned upon differential rent No. I. The minimum product raised by a capital of 2½ pounds sterling upon the worst
soil is here assumed to be 1 quarter. Take it then that the
tenant using soil of class D invests in this same soil, aside
from the 2½ pounds sterling which raise 4 quarters and pay
a differential rent of 3 quarters, still another capital of 2½
pounds sterling, which raise only 1 quarter, like the same
capital upon the worst soil A. This would be a rentless investment, which would pay him only the average profit.
There would be no surplus profit, which could be converted
into rent. On the other hand, this decreasing yield of the
second investment of capital in D would not have any influence on the rate of profit. It would be the same as though
2½ pounds sterling had been invested in another acre of the
soil of class A, a circumstance which would in no way affect
the surplus profit, nor for that reason the differential rent
of the classes A, B, C, and D. But for the tenant this additional investment of 2½ pounds sterling in D would have
been quite as profitable as the investment of the original 2½
pounds sterling had been per acre of D, according to our assumption, although this had raised 4 quarters. Furthermore,
if two other investments of 2½ pounds sterling each should
yield an additional product of 3 quarters and 2 quarters respectively, another decrease would have taken place compared
with the product of the first investment of 2½ pounds sterling in D, which amounted to 4 quarters and paid a surplus
profit of 3 quarters. But it would be merely a decrease in

the amount of surplus profit, and would not affect either the average profit or the regulating price of production. It would have such an effect only if the additional production yielding this decreasing surplus profit should make the production upon A superfluous and throw class A out of cultivation. In that case the decreasing fertility of the additional investments of capital in class D would be accompanied by a fall of the price of production, for instance from 3 pounds sterling to $1\frac{1}{2}$ pounds sterling, and the class B would become the rentless regulator of the market price.

The product of D would not be $4 + 1 + 3 + 2 = 10$ quarters, whereas it was only 4 quarters formerly. But the price per quarter as regulated by B would have fallen to $1\frac{1}{2}$ pounds sterling. The difference between D and B would be $10 - 2 = 8$ quarters, at $1\frac{1}{2}$ pounds sterling per quarter, or 12 pounds sterling, whereas the money rent in D used to be 9 pounds sterling. This should be noted. Calculated per acre, the amount of the rent would have risen by $33\frac{1}{3}\%$ in spite of the decreasing rate of the surplus profits on the two additional capitals of $2\frac{1}{2}$ pounds sterling each.

We see by this to what highly complicated combinations differential rent in general, and particularly form II coupled with form I, may give rise, whereas Ricardo, for instance, treats it very onesidedly and as a simple matter. One may meet, as in the above case, with a fall of the regulating market price and at the same time with a rise of the rent upon superior soils, so that both the absolute product and the absolute surplus product grow. (In differential rent No. I, in a descending line, the relative surplus product and thus the rent per acre may increase, although the absolute surplus product per acre may remain constant or even decrease.) But at the same time the fertility of the investments of capital made successively in the same soil decreases, although a large portion of them falls upon the superior lands. From a certain point of view — both as concerns the product and the prices of production — the productivity of labor has risen. But from another point of view it has decreased, because the rate of surplus profit and the surplus product per acre decrease for the various investments of capital in the same soil.

Differential rent No. II, with a decreasing fertility of the successive investments of capital, would be necessarily accompanied with a rise of the price of production and an absolute decrease of the productivity only in the case that these investments of capital could be made on none but the worst soil A. If one acre of A, which raised with an investment of a capital of $2\frac{1}{2}$ pounds sterling 1 quarter at a price of production of 3 pounds sterling, should raise only a total of $1\frac{1}{2}$ quarters with an additional investment of $2\frac{1}{2}$ pounds sterling, or a total investment of 5 pounds sterling, then the price of production of this $1\frac{1}{2}$ quarter would be 6 pounds sterling, or that of one quarter 4 pounds sterling. Every decrease of the productivity with a growing investment of capital would imply a relative decrease of the product per acre in such a case, whereas it would signify only a decrease of the surplus product upon superior soils.

The nature of the matter will carry with it the fact that with the development of intensive culture, i. e., with successive investments of capital upon the same soil, mainly the superior soils will show this tendency, or will show it to a greater degree. (We are not speaking now of permanent improvements, by which a hitherto useless soil is converted into useful soil.) The decreasing fertility of the successive investments of capital must, therefore, have principally the effect indicated above. The better soil is chosen, because it offers the best prospects that the capital invested in it will be profitable, since this soil contains the greater quantity of the useful elements of fertility, which need but be utilised.

When after the abolition of the corn laws the cultivation in England was made still more intensive, a great deal of the former wheat land was used for other purposes, particularly for cattle pastures, while the tracts best adapted to wheat and fertile were drained and otherwise improved. The capital for wheat culture was thus concentrated into a more limited area.

In this case — and all possible surplus rates between the highest surplus product of the best soil and the product of the rentless soil A coincide here, not with a relative, but with an absolute increase of the surplus product per acre — the newly formed surplus profit (eventually rent) does not represent a portion of a former average profit converted into rent (not a portion of the product in which the average profit formerly incorporated itself) but an additional surplus profit, which converted itself out of this form into rent.

Only in the case in which the demand for cereals would increase to such an extent, that the market price would rise above the price of production of A, so that for this reason the surplus product of A, B, or any other class of soil could be supplied only at a higher price than 3 pounds sterling, would the decrease of the results of an additional investment of capital in A, B, C and D be accompanied by a rise of the price of production and of the regulating market price. To the extent that this would last for a certain length of time without calling forth the cultivation of additional soil (which should be at least of the quality of A), or without bringing on a cheaper supply through other circumstances, wages would rise in consequence of the dearness of bread, other circumstances remaining the same, and the rate of profit would fall accordingly. In this case it would be immaterial, whether the increased demand would be satisfied by drawing upon inferior soil than A, or by additional investments of capital, no matter upon which of the four classes of soil. Differential rent would then rise in connection with a falling rate of profit.

This one case, in which the decreasing fertility of additional capitals invested in already cultivated soils may lead to an increase of the price of production, a fall in the rate of profit, and a formation of higher differential rents — for this rent would rise under the given circumstances upon all classes of soil just as though inferior soil than A were regulating the market — has been stamped by Ricardo as the only case, the normal case, to which he reduces the entire formation of differential rent No. II.

This would also be the case, if only the class A of soils were cultivated, and if successive investments of capital upon it were not accompanied by a proportional increase of the product.

Here then differential rent No. I is entirely lost sight of when analysing differential rent No. II.

With the exception of this case, in which the supply from the cultivated classes of soil is insufficient, so that the market price stands continually higher than the price of production, until new soil of an inferior character is taken under cultivation in addition to the others, or until the total product of the additional capitals invested in the various classes of soil can be supplied only at a higher price of production than the hitherto customary one, with the exception of this case the proportional decrease in the productivity of the additional capitals leaves the regulating price of production and the rate of profit unchanged. For the rest three cases are possible.

a) If the additional capital upon any one of the classes of soil A, B, C or D yields only the rate of profit determined by the price of production of A, then no surplus profit, and therefore no rent, is formed, any more than there would be, if additional soil of the A class had been cultivated.

b) If the additional capital yields a larger product, then a new surplus profit (potential rent) is, of course, formed, provided the regulating price remains the same. This is not necessarily the case, namely it is not the case when this additional production throws the soil A out of cultivation and thus out of the succession of the competing soils. In this case the regulating price of production falls. The rate of profit would rise, if a fall in wages were connected with this, or if the cheaper product were to enter into the constant capital as one of its elements. If the increased productivity of the additional capital had taken place upon the best soils C and D, it would depend entirely upon the degree of the increased productivity and the mass of the additional capitals to what extent a formation of increased surplus profit (and thus increased rent) would be connected with the fall in prices and the rise of the rate of profit. This rate may also rise without a fall in wages, by a cheapening of the elements of constant capital.

c) If the additional investment of capital takes place with decreasing surplus profits, but in such a way that the product of such additional investment still leaves a surplus above the product of the same capital in A, a new formation of surplus profits takes place under all circumstances, unless the increased supply throws the soil A out of cultivation. This new formation of surplus profit may take place simultaneously upon all four soils, D, C, B and A. But if the worst soil A is crowded out of cultivation, then the regulating price of production falls, and it will depend upon the proportion between the reduced price of 1 quarter and the increased number of quarters yielding a surplus profit, whether the surplus profit expressed in money, and consequently the differential rent, shall rise or fall. But at any rate we meet here with the peculiarity, that in spite of decreasing surplus profits of successive investments of capital the price of production may fall, instead of rising, as it seems it ought to do at first sight.

These additional investments of capital with decreasing surplus products correspond entirely to the case, in which four new and separate capitals would be invested in soils having a fertility ranging between A and B, B and C, C and D, for instance four capitals of $2\frac{1}{2}$ pounds sterling each and yielding $1\frac{1}{2}$, $2\frac{1}{3}$, $2\frac{2}{3}$, and 3 quarters respectively. Surplus profits (potential rents) would form upon all these kinds of soil for all four additional capitals, although the rate of surplus profit, compared with the surplus profit of the same investment of capital, on the corresponding better soil, would have decreased. And it would be immaterial, whether these four capitals were invested in D, etc., or distributed between D and A.

We now come to one essential difference between the two forms of differential rent.

With a constant price of production and constant differences, the rental and the average rent per acre, or the average rent per capital, may rise under differential rent No. I. But the average is a mere abstraction. The actual amount of the rent, calculated per acre or per capital, remains the same here.

On the other hand, under the same conditions, the amount of the rent calculated per acre may rise, although the rate of rent, measured by the invested capital, remains the same. Let us assume that production is doubled by the investment of 5 pounds sterling in each of the soils A, B, C and D instead of $2\frac{1}{2}$ pounds sterling, a total of 20 pounds sterling instead of 10 pounds sterling, with the relative fertilities unchanged. This would be the same as though 2 acres instead of 1 were being cultivated, with the same cost, on each one of these classes of soil. The rate of profit would remain the same, also its ratio to the surplus profit or the rent. But if A were raising 2 quarters now, and B, 4, C, 6, D, 8, the price of production would nevertheless remain at 3 pounds sterling per quarter because this increment is not due to a doubled fertility of the same capital, but to the same proportional fertility of a doubled capital. The two quarters of A would now cost 6 pounds sterling, just as one quarter used to cost 3 pounds sterling. The profit would have doubled on all four classes of soils, but only because the invested capital did. But in the same proportion the rent would also have become doubled. It would now be two quarters for B instead of one, four for C instead of two, and six for D instead of three. And corresponding to this the money rent for B, C, and D would now be 6 pounds sterling, 12 pounds sterling, and 18 pounds sterling respectively. Like the product per acre, so the rent in money per acre would be doubled, and consequently the price of the land also, in which this rent is capitalised. If calculated in this manner, the amount of the rent in grain and money rises, and thus the price of land, because the standard by which the calculation is made, the acre, is a tract of a constant magnitude. On the other hand, calculating it as the rate of rent on the invested capital, no change has taken place in the proportional amount of the rent. The total rental of 36 is proportioned to the invested capital of 20 as the rental of 18 was proportioned to the invested capital of 10. The same holds good for the ratio of the money rent of all classes of soil to the capital invested in them, for instance, 12 pounds sterling of rent in C are proportioned to 5 pounds sterling of capital, as 6 pounds sterling of rent used to be proportioned to $2\frac{1}{2}$ pounds sterling of capital. No new differences arise here between the invested capitals, but new surplus profits arise, because the additional capital is invested in one of the rent paying soils, or in all of them, with the same proportional product. If this double investment were made only in one of these soils, for instance in C, the differential rent, calculated per capital, would remain the same between C, B, and D. For while its mass is doubled in C, so is the invested capital.

This shows that the amount of rent in products and money, and with it the price of the land, may rise while the price of production, the rate of profit, and the differences of fertility remain unchanged (and with them remain unchanged the rate of surplus profit or the rent, calculated on the capital).

The same may take place with decreasing rates of surplus profits and of rent, that is, with a decreasing productivity of the rent paying additional investments of capital. If the second investments of capital of $2\frac{1}{2}$ pounds sterling had not doubled the product, but B would raise only $3\frac{1}{2}$ quarters, C, 5 quarters, and D, 6 quarters, then the differential rent for the second capital of $2\frac{1}{2}$ pounds sterling in B would be only $\frac{1}{2}$ quarter instead of one quarter, in C, one quarter instead of two, and in D, two quarters instead of three. The proportions between rent and capital for the two successive investments would then be as follows:

First Investment	Second Investment
B: Rent 3 p/st., Capital 2 1 2 p st.	Rent 1 1 2 p/st., Capital 2 1/2 p/st.
C: Rent 6 p/st., Capital 2 1 2 p st.	Rent 3 p/st., Capital 2 1/2 p/st.
D: Rent 9 p st., Capital 2 1 2 p st.	Rent 6 p/st., Capital 2 1/2 p/st.

In spite of this decreased rate of the relative productivity of capital and thus of surplus profit, calculated per capital, the rent in grain and money would have risen in B from one to one and a half quarter (from 3 to $4\frac{1}{2}$ pounds sterling), in C, from two quarters to three (from 6 pounds sterling to 9 pounds sterling), and in D, from three quarters to five (from

9 pounds sterling to 15 pounds sterling)'. In this case the
differences for the additional capitals, compared with the
capital invested in A, would have decreased, the price of production would have remained the same, but the rent per acre,
and consequently the price of the land per acre, would have
risen.

The combinations of differential rent No. II, which are
conditioned upon differential rent·No. I as their basis, are
analysed in the following chapters.

CHAPTER XLI.

DIFFERENTIAL RENT II.— FIRST CASE: CONSTANT PRICE OF PRODUCTION.

THIS assumption implies that the market price is regulated
the same as ever by the capital invested in the worst soil A.

1) If the additional capital invested in any one of the rent
paying soils B, C, D produces no more than the same capital
upon the soil A, in other words, if it pays only the average
profit by means of the regulating price of production, but no
surplus profit, then the effect upon the rent is nil. Everything remains as it is. It is the same as though any number
of acres of the A quality, of the worst soil, had been added to
the cultivated area.

2) The additional capital brings forth upon every one of
the different soils additional products proportional to their
magnitude; in other words, the volume of production grows
according to the specific fertility of every class of soil, in proportion to the magnitude of the additional capital. We
started out in chapter XXXIX from the following Table I:

Class of Soil	Acres	Capital P/st.	Profit P/st.	Cost of Prod. P/st.	Prod-uct Qrs.	Selling Price P/st.	Yield	Rent Qrs.	Rent P/st.	Rate of Surplus Profit
A	1	2 1/2	1/2	3	1	3	3			0%
B	1	2 1/2	1/2	3	2	3	6	1	3	12%
C	1	2 1/2	1/2	3	3	3	9	2	6	24%
D	1	2 1/2	1/2	3	4	3	12	3	9	36%
Totals	4	10		12	10		30	6	18	

This table is now transformed into *Table II.*

Class of Soil	Acres	Capital P. st.	Profit P. st.	Cost of Prodc'n P. st.	Prod-uct Qrs.	Selling Price P. St.	Yield	Rent		Rate of Surplus Profit
								Qrs.	P.st	
A	1	2 1/2 + 2 1/2 = 5	1	6	2	3	6			
B	1	2 1/2 + 2 1/2 = 5	1	6	4	3	12	2	6	120%
C	1	2 1/2 + 2 1/2 = 5	1	6	6	3	18	4	12	240%
D	1	2 1/2 + 2 1/2 = 5	1	6	8	3	24	6	18	360%
Total	4	20			20		60	12	36	

It is not necessary in this case that the investment of capital should be doubled in all classes of soil, as it does in this
Table. The law is the same, so long as additional capital is
invested in one, or several, of the rent paying soils, no matter in what proportion. It is only necessary that production
should increase upon every kind of soil in the same ratio as
the capital. The rent rises here merely in consequence of an
increased investment of capital in the soil, and in proportion
to this increase. This increase of the product and of the rent
in consequence of, and proportionately to, the increased investment of capital is just the same, so far as the quantity of
the product and of the rent is concerned, as though the cultivated area of the rent paying lands of the same quality had
been increased and taken under cultivation with the same investment of capital as that previously invested in the same
classes of land. In the case of Table II, for instance, the
result would remain the same, if the additional capital of 2½
pounds sterling per acre were invested in one additional acre
each of B, C and D.

This assumption, furthermore, does not imply a more productive investment of capital, but only an investment of more
capital upon the same area with the same success as before.

All proportional relations remain the same here. True,
if we do not consider the proportional differences, but the
purely arithmetical ones, then the differential rent may
change upon the various classes of soil. Let us assume, for
instance, that the additional capital has been invested only in
B and D. In that case the difference between D and A is
7 quarters, whereas it was only 3 before; the difference between B and A is 3 quarters, whereas it was one; that be-

tween C and B is minus one, whereas it was plus one, etc. But this arithmetical difference, which is decisive in differential rent I, so far as it expresses the difference of productivity with equal investments of capital, is here quite immaterial, because it is a consequence of different additional investments, or of no additional investments, of capital, while the difference for each aliquot part of capital upon the various lands remains unchanged.

3) The additional capitals bring forth surplus products and thus form surplus profits, but at a decreasing rate, not in proportion to their increase. *Table III.*

Class of Soil	Acres	Capital P. st.	Profit P. st.	Cost of Prod'n P. st.	Product Qrs.	Sell-Price P. st.	Yield P. st.	Rent		Rate of S'rpls profit
								Qrs.	P. st.	
A	1	2½	¼	3	1	3	3	0	0	0%
B	1	2½ + 2½ = 5	1	6	2 + 1½ = 3½	3	10½	1½	4½	90%
C	1	2½ + 2½ = 5	1	6	3 + 2 = 5	3	15	3	9	180%
D	1	2½ + 2½ = 5	1	6	4 + 3½ = 7½	3	22½	5½	16½	330%
		17½	3½	21	17		51	10	30	

In the case of this third assumption it is again immaterial, whether the additional second investments of capital are uniformly distributed over the various classes of soil or not; whether the decreasing production of surplus profit proceeds in equal or unequal proportions; whether the additional investments of capital fall all of them upon the same rent paying class of soil, or whether they are distributed equally or unequally over soils of different quality paying rent. All these circumstances are immaterial for the law which we are developing here. The only premise is that additional investments of capital must yield a surplus profit upon any one of the rent paying soils, but in a decreasing ratio to the amount of the increase of capital. The limits of this decrease move in the above illustration of Table III between 4 quarters = 12 p.st., the product of the first investment of capital upon the best soil D, and 1 quarter = 3 p.st., the product of the same investment of capital upon the worst soil A. The product of the best soil on the first investment of capital forms the maximum boundary, and the product of the same investment of capital in the worst soil A, which pays no rent and yields no surplus profit, forms the minimum limit of the product, which the successive investments of capital yield upon any of the various classes of soils producing a surplus profit with successive investments of capital and a decreasing productivity. Just as assumption No. II corresponds to a condition, in which new pieces of the same quality are added to the cultivated area among the superior soils, so that the quantity of any one of the cultivated soils is increased, so assumption No. III corresponds to a condition, in which additional pieces of soil are cultivated in such a way that their various degrees of fertility are distributed among soils between D and A, among soils from the best to the worst kind. If the successive investments of capital take place exclusively upon the soil D, they may include the existing differences between D and A, likewise those between D and C and those between D and B. If all the successive investments are made upon soil C, they will comprise only differences between C and A and C and B; if made exclusively upon B, only differences between B and A.

But this is the law: **That** the rent increases absolutely upon all these classes of soil, although not in proportion to the additional capital invested.

The rate of surplus profit, considering both the additional capital and the total capital invested in the soil, decreases; but the absolute magnitude of the surplus profit increases. In like manner the decreasing rate of profit on capital in general is generally accompanied by an absolutely increasing mass of profit. Thus the average surplus profit of the investment of capital upon B amounts to 90% on the capital, whereas it amounted to 120% on the first investment of capital. But the total surplus profit increases from one quarter to one and a half quarter, or from 3 pounds sterling to $4\frac{1}{2}$ pounds sterling. Considering the total rent by itself — and not comparing it with the doubled magnitude of the advanced capital — it has risen absolutely. The differences of the rents of the various kinds of soil and their relative proportions may vary here; but this variation in the differences is here a consequence, not a cause, of the increase of the rents compared to one another.

4) The case, in which the additional investments of capital upon the superior soils bring forth a greater product than the original ones, requires no further analysis. It is a matter of course that under this assumption the rent per acre will rise, and will do so at a greater rate than the additional capital, no matter upon which kind of soil the investment may have been made. In this case the additional investment of capital is accompanied by improvements. This includes the case, in which an additional investment of less capital produces the same or a greater result than did formerly an investment of more capital. This case is not quite identical with the former one, and this is a distinction, which is important in all investments of capital. For instance, if 100 make a profit of 10, and 200, employed in a certain form, make a profit of 40, then the profit has risen from 10% to 20%, and to that extent it is the same as though 50, employed in a more effective form, make a profit of 10 instead of 5. We assume here that the profit is combined with a proportional increase of the product. But the difference is this, that I must double the capital in the one case, whereas in the other I produce the double effect by the same capital. It is by no means the same whether I bring forth the same product as before with half as much living and materialized labor, or twice the product as before with the same labor, or four times the former product with twice the labor. In the first case, labor in a living or materialised form is released, which may be employed otherwise; the power to dispose of capital and labor increases. The release of capital (and labor) is in itself an augmentation of wealth; it has just the same effect as though this additional capital had been obtained by accumulation, but it saves the labor of accumulation.

Take it that a capital of 100 has produced a product of ten yards. The 100 may include both constant capital, living labor and profit. In that case one yard costs 10. Now if I can produce 20 yards with the same capital of 100, then one yard costs 5. On the other hand, if I can produce 10 yards with a capital of 50, then one yard likewise costs 5, and a capital of 50 is released, assuming the former supply of commodities to be sufficient. Again, if I have to invest 200 of capital in order to produce 40 yards, then one yard also costs 5. The determination of the value, or price, does not indicate such differences as these, neither does the mass of products proportional to the investment of capital. But in the first case, capital is released; in the second case additional capital is saved to the extent that a duplication of production would be required; in the third case the increased product can be obtained only by an augmentation of the invested capital, although not in the same proportion as it would be if the increased product had to be supplied by the old productive power. (This belongs in Part I.)

From the point of view of capitalist production the employment of constant capital is always cheaper than that of variable capital, not where it is a question of increasing the surplus-value, but of reducing the cost price. For a saving of costs even in the element creating the surplus-value, labor, performs this service for the capitalist and makes profit for him, so long as the regulating price of production remains the same. This presupposes in fact the existence of a development of credit and of an abundance of loan capital corresponding to the capitalist mode of production. On the one hand I employ 100 pounds sterling of additional constant capital, if 100 pounds sterling are the product of five laborers during one year; on the other hand, 100 pounds sterling in variable capital. If the rate of surplus-value is 100%, then the value created by those five laborers is 200 pounds sterling; on the other hand, the value of 100 pounds sterling of constant capital is 100 pounds sterling, or perhaps 105 pounds sterling in its capacity as loan capital, if the rate of interest is 5%. The same sums of money express largely different values in product, according to whether they are advanced to production as values of constant or variable capital. Furthermore, as concerns the cost of the commodities from the point of view of the capitalist, there is also this difference that of 100 pounds sterling of constant capital only the wear and tear passes into the value of the product to the extent that this money is invested in fixed capital, whereas 100 pounds sterling invested in wages pass wholly into the values of commodities and must be reproduced in them.

In the case of colonists and of independent small producers in general, who have no command at all over capital or at least command it only at a high rate of interest, that part of the product which stands in place of wages is their revenue, whereas it constitutes an investment of capital for the capitalist. The colonist, therefore, regards this expenditure of labor as the indispensable prerequisite of his product, which is the thing that interests him first of all. As for his surplus-labor, after deducting that necessary labor, it is evidently realised in a surplus-product; and as soon as he can sell this, or even use it for himself, he looks upon it as something that cost him nothing, because it cost him no materialised labor. It is only the expenditure of materialised labor which appears to him as an outlay of wealth. Of course, he tries to sell as high as possible; but even a sale below value and below the capitalist price of production still appears to him as a profit, unless this profit is claimed beforehand by debts, mortgages, etc. But for the capitalist the investment of both variable and constant capital represents an outlay of capital. The relatively larger outlay of the capitalist reduces the cost-price, and in fact the value of commodities, provided other circumstances remain the same. Hence, although the profit arises only from surplus-labor, consequently only from the employment of variable capital, still it may seem to the individual capitalist that living labor is the most expensive element of his cost of production, which should be reduced to a minimum above all others. This is but a capitalistically distorted form of the correct view that the relatively greater use of past labor, compared to living labor, signifies an increase in the productivity of social labor and a greater social wealth. From the point of view of competition, everything appears thus distorted and inverted.

Assuming the prices of production to remain unchanged, additional investments of capital may be made with an unaltered, an increasing, or a decreasing productivity upon the better soils, that is upon all soils from B upward. Upon soil A this would be possible, under the conditions assumed by us, only in the case that productivity should remain the same, in which case this land continues to pay no rent, or in the case that productivity increases in which case a portion of the capital invested in A would produce rent, while the remainder would not. But it would be impossible, if the productivity upon A were to decrease, for in that case the price of production would not remain unchanged, but would rise. But under all these circumstances the surplus-product and the surplus-profit corresponding to it increases per acre, and with them eventually the rent, in grain or in money, regardless of whether the surplus-product yielded by them is proportional to their magnitude, or above or below this proportion, regardless of whether the rate of the surplus-profit of capital remains constant, rises or falls when this capital increases. The growth of the mere mass of surplus-profit, or of the rent calculated per acre, that is, an increasing mass calculated on the same unaltered unit, in the present case on a definite quantity of land, such as an acre or an hectare, expresses itself as an increasing ratio. Hence the magnitude of the rent, calculated per acre, increases under such circumstances simply in consequence of the increase of the capital invested in the soil. This takes place when the prices of production remain the same, no matter whether the productivity of the additional capital stays unaltered, or decreases, or increases. These last named circumstances modify the volume, in which the level of the rent per acre rises, but not the fact of this increase itself. This is a phenomenon, which is peculiar to differential rent No. II and distinguishes it from differential rent No. I. If the additional investments of capital, instead of being made successively one after another upon the same soil, were made side by side upon new additional soil of the corresponding quality, the mass of the rental would have increased, and, as previously shown, the average rent of the cul-

tivated total area would likewise have increased, but not the
size of the rent per acre.   When results remain the same so
far as the mass and value of the total production and of the
surplus product are concerned, the concentration of capital
upon a smaller area of land develops the size of the rent per
acre, whereas its distribution over a larger area, under the
same circumstances, and other circumstances remaining the
same, does not produce this effect.   But the more the capitalist mode of production develops, the more develops also the
concentration of capital upon the same area of land, and the
higher rises the rent calculated per acre.   Consequently, if
we have two countries, in which the prices of production are
identical, the differences of the various kinds of soil the same,
and the same amount of capital invested, but in such a way
that the investment is made in the form of successive outlays
upon a limited area in one country, whereas in the other
country it is made more in the shape of co-ordinated outlays
upon a wider area, then the rent per acre, and with it the
price of land, would be higher in the first and lower in the second country, although the mass of the rent would be the same
in both countries.   The difference in the size of the rent could
not be explained in such a case out of the natural fertility of
the various kinds of soil, nor out of the quantity of employed
labor, but solely out of the different ways in which the capital
is invested.

In speaking of a surplus-product in this case, we mean that
aliquot part of the product, in which the surplus-profit presents
itself.   Ordinarily we mean by surplus-product that portion
of the product, in which the total surplus-value is materialised, or in some cases that portion, in which the average profit
presents itself.   The specific significance, which this term assumes in the case of rent-paying capital, gives rise to misunderstanding, as we have shown in another place.

CHAPTER XLII.

DIFFERENTIAL RENT II.— SECOND CASE: FALLING PRICE
OF PRODUCTION.

THE price of production may fall, when the additional investments of capital take place with an unaltered, a falling, or a rising rate of productivity.

I. *The Productivity of the Additional Investment of
Capital Remains the Same.*

In this case the assumption is that the product increases in the same proportion as the capital invested in the various soils and in accordance with their respective qualities. This implies, always assuming the differences of the various soil to remain unaltered, that the surplus-product increases in proportion to the increased investment of capital. This case, then, excludes any additional investment of capital upon soil A which might affect the differential rent. Upon this soil the rate of surplus-profit is 0; it remains 0, since we have assumed that the productive power of the additional capital and therefore the rate of surplus-profit remain the same.

But under these conditions the regulating price of production can fall only, because instead of the price of production of A that of the next best soil B, or of any better soil than A, becomes the regulator; so that the capital is withdrawn from A, or perhaps from B and A, in case the price of production of C should become the regulating one and all inferior soil should be eliminated from the competition of the wheat raising soils. The prerequisite for this would be, under the assumed conditions, that the additional product of the additional investments of capital should satisfy the demand, so that the product of the inferior soils A, etc., would become superfluous for the formation of a full supply.

Take, for instance, Table II, but in such a way that 18 quarters instead of 20 will satisfy the demand. Soil A would drop out; D and its price of production of 30 shillings would become regulating. In that case the differential rent would assume the following form:

Table IV.

Soils	Acres	Capital £	Profit £	Cost of Production £	Product Quarters	Selling Price Per Quarter £	Yield	Rent		Rate of Surplus Profit
								in grain Qrs.	in money £	
B	1	5	1	6	4	1½	6	0	0	0
C	1	5	1	6	6	1½	9	2	3	60%
D	1	5	1	6	8	1½	12	4	6	120%
T'ls	3	15	3	18	18		27	6	9	

In other words, compared to Table II the ground-rent would have fallen in money from 36 pounds sterling to 9 pounds sterling and in grain from 12 quarters to 6 quarters, whereas the total output would have fallen only by 2, from 20 to 18. The rate of surplus-profit, calculated on the capital, would have fallen by one-half, from 180% to 90%. The fall of the price of production in this case is accompanied by a decrease of the rent in grain and money.

Compared to Table I there is merely a decrease in the money rent; the rent in grain in both cases is 6 quarters. But in the one case these bring 18 pounds sterling, in the other only 9 pounds sterling. So far as the soils C and D are concerned, the rent in grain compared to Table I remains the same. In fact, owing to the additional production put forth by the uniformly working additional capital, the product of A has been pushed out of the market, the soil A has been eliminated from the competition of the producing agents, and a new differential rent No. 1 has thus been formed, in which the better soil B plays the same role as formerly the inferior soil A. Consequently the rent of B disappears on the one side; on the other side nothing has been altered in the differences of B, C and D by the investment of additional capital, according to our assumption. For this reason that part of the product, which is converted into rent, is reduced.

If the above result, the satisfaction of the demand with A left out, should have been accomplished by the investment of more than double the capital upon C or D, or upon both, then the matter would assume a different aspect. Let us suppose, that a third investment of capital is made upon C.

Table IV a.

Soils	Acres	Capital £	Profit £	Cost of Production £	Product Qrs.	Selling Price £	Yield £	Rent Grain Qrs.	Rent Money £	Rate of Surplus Profit
B	1	5	1	6	4	1½	6	0	0	0
C	1	7½	1½	9	9	1½	13½	3	4½	60%
D	1	5	1	6	8	1½	12	4	6	120%
T'ls	3	17½	3½	21	21		31½	7	10½	

In this case, compared to Table IV, the product of C has risen from 6 quarters to 9, the surplus product from 2 quarters to 3, the money rent from 3 pounds sterling to 4½ pounds sterling. Compared to Table II, in which the money rent was 12 pounds sterling, and Table I, in which it was 6 pounds sterling, it has fallen off. The total rental in grain is 7 quarters. It has fallen compared to Table II, in which it was 12 quarters, but has risen compared to Table I, in which it was 6 quarters. In money the rent is 10½ pounds sterling and has fallen compared to both of the other Tables, in which it was 18 and 36 pounds sterling respectively.

If the third investment of capital, amounting to 2½ pounds sterling, had been applied to soil B, it would indeed have altered the quantity of production, but would not have touched the rent, since the successive investments, according to our assumption, do not produce any differences upon the same soil, and soil B does not produce any rent.

Again, if we assume that the third investment of capital takes place upon D instead of C, we get

Table IV b.

Sois	Acres	Capital £	Profit £	Cost of Production £	Product Qrs.	Selling Price £	Rent Yield £	Rent Qrs.	£	Rate of Surplus Profit
B	1	5	1	6	4	1½	6	0	0	0
C	1	5	1	6	6	1½	9	2	3	60%
D	1	7½	1½	9	12	1½	18	6	9	120%
T'ls	3	17½	3½	21	22		33	8	12	

Here the total product is 22 quarters, more than double that of Table I, although the invested capital is only 17½ pounds sterling as against 10 pounds sterling, in other words, not twice the size. The total product is also larger by 2 quarters than that of Table II, although the capital in it is larger, namely 20 pounds sterling.

Compared to Table I, the rent in grain upon soil D has increased from 2 quarters to 6, whereas the money rent has remained the same, 9 pounds sterling. Compared to Table II the grain rent of D is the same, namely 6 quarters, but the money rent has fallen from 18 pounds sterling to 9 pounds sterling.

Comparing the total rents, the grain rent of IV b is 8 quarters, larger than that of I which is 6 and than that of IV a which is 7 quarters; but it is smaller than that of II which is 12 quarters. The money rent of IV b, 12 pounds sterling, is larger than that of IV a, which is 10½ pounds sterling, and smaller than that of Table I, which is 18 pounds sterling and that of Table II, which is 36 pounds sterling.

In order that the total rental under the conditions of Table IV b, after the elimination of the rent upon B, may be equal to that of Table I, we need 6 pounds sterling of surplus product more, that is, 4 quarters at 1½ pounds sterling, which is the new price of production. Then we shall have once more a total rental of 18 pounds sterling, the same as in Table I. The magnitude of the required additional capital will differ, according to whether we invest it upon C or D, or distribute it between these two.

In the case of C 5 pounds sterling of capital result in a

surplus product of 2 pounds sterling, consequently 10 pounds sterling of additional capital will result in 4 quarters of additional surplus product. In the case of D 5 pounds sterling of additional capital would suffice for the purpose of producing 4 quarters of additional grain rent, under the conditions assumed here, namely that the productivity of the additional investments of capital will remain the same. We should then get the following Tables:

Table IV c.

Soils	Acres	Capital £	Profit £	Cost of Prod'n £	Product Qrs.	Selling Price £	Yield £	Qrs.	£	Rate of Surplus Profit
B	1	5	1	6	4	1½	6	0	0	0
C	1	15	3	18	18	1½	27	6	9	60%
D	1	7½	1½	9	12	1½	18	6	9	120%
T't'ls	3	27½	5½	33	34		51	12	18	

Table IV d.

Soils	Acres	Capital £	Profit £	Cost of Production £	Product Qrs.	Selling Price £	Yield £	Qrs.	£	Rate of Surplus Profit
B	1	5	1	6	4	1½	6	0	0	0
C	1	5	1	6	6	1½	9	2	3	60%
D	1	12½	2½	15	20	1½	30	10	15	120%
Totals	3	22½	4½	27	30		45	12	18	

The total money rental would be exactly one-half of what it was in Table II, where the additional capitals were invested under conditions, in which the prices of production remained the same.

The most important thing is to compare the above Tables with Table I.

We find that the total money rental has remained the same, namely 18 pounds sterling, while the price of production has fallen by one-half, from 60 shillings to 30 shillings per quarter, and that the grain rent has been correspondingly duplicated, from 6 quarters to 12. The rent upon B has disappeared; the money rent has risen by one-half in IV c, but fallen by one-half in IV d; upon D the money rent has remained the same, 9 pounds sterling, in IV c, and has risen

from 9 pounds sterling to 15 pounds sterling in IV d.   The
production has risen from 10 quarters to 34 in IV c, and to
30 quarters in IV d; the profit from 2 pounds sterling to
$5\frac{1}{2}$ pounds sterling in IV c and to $4\frac{1}{2}$ pounds sterling in IV d.
The total investment of capital has risen in one case from 10
pounds sterling to $27\frac{1}{2}$ pounds sterling, and in the other from
10 pounds sterling to $22\frac{1}{2}$ pounds sterling, in either case by
more than one-half.   The rate of rent, that is, the rent
calculated on the invested capital, is everywhere the same in
all the Tables from IV to IV d for the respective kinds of
soils, for this was implied by the assumption that every kind
of soil should retain the same rate of productivity with the
two successive investments of capital.   But compared to
Table I, this rate has fallen, both for the average of all kinds
of soil and for each one of them individually.   In Table I
it was 180% on an average, whereas in IV c it is $(18 \div$
$27\frac{1}{2}) \times 100 = 65\frac{5}{11}\%$ and in IV d it is $(18 \div 22\frac{1}{2}) \times 100$
$= 80\%$.   The average money rent per acre has risen. -
Formerly, in Table I, its average was $4\frac{1}{2}$ pounds sterling per
acre upon all four acres, whereas now, in IV c and IV d, it is
6 pounds sterling per acre upon the three acres.   Its average
upon the rent paying soil was formerly 6 pounds sterling,
whereas now it is 9 pounds sterling per acre.   Hence the
money value of the rent per acre has risen, and represents
now double the grain product that it did formerly; but the
12 quarters of grain rent are now less than one-half of the
total product of 33 and 27 quarters respectively, whereas in
Table I the 6 quarters represent $\frac{3}{5}$ths of the total product of 10
quarters.   Consequently, although the rent as an aliquot part
of the total product has fallen, and has also fallen when calculated on the invested capital yet its money-value, calculated
per acre, has risen and still more its value as a product.   If
we take soil D in Table IV d, we find that the cost of production expended in it amounts to 15 pounds sterling, of which
$12\frac{1}{2}$ pounds sterling are invested capital.   The money rent is
15 pounds sterling.   In Table I, for the same soil D, the cost
of production was 3 pounds sterling, the invested capital $2\frac{1}{4}$
pounds sterling the money rent 9 pounds sterling, that is, the

money rent amounted to three times the cost of production and almost four times the capital. In Table IV d, the money rent for D, 15 pounds sterling, is exactly equal to the cost of production and only by $\frac{1}{5}$th larger than the capital. Nevertheless the money rent per acre is two-thirds larger, namely 15 pounds sterling instead of 9 pounds sterling. In Table I the grain rent of 3 quarters constitutes three quarters of the total product of 4 quarters; in Table IV d it is 10 quarters, or one-half of the total product of 20 quarters of one acre of D. This shows that the money value and grain value of the rent per acre may rise, although it forms a smaller aliquot part of the total yield and has fallen in proportion to the invested capital.

The value of the total product in Table I is 30 pounds sterling. The rent is 18 pounds sterling, more than one-half of it. The value of the total product of IV d is 45 pounds sterling, the rent is 18 pounds sterling, or less than one-half of it.

The reason, why in spite of the fall of the price by $1\frac{1}{2}$ pounds sterling per quarter, a fall of 50%, and in spite of the reduction of the competing soil from 4 acres to 3, the total rent remains the same and the grain rent is doubled, while on a calculation per acre both the grain rent and money rent rise, is that more surplus product is created. The price of grain falls by 50%, the surplus product increases by 100%. But in order to accomplish this result, the total production under the conditions assumed by us must be trebled, and the investment of capital upon the superior soils must be more than doubled. In what proportion this last factor must increase, depends in the first place upon the distribution of the additional investments of capital among the superior and best kinds of soil, always assuming that the productivity of the capital upon every kind of soil increases proportionately to its size.

If the fall of the price of production were smaller, less additional capital would be required for the production of the same money rent. If the supply required for the purpose of throwing soil A out of cultivation — and this depends not merely upon the product per acre of A, but also upon the proportional share taken by A in the entire cultivated area — were larger, and with it also the amount of additional capital required upon better soils than A, then, other circumstances remaining the same, the money rent and the grain rent would have increased still more, although both of them would disappear upon the soil B.

If the eliminated capital of A had been 5 pounds sterling, we should have to compare Tables II and IV d: The total product would have increased from 20 quarters to 30. The money rent would be only half as large, that is, 18 pounds sterling instead of 36 pounds sterling; the grain rent would be the same, namely 12 quarters.

If a total product of 44 quarters, valued at 66 pounds sterling, could be produced upon D with a capital of $27\frac{1}{2}$ pounds sterling — corresponding to the old rate of D, 4 quarters per $2\frac{1}{2}$ pounds sterling of capital — then the total rental would once more reach the level of Table II, and we should get the following diagram:

Soils	Capital p. st.	Product quarters	Grain Rent quarters	Money Rent p. st.
B	5	4	0	0
C	5	6	3	3
D	27½	44	22	33
Totals	37½	54	25	36

The total production would be 54 quarters as against 20 quarters in Table II, and the money rent would be the same, 36 pounds sterling. But the total capital would be $37\frac{1}{2}$ pounds sterling, whereas it was 20 in Table II. The invested total capital would almost be doubled, while production would be nearly trebled; the grain rent would have been doubled, the money rent would have remained the same. Hence, if the price falls as a result of the investment of additional money-capital, while productivity remains the same, upon the better soils which pay rent, that is, all soils above A, then the total capital has a tendency not to increase in the same proportion as the production and the grain rent; so that the increase of the grain rent may offer

2Z

a compensation for the loss in money rent due to the falling price. The same law also manifests itself through the fact that the invested capital must be larger in proportion as it is more largely invested upon C than D, upon the soils paying a smaller rent rather than upon the soils paying a larger rent. The point is simply this: In order that the money rent may remain the same or rise, a certain additional quantity of surplus product must be created, and this requires less capital in proportion as the productivity of the soils yielding a surplus product is greater. If the difference between B and C, C and D were still greater, still less additional capital would be required. The proportion is determined 1) by the proportion in which the price falls, in other words, by the difference between soil B, which is not paying any rent now, and soil A, which formerly was the soil that did not pay any rent; 2) by the proportion between the differences of the better soils from B upward; 3) by the amount of newly invested additional capital, and 4) by its distribution among the different qualities of soil.

In fact, we see that this law expresses merely the same thing which we ascertained already in the case of the first illustration: When the price of production is given, no matter what may be its figure, the rent may increase in consequence of additional investments of capital. For owing to the elimination of A, we have now a new differential rent No. I with B as the worst soil and $1\frac{1}{2}$ pounds sterling per quarter as the new price of production? This applies to Tables IV as well as to Table II. It is the same law, only that we have as a basis soil B instead of A, and a price of production of $1\frac{1}{2}$ pounds sterling instead of 3 pounds sterling.

The important thing here is this: To the extent that so and so much additional capital was necessary for the purpose of withdrawing the capital from soil A and satisfying the supply without it, we find that this may be accompanied by an unaltered, a rising, or a falling rent per acre, if not upon all soils, then at least upon some and so far as the average of the cultivated lands is concerned. We have seen that the grain rent and the money rent do not maintain a uniform ratio to one another. However, it is merely due to tradition that grain rent is still playing any role at all in political economy. One might demonstrate equally well that a manufacturer can buy much more of his own yarn with his profit of 5 pounds sterling than he could formerly with a profit of 10 pounds sterling. It shows at any rate, that the landlords, when they are at the same time owners or partners of manufacturing establishments, sugar factories, distilleries, etc., may still make a considerable profit even when the money rent is falling, in their capacity as producers of their own raw materials.[127]

II. *The Rate of Productivity of the Additional Capitals Decreases.*

This does not carry anything new into the problem, in so far as the price of production may also fall in this case as in the previously considered one, when additional investments of capital upon better soils than A make the product of A superfluous and withdraw the capital from A, or lead to the employment of A for the production of other things. We have analysed this eventuality exhaustively. We have shown that in this case the rent in grain and money per acre may increase, decrease, or remain unchanged.

For the purpose of easy comparison we reproduce

[127] The above Tables IV a to IV d had to be figured over on account of an error of calculation which ran through all of them. While this did not affect the theoretical conclusions drawn from these Tables, it carried monstrous figures concerning the production per acre into them. Even these would not be objectionable on principle. In all maps showing geographical conditions in relief or giving a view of altitudes in profile it is customary to choose a much larger scale for the vertical than for the horizontal lines. Nevertheless, should any one feel that his agrarian heart is injured thereby, he is at liberty to multiply the number of acres with any figure that will satisfy him. One might also choose 10, 12, 14, 16 bushels (8 bushels = 1 quarter) per acre instead of 1, 2, 3, 4 quarters in Table I, and in that case the figures of the other Tables which are developed out of them would remain within the limits of probability; it will be found that the result, the proportion of increase in the rent compared to the increase in capital, comes to the same thing. This has been done in the following Tables, which were added by the editor.— F. E.

Table I.

Soils	Acres	Capital P. St.	Product P. St.	Cost of Production per Quarter	Product Qrs.	Grain Rent Qrs.	Money Rent P. St.	Rate of Surplus Profit
A	1	2½	½	3	1	0	0	0
B	1	2½	½	1½	2	1	3	120%
C	1	2½	½	1	3	2	6	240%
D	1	2½	½	¾	4	3	9	360%
Totals	4	10			10	6	18	180% Average

Now let us assume that the figure of 16 quarters, supplied by B, C, D, with a decreasing rate of productivity, suffices to throw A out of cultivation. In that case Table III is transformed into the following

Table V.

Soils	Acres	Capital P. St	Profit P. St.	Product quarters	Selling Price P. St	Yield P. St.	Grain Rent Qrs.	Money Rent P. St.	Rate of Surplus Profit
B	1	2½+2½	1	2+1½= 3½	1 5/7	6	0	0	0
C	1	2½+2½	1	3+2 = 5	1 5/7	8 4/7	1 1/2	2 4/7	51 2/5%
D	1	2½+2½	1	4+3½= 7½	1 5/7	12 6/7	4	6 6,7	187 1/5%
Totals	3	15		16		27 3/7	5 1/2	9 3,7	Average 94 3/10

Here the rate of productivity of the additional capitals is decreasing, and the decrease is different upon different soils, while the regulating price of production has fallen from 3 pounds sterling to $1\frac{5}{7}$ pounds sterling. The investment of capital has risen by one-half, from 10 pounds sterling to 15 pounds sterling. The money rent has fallen by almost one-half, from 18 pounds sterling to $9\frac{3}{7}$ pounds sterling, while the grain rent has fallen only by one-twelfth, from 6 quarters to $5\frac{1}{2}$ quarters. The total product has risen from 10 to 16, or by 160%. The grain rent constitutes a little more than one-third of the total product. The advanced capital has a ratio of 15 to $9\frac{3}{7}$ to the money rent, whereas formerly this ratio was 10 to 18.

III. *The Rate of Productivity of the Additional Capitals Increases.*

This differs from Case I in the beginning of this chapter, in which the price of production falls while the rate of productivity remains the same, merely by the fact that soil A is thrown more quickly out of competition, if an increase of the product is required to effect this.

This may work its effects differently, according to the distribution of the investments over the various soils, no matter whether productivity be rising or falling. In proportion as these different effects balance the differences, or accentuate them, the differential rent of the better soils, and with it the total rental, will fall or rise, as we have seen in discussing differential rent No. I. For the rest, everything depends upon the size of the area and of the capital, which are thrown out of competition together with soil A, and upon the relative advance of capital required with a rising productivity for the purpose of supplying the capital which is to cover the demand.

The only point which it is worth while to analyse here, and which alone carries us back to the investigation of the way in which this differential profit is converted into differential rent, is the following:

In the first case, in which the price of production remains the same, the additional capital which may be invested in the soil A is immaterial for the differential rent as such, since this soil A does not yield any rent now any more than it did before, the price of its product remains the same and continues to regulate the market.

In the second case of Variant No. I, in which the price of production falls while the rate of productivity remains the same, soil A will necessarily be thrown out, and still more so in Variant No. II, in which both the price and production and the rate of productivity fall, since otherwise the additional capital upon soil A would have to raise the price of production. But here, in Variant No. III of the second case, in which the price of production falls, because the productivity of the additional capital rises, this additional capital may eventually be invested upon the soil A as well as upon the better soils.

We will assume that an additional capital of $2\frac{1}{2}$ pounds sterling, when invested upon the soil A, produces $1\frac{1}{5}$ quarter instead of 1 quarter.

Table VI.

Soils	Acres	Capital P. St.	Profit P. St.	Cost of Prod'n P.St	Product Qrs.	Selling Price P. St.	Yield P. St.	Rent		Rate of Surplus Profit
								Qrs.	P. St.	
A	1	2½+2½= 5	1	6	1+1 1.5=2 1.5	2 8/11	6	0	0	0
B	1	2½+2½= 5	1	6	2+2 2/5=4 2.5	2 8/11	12	2 1 5	6	120%
C	1	2½+2½= 5	1	6	3+3 3/5=6 3/5	2 8/11	18	4 2.5	12	240%
D	1	2½+2½= 5	1	6	4+4 4.5=8 4 5	2 8/11	24	6 3/5	18	360%
T'ls	4	20	4	24	22		60	13 1/5	36	Av'rage 240%

This Table VI should be compared with both Basic Tables I and Table II, in which the double investment of capital is combined with a constant productivity proportional to the investment of capital.

According to our assumption the regulating price of production falls. If it were to remain constant, at 3 pounds sterling, then the worst soil which used to pay no rent with an investment of $2\frac{1}{2}$ pounds sterling, would then yield a rent, although no worse soil would have been drawn into cultivation. This would have been accomplished by increasing the productivity of this soil, but only for a part, not for the original capital invested in it. The first 3 pounds sterling of cost of production bring 1 quarter; the second bring $1\frac{1}{5}$ quarter; but the entire product of $2\frac{1}{5}$ quarters is now sold at its average price.

Since the rate of productivity increases with the additional investment of capital, this implies an improvement. This may consist of a general increase of the capital per acre (more fertilizer, more mechanical labor, etc.), or it may be due exclusively to this additional investment that any difference in the quality and productiveness of the investment is brought about. In both cases the investment of 5 pounds sterling of capital per acre brings forth a product of $2\frac{1}{5}$ quarters, whereas

the investment of one-half of this capital, or $2\frac{1}{2}$ pounds sterling, brought forth a product of only 1 quarter. The product
of the soil A, leaving aside the question of transient market
conditions, could not continue to be sold at a higher price of
production instead of at the new average price unless a considerable area of the class A would remain under cultivation
with a capital of only $2\frac{1}{2}$ pounds sterling. But as soon as
the new scale of 5 pounds sterling of capital per acre would
become universal, and with it an improvement of cultivation,
the regulating price of production would have to fall to 2 8-11
pounds sterling. The difference between the two portions of
capital would disappear, and in that case the cultivation of
one acre of soil A with a capital of only $2\frac{1}{2}$ pounds sterling
would be abnormal, would not correspond to the new conditions of production. It would then no longer be a difference
between the yields of different portions of capital upon the
same acre, but between a sufficient and an insufficient investment of capital per acre. This shows, 1), that an insufficient capital in the hands of a large number of capitalist
farmers (it must be a large number, for a small number would
simply be compelled to sell below their price of production)
produces the same effect as a differentiation of soils in a descending line. The inferior cultivation upon inferior soil
increases the rent upon the superior soils; it may even create
a rent upon better cultivated soil of the inferior kind, which
would otherwise yield no rent. It shows, 2), that differential rent, to the extent that it arises from successive investments of capital in the same total area, resolves itself in reality into an average, in which the effects of the different investments of capital are no longer visible and distinguishable,
so that the worst soil does not yield any rent, but rather, a),
the average price of the total product of, say, one acre of A
is made the new regulating price, and, b), the effects of the
different investments of capital appear as changes in the total
quantity of capital per acre, which is required under the new
conditions for the adequate cultivation of the soil, and thus
the individual successions of invested capital as well as their
respective effects are indistinguishably amalgamated. It is

the same with the individual differential rents of the superior kinds of soil. In every case they are determined by the difference of the average products of the various soils, compared to the product of the worst soil, with the increase of capital which has become the normal one.

No soil yields any product without an investment of capital. Even in the case of simple differential rent, or differential rent No. I, some capital must be invested. When we say that one acre of class A, which regulates the price of production, gives so and so much of a product at that and that price, and that the superior soils B, C and D yield so much differential product and so much money rent at the regulating price of production, it is always understood that a certain amount of capital is invested in A which is normal under the prevailing conditions. In the same way a certain minimum capital is required for every individual line of industry, in order that commodities may be produced at their price of production.

If this minimum is altered in consequence of successive investments of capital which are accompanied by improvements, it is done gradually. So long as a certain number of acres, say, of A, do not receive this additional first capital, a rent is created upon the better cultivated portions of A by the unaltered price of production, and the rent of all superior soils, such as B, C, D, is raised. But as soon as the new method of cultivation has become general enough to be the normal one, the price of production falls; the rent of the superior soils declines then, and that portion of the soil A, which does not enjoy the normal running capital, must sell its product below its individual price of production, and therefore below the average profit.

In the case of a falling price of production this happens also, even assuming the productivity of the additional capital to be decreasing, as soon as the required total product is supplied in consequence of increased investments of capital by the superior classes of soil, so that the running capital is withdrawn, say, from A and A does not compete any longer in the production of this one staple, say wheat. The quantity of capital, which is now required on an average as an investment upon the new regulating soil, B, is now considered the normal one; and when we speak of the different fertility of the soils, it is understood that this new normal quantity of capital is employed per acre.

On the other hand, it is evident that this average investment of capital, for instance 8 pounds sterling per acre in England before 1848, and 12 pounds sterling after that year, will form the standard in the making of leases for land. For any capitalist farmer spending more than that the surplus profit does not assume the form of rent during the time of his contract. Whether this takes place after the expiration of his contract, will depend upon the competition of the capitalist farmers, who are in a position to make the same extra advance. We are not speaking here of such permanent improvements of the soil as continue to guarantee an increased product with the same or with even a decreasing investment of capital. Such improvements, although products of capital, have the same effect as the natural differences of quality of the land.

We see, then, that an element must be considered in the case of differential rent No. II, which does not appear in differential rent No. I as such, since this last rent may continue independently of any change in the normal investment of capital per acre. It is on one hand the obliteration of the results of different investments of capital upon the regulating soil A, the product of which now appears simply as a normal average product per acre. It is on the other hand the change in the average minimum, or in the average magnitude of invested capital per acre, so that this change presents itself as a quality of the soil. It is finally the difference in the manner of transforming surplus profit into the form of rent.

Table VI shows furthermore, compared with Tables I and II, that the grain has increased more than double as compared to I, and by 1⅕ quarters as compared to II; while the money rent has doubled as compared to I, but has not changed as compared with II. It would have increased considerably, if (other conditions remaining the same) the additional capital had been placed more upon the superior soils, or if the effects of the addition of capital to A had been less appreciable, so that the regulating average price of the quarter from A had stood higher.

If the increase of productivity by means of additional capital should produce different results upon different soils, it would cause a change in their differential rents.

At any rate we have demonstrated, that the rent per acre, for instance with a doubled capital, may not only be doubled, but more than doubled, while the price of production is falling in consequence of an increased rate of productivity of the additional capitals (as soon as the productivity grows at a greater rate than the advance of capital). But it may also fall, if the price of production should fall much lower as a result of a more rapid increase of productivity upon the soil A.

Let us assume that the additional investments of capital, for instance upon B and C, do not increase the productivity as much as they do upon A, so that the proportional differences would decrease for B and C, and the increase of the product did not make up for the fall in price, then, compared to Table II, the rent upon D would rise, and would fall upon B and C:

Table VI a.

Soils	Acres	Capital P. St.	Profit	Product per Acre quarters	Selling Price P St.	Yield P.St.	Grain Rent Qrs.	Money Rent P. St.
A	1	2½+2½= 5	1	1+ 3 = 4	1½	6	0	0
B	1	2½+2½= 5	1	2+ 2½= 4½	1½	6¾	½	¾
C	1	2½+2½= 5	1	3+ 5 = 8	1½	12	4	6
D	1	2½+2½= 5	1	4+12 =16	1½	24	12	18
Totals	4	20		32½			16½	24¾

Finally, the money rent would rise, if more additional capital were invested upon the superior soils under the same proportional increase of fertility than upon A, or if the additional investments of capital upon the superior soils worked with an increasing rate of productivity. In both cases the differences would increase.

The money rent falls, when the improvement due to additional investments of capital which reduces the differences all over, or in part, affects A more than B and C. It falls so much the more, the less the productivity of the superior soils increases. It depends upon the proportion of inequality in the effects, whether the grain rent shall rise, fall, or remain stationary.

The money rent rises, and so does the grain rent, assuming the proportional difference in the additional fertility of the different soils to remain unaltered, when more capital is added to the rent paying soils than to the rentless soil A, and more capital placed upon the soils with high than those with low rents, or when the fertility, assuming the same additional capital to be used, increases more upon the better and best soils than upon A, and at that in proportion as this increase in fertility is greater upon the better classes of soil than upon the lesser ones.

But under all circumstances the rent rises relatively, when the increased productive power is a result of an addition of capital, and not merely a result of increased fertility with an unaltered investment of capital. This is the absolute point of view, which shows that here, as in former cases, the rent and the increased rent per acre (as in the case of differential rent I upon the entire cultivated area — the amount of the average rental) are a result of an increased investment of capital in the soil, no matter whether this capital does its work with a constant rate of productivity at constant or decreasing prices, or with a decreasing rate of productivity at constant or falling prices, or with an increasing rate of productivity at falling prices. For our assumption of a constant price with a constant, falling, or rising rate of productivity of the additional capitals, and of a falling price with a constant, falling, or rising rate of productivity, resolves itself into a constant rate of productivity of the additional capital at constant or falling prices, a falling rate of productivity at constant or falling prices, and a rising rate of productivity at constant and falling prices. Although the rent may remain stationary or may fall in all these cases, it would fall more, if the additional investment of capital, other circumstances remaining the same; were not a prerequisite of an increased fertility. An addition of capital, then, is always the cause of the relative magnitude of this rent, although it may have decreased absolutely.

CHAPTER XLIII.

DIFFERENTIAL RENT NO. II.— THIRD CASE: RISING PRICE OF PRODUCTION.

[A rising price of production presupposes that the productivity of the least productive quality of land, which pays no rent, decreases. The regulating price of production cannot rise above 3 pounds sterling per quarter, unless the $2\frac{1}{2}$ pounds sterling invested in soil A produce less than one-quarter, or the 5 pounds sterling less than two-quarters, or unless, even inferior soil than A has to be taken under cultivation.

If the productivity of the second investment of capital should remain the same, this would be possible only in the case that the productivity of the first investment of capital would have decreased. This case occurs often enough. It happens, for instance, when the top soil, exhausted and superficially plowed, produces inferior crops with the old style of cultivation, and when the subsoil, thrown up by deeper plowing, produces better crops than formerly under a more rational treatment. But strictly speaking this special case does not belong here. The falling off in the productivity of the first investment of $2\frac{1}{2}$ pounds sterling implies for the superior soils, even when conditions with them should be analogous, a decrease of the differential rent No. I; but here we are considering only differential rent No. II. Since the present special case cannot occur without the previous existence of differential rent No. II, but represents in fact a reaction of a certain modification of differential rent No. I upon No. II, we will give an illustration of it.

TABLE VII.

Soils	Acres	Invested Capital P. St.	Profit	Cost of Prod'n P. St.	Product Qrs.	Selling Price P. St.	Yield P. St.	Grain Rent Qrs.	Money Rent P. St.	Rate of Rent
A	1	2½+2½	1	6	½+1¼ = 1¾	3 3/7	6	0	0	0
B	1	2½+2½	1	6	1 +2½ = 3½	3 3/7	12	1¾	6	120%
C	1	2½+2½	1	6	1½+3¾ = 5¼	3 3/7	18	3½	12	240%
D	1	2½+2½	1	6	2 +5 = 7	3 3/7	24	5¼	18	360%
T'tl		20			17½		60	10½	36	Av'rage 240%

The money rent, and the yield in money, are the same as in Table II. The increased regulating price of production makes up exactly for what has been lost in the quantity of the product; since both of them vary in an inverse proportion, it is a matter of course that the product of both will remain the same.

In the above case we had assumed that the productive power of the second investment of capital was higher than the original productivity of the first investment. The matter remains the same, if we assume that the second investment has only the same productivity as that of the first, as shown in the following:

TABLE VIII.

Soils	Acres	Invested Capital P. St.	Profit P. St.	Cost of Produc'n P. St.	Product Qrs.	Selling Price P. St.	Yield P. St.	Grain Rent Qrs.	Money Rent P. St.	Rate of Surplus Profit
A	1	2½+2½ = 5	1	6	½+1 = 1½	4	6	0	0	0
B	1	2½+2½ = 5	1	6	1 +2 = 3	4	12	1½	6	120%
C	1	2½+2½ = 5	1	6	1½+3 = 4½	4	18	3	12	240%
D	1	2½+2½ = 5	1	6	2 +4 = 6	4	24	4½	18	360%
		20			15	.	60	9	36	Average 240%

Here likewise the rising of the price of production at the same ratio fully compensates for the decrease in the productivity both in the yield and rent in money.

The third case shows itself in its pure form only when the second investment of capital declines in its productivity, while that of the first remains constant, as assumed everywhere in the first and second cases. Here differential rent No. I is not touched, the change affects only that part which arises from differential rent No. II. We give below two illustrations: In the first we assume that the productivity of the second investment of capital has been reduced by one-half, in the second by one-fourth.

TABLE IX.

Soils	Acres	Invested Capital P. St.	Profit P. St.	Cost of Produc'n P. St.	Product Qrs.	Selling Price P. St.	Yield P. St.	Grain Rent Qrs.	Money Rent P. St.	Rate of Rent
A	1	2 1/2+2 1/2= 5	1	6	1+ 1/2= 1 1/2	4	6	0	0	0
B	1	2 1/2+2 1/2= 5	1	6	2+1 = 3	4	12	1 1/2	6	120%
C	1	2 1/2+2 1/2= 5	1	6	3+1 1/2= 4 1/2	4	18	3	12	240%
D	1	2 1/2+2 1/2= 5	1	6	4+2 = 6	4	24	4 1/2	18	360%
T'tl		20			15		60			Av'rage 240%

Table IX is the same as Table VIII, only that the decrease in productivity in VIII falls upon the first investment of capital, and in IX upon the second investment of capital.

TABLE X.

Soils	Acres	Invested Capital P. St,	Profit P. St.	Cost of Produc'n P. St.	Product Qrs.	Selling Price P. St.	Yield P. St.	Grain Rent Qrs.	Money Rent P. st.	Rate of Rent
A	1	2 1/2+2 1/2= 5	1	6	1+ 1/4= 1 1/4	4 4/5	6	0	0	0
B	1	2 1/2+2 1/2= 5	1	6	2+ 1/2= 2 1/2	4 4/5	12	1 1/4	6	120%
C	1	2 1/2+2 1/2= 5	1	6	3+ 3/4= 3 3/4	4 4/5	18	2 1/2	12	2+0%
D	1	2 1/2+2 1/2= 5	1	6	4+1 = 5	4 4/5	24	3 3/4	18	360%
T'tl		20			12 1/2		60	7 1/2		Av'rage 240%

In this table, likewise, the total yield, the money rental, and the rate of rent remain the same as in Tables II, VII and VIII, because the product and the selling price have once more varied in an inverse proportion, while the invested capital has remained the same.

But how do matters stand in the other case, which is possible with a rising price of production, namely in the case that a soil, which so far was too poor to be cultivated, is taken under cultivation?

Let us suppose that such a soil, which we will designate by *a,* is entering into competition. Then the hitherto rentless soil A would yield a rent, and the foregoing Tables VII, VIII and X would assume the following forms:

TABLE VIIa.

Soils	Acres	Capital P. St.	Profit P. St.	Cost of Produc'n P. St.	Product Qrs.		Selling Price P. St.	Yield P. St.	Grain Rent Qrs.	Money Rent P. St.	Increase
a	1	5	1	6		1½	4	6	0	0	0
A	1	2 1/2+2 1/2	1	6	½+1¼ =	1¾	4	7	1/4	1	1
B	1	2 1/2+2 1/2	1	6	1 +2½ =	3½	4	14	2	8	1+7
C	1	2 1/2+2 1/2	1	6	1½+3¾ =	5¼	4	21	3 3/4	15	1+2×7
D	1	2 1/2+2 1/2	1	6	2 +5 =	7	4	28	5 1/2	22	1+3×7
T'ls				30		19		76	11 1/2		

TABLE VIIIa.

Soils	Acres	Capital P. St.	Profit	Cost of Produc'n P. St.	Product Qrs.		Selling Price P. St.	Yield P. St.	Grain Rent Qrs.	Money Rent P. St.	Increase
a	1	5	1	6		1¼	4 4/5	6	0	0	0
A	1	2½+2½	1	6	1 + ½=	1½	4 4/5	7 1/5	1/4	1 1/5	1 1/5
B	1	2½+2½	1	6	1 +2 =	3	4 4/5	14 2/5	1 3/4	8 2/5	1 1/5+7 1/5
C	1	2½+2½	1	6	1½+3 =	4½	4 4/5	21 3/5	2 1/4	15 3/5	1 1/5+2×7 1/5
D	1	2½+2½	1	6	2 +4 =	6	4 4/5	28 4/5	4 3/4	22 4/5	1 1/5+3×7 1/5
T'ls				30		16¼		78	9	48	

TABLE Xa.

Soils	Acres	Capital P. St.	Profit	Cost of Produc'n P. St.	Product Qrs.		Selling Price P. St.	Yield P. St.	Grain Rent Qrs.	Money Rent P. St.	Increase
a	1	5	1	6		1⅛	5⅓	6	0	0	0
A	1	2 1/2+2 1/2	1	6	1+ ¼=	1¼	5⅓	6⅔	⅛	⅔	⅔
B	1	2 1/2+2 1/2	1	6	2+ ½=	2½	5⅓	13⅓	1⅜	7⅓	⅔+6⅔
C	1	2 1/2+2 1/2	1	6	3+ ¾=	3¾	5⅓	20	2⅝	14	⅔+2×6⅔
D	1	2 1/2+2 1/2	1	6	4+1 =	5	5⅓	26⅔	3⅞	20⅔	⅔+3×6⅔
T'ls				30		13⅝		72⅔	8	42⅔	

By the interpolation of soil *a* there arises a new differential rent No. I. Upon this new basis differential rent No. II likewise develops in an altered form. The soil *a* has a different fertility in every one of the above three Tables. The series of successively increasing productivities begins only with soil A. The series of rising rents corresponds to this. The rent of the least rent producing soil forms a constant magnitude, which is simply added to all higher rents; only after the deduction of this constant magnitude does the series of differences clearly appear among the higher rents, and so does its parallelism with the succession of fertilities of the various kinds of soil. In all Tables, the fertilities from A to D have a proportion of $1 : 2 : 3 : 4$, and the rents are correspondingly in VIIa as $1 : 1 + 7 : 1 + 2 \times 7 : 1 + 3 \times 7$, in VIIIa as $1\frac{1}{5} : 1\frac{1}{5} + 7\frac{1}{5} : 1\frac{1}{5} : 2 \times 7\frac{1}{5} : 1\frac{1}{5} + 3 \times 7\frac{1}{5}$, and in Xa as $\frac{2}{3} : \frac{2}{3} + 6\frac{2}{3} : \frac{2}{3} + 2 \times 6\frac{2}{3} : \frac{2}{3} + 3 \times 6\frac{2}{3}$. In brief, if the rent of $A = n$, and the rent of the soil of next higher fertility $= n + m$, then the series is as $n : n + m : n + 2m : n + 3m$, etc.— F. E.]

[Since the foregoing third case had not been elaborated in the manuscript, only its title being there, the editor had to supplement the work as he did above. It remains now to draw the general conclusions following from the entire foregoing analysis of differential rent in its three principal cases and nine subcases. The illustrations chosen in the manuscript do not suit this purpose very well. In the first place, they compare pieces of land, equal portions of which have yields at the ratio of $1 : 2 : 3 : 4$. These are differences, which strongly exaggerate and which lead to utterly forced results in the further development of the assumptions and calculations made upon this basis. In the second place, these proportions create a wrong impression. If degrees of fertility of the proportion $1 : 2 : 3 : 4$, etc., produce rents in a series of $0 : 1 : 2 : 3 : 4$, etc., one feels tempted to derive the second series from the first and to explain the duplication, triplication, etc., of the rents out of the duplication, triplication, etc., of the total yields. But this would be wholly incorrect. The rents show proportions like that of $0 : 1 : 2 : 3 : 4$ even when the degrees of fertility are proportioned as $n : n + 1 : n +$

2 : n + 3 : n + 4; the rents are not proportioned as the degrees of fertility, they are rather proportioned as the differences of fertility, beginning with the rentless soil as a zero point.

The tables of the original had to be given for the illustration of the text. But in order to obtain a suitable basis for the following results of our analysis, I present below a new series of tables, in which the yields are indicated in bushels ($\frac{1}{8}$ quarter or 36.35 liters) and shillings.

The first of these tables, Table XI, corresponds to the former Table I. It shows the yields and rents for five qualities of soil, A to E, with a first investment of a capital of 50 shillings, which makes a profit of 10 shillings, so that the total cost of production per acre is 60 shillings. The yields in grain are placed at low figures, 10, 12, 14, 16, 18 bushels per acre. The resulting regulating price of production is 6 shillings per bushel.

The following 13 tables correspond to the three cases of differential rent No. II, with an additional investment of a capital of 50 shillings per acre upon the same soil, with a constant, falling and rising price of production. Every one of these cases, again, is represented as it turns out, 1) with a constant, 2) with a falling, 3) with a rising productivity of the second investment of capital as compared to the first. This results furthermore in a few other cases, which are presented separately.

In case I, with a constant price of production, we have:
Variant No. 1: The productivity of the second investment of capital remains the same (Table XII.)
Variant No. 2: The productivity declines. This can take place only when soil A receives no second investment of capital, and it may take place in such a way that
a) the soil B likewise produces no rent (Table XIII), or,
b) the soil B does not lose all rent (Table XIV).
Variant No. 3: The productivity increases. (Table XV.) This case likewise excludes a second investment of capital upon soil A.

3A

In case II, with a falling price of production, we have:

Variant No. 1:   The productivity of the second investment
of capital remains the same (Table XVI).

Variant No. 2:   The productivity declines (Table XVII).
These two variants are conditioned upon the throwing of soil A out of competition, and soil B producing
no rent and regulating the price of production.

Variant No. 3:   The productivity increases (Table XVIII).
In this case the soil A remains the regulator.

In case III, with a rising price of production, two eventualities are possible; soil A may remain without rent and
regulate the price, or, an inferior class of soil than A enters
into competition and regulates the price, in which case A produces a rent.

First eventuality: Soil A remains the regulator.

Variant No. 1:   The productivity of the second investment
remains the same (Table XIX). This will happen
under the conditions assumed by us only when the
productivity of the first investment decreases.

Variant No. 2:   The productivity of the second investment
decreases (Table XX). This does not exclude the
possibility that the first investment may retain the
same productivity.

Variant No. 3:   The productivity of the second investment
(Table XIX) increases; this, again, presupposes a
falling productivity of the first investment.

Second eventuality: An inferior quality of soil (designated
as *a*) enters into competition; soil A yields a rent.

Variant No. 1:   The productivity of the second investment
remains the same (Table XXII).

Variant No. 2:   The productivity declines (Table XXIII).

Variant No. 3:   The productivity increases (Table XXIV).

These three variants appear under the general conditions
of the problem and require no further remarks.

We herewith produce the Tables.

Table XI.

Soils	Cost of Production	Product Bushels	Selling Price	Yield Shillings	Rent Shillings	Increase of Rent
A	60	10	6	60	0	0
B	60	12	6	72	12	12
C	60	14	6	84	24	2×12
D	60	16	6	96	36	3×12
E	60	18	6	108	48	4×12
Total					120	10×12

When a second investment is placed upon the same soil, we have the following eventualities:

First Case: The Price of production remains unaltered.
Variant No. 1: The productivity of the second investment remains the same.

Table XII.

Soils	Cost of Production	Product Bushels	Selling Price	Yield Shillings	Rent Shillings	Increase of Rent
A	60+60= 120	10+10= 20	6	120	0	0
B	60+60= 120	12+12= 24	6	144	24	24
C	60+60= 120	14+14= 28	6	168	48	2×24
D	60+60= 120	16+16= 32	6	192	72	3×24
E	60+60= 120	18+18= 36	6	216	96	4×24
Total					240	10×24

Variant No. 2: The productivity of the second investment of capital declines; soil A receives no second investment.

a) If soil B ceases to yield a rent.

Table XIII.

Soils	Cost of Production	Product Bushels	Selling Price Shillings	Yield Shillings	Rent Shillings	Increase of Rent
A	60	10	6	60	0	0
B	60+60= 120	12+ 8 =20	6	120	0	0
C	60+60= 120	14+ 9½=23½	6	140	20	20
D	60+60= 120	16+10⅔=26⅔	6	160	40	2×20
E	60+60= 120	18+20 =38	6	180	60	3×20
Total					120	6×20

b) If soil B does not lose all the rent.

Table XIV.

Soils	Cost of Production	Product Bushels	Selling Price Shillings	Yield Shillings	Rent Shillings	Increase of Rent
A	60	10	6	60	0	0
B	60+60=120	12+ 9 =21	6	126	6	6
C	60+60=120	14+10½=24½	6	147	27	6+21
D	60+60=120	16+12 =28	6	168	48	6+2×21
E	60+60=120	18+13½=31½	6	189	69	6+3×21
Total					150	4×6+6×21

Variant No. 3: The productivity of the second investment of capital increases; no second investment upon soil A.

Table XV.

Soils	Cost of Production	Product Bushels	Selling Price Shillings	Yield Shillings	Rent	Increase of Rent
A	60	10	6	60	0	0
B	60+60=120	12+15 =27	6	162	42	42
C	60+60=120	14+17½=31½	6	189	69	42+27
D	60+60=120	16+20 =36	6	216	96	42+2×27
E	60+60=120	18+22½=40½	6	243	123	42+3×27
Total					330	4×42+6×27

Second Case: The price of production declines.
Variant No. 1: The productivity of the second investment of capital remains the same. Soil A is thrown out of competition, soil B loses its rent.

Table XVI.

Soils	Cost of Production Shillings	Product Bushels	Selling Price	Yield Shillings	Rent Shillings	Increase of Rent
B	60+60=120	12+12=24	5	120	0	0
C	60+60=120	14+14=28	5	140	20	20
D	60+60=120	16+16=32	5	160	40	2×20
E	60+60=120	18+18=36	5	180	60	3×20
Total					120	6×20

Variant No. 2: The productivity of the second investment of capital declines; soil A is thrown out of competition, soil B loses its rent.

Table XVII.

Soils	Cost of Production Shillings	Product Bushels	Selling Price	Yield Shillings	Rent Shillings	Increase of Rent
B	60+60=120	12+ 9 =21	5 5/7	120	0	0
C	60+60=120	14+10½=24½	5 5/7	140	20	20
D	60+60=120	16+12 =28	5 5/7	160	40	2×20
E	60+60=120	18+13½=31½	5 5/7	180	60	3×20
Total					120	6×20

Variant No. 3: The productivity of the second investment of capital increases; soil A remains in the competition. Soil B produces rent.

Table XVIII.

Soils	Cost of Production Shillings	Product Bushels	Selling Price Shillings	Yield Shillings	Rent Shillings	Increase of Rent
A	60+60=120	10+15=25	4 4/5	120	0	0
B	60+60=120	12+18=30	4 4/5	144	24	24
C	60+60=120	14+21=35	4 4/5	168	48	2×24
D	60+60=120	16+24=40	4 4/5	192	72	3×24
E	60+60=120	18+27=45	4 4/5	216	96	4×24
Total					240	10×24

Third Case: The price of production rises.

A) If soil A remains without rent and continues to regulate the price.

Variant No. 1: The productivity of the second investment of capital remains the same; this implies a decreasing productivity of the first investment of capital.

Table XIX.

Soils	Cost of Production Shillings	Product Bushels	Selling Price	Yield Shillings	Rent Shillings	Increase of Rent
A	60+60=120	5+12½=17½	6 6/7	120	0	0
B	60+60=120	6+15 =21	6 6/7	144	24	24
C	60+60=120	7+17½=24½	6 6/7	168	48	2×24
D	60+60=120	8+20 =28	6 6/7	192	72	3×24
E	60+60=120	9+22½=31½	6 6/7	216	96	4×24
Total					240	10×24

Variant No. 2: The productivity of the second investment of capital decreases; this does not exclude a constant productivity of the first investment.

Table XX.

Soils	Cost of Production Shillings	Product Bushels	Selling Price Shillings	Yield Shillings	Rent Shillings	Increase of Rent
A	60+60=120	10+5=15	8	120	0	0
B	60+60=120	12+6=18	8	144	24	24
C	60+60=120	14+7=21	8	168	48	2×24
D	60+60=120	16+8=24	8	192	72	3×24
E	60+60=120	18+9=27	8	216	96	4×24
Total					240	10×24

Variant No. 3: The productivity of the second investment of capital rises, which implies, under the assumed conditions, a declining productivity of the first investment.

Table XXI.

Soils	Cost of Production Shillings	Product Bushels	Selling Price	Yield Shillings	Rent Shillings	Increase of Rent
A	60+60=120	5+12½=17½	6 6/7	120	0	0
B	60+60=120	6+15 =21	6 6/7	144	24	24
C	60+60=120	7+17½=24½	6 6/7	168	48	2×24
D	60+60=120	8+20 =28	6 6/7	192	72	3×24
E	60+60=120	9+22½=31½	6 6/7	216	96	4×24
Total					240	10×24

B) If an inferior soil (designated as *a*) becomes the regulator of prices and soil A produces a rent. This admits of a constant productivity of the second investment in the case of all variants.

Variant No. 1: The productivity of the second investment of capital remains the same.

Table XXII.

Soils	Cost of Production Shillings	Product Bushels	Selling Price	Yield Shillings	Rent Shillings	Increase of Rent
a	120	16	7½	120	0	0
A	60+60=120	10+10=20	7½	150	30	30
B	60+60=120	12+12=24	7½	180	60	2×30
C	60+60=120	14+14=28	7½	210	90	3×30
D	60+60=120	16+10=32	7½	240	120	4×30
E	60+60=120	18+18=36	7½	270	150	5×30
Total					450	15×30

Variant No. 2: The productivity of the second investment of capital declines.

Table XXIII.

Soils	Cost of Production Shillings	Product Bushels	Selling Price	Yield Shillings	Rent Shillings	Increase of Rent
a	120	15	8	120	0	0
A	60+60=120	10+ 7½=17½	8	140	20	20
B	60+60=120	12+ 9 =21	8	168	48	20×28
C	60+60=120	14+10½=24½	8	196	76	20+2×28
D	60+60=120	16+12 =28	8	224	104	20+3×28
E	60+60=120	18+13½=31½	8	252	132	20+4×28
Total					380	5×20+10×28

Variant No. 3: The productivity of the second investment increases.

Table XXIV.

Soils	Cost of Production Shillings	Product Bushels	Selling Price	Yield Shillings	Rent Shillings	Increase of Rent
a	120	16	7½	120	0	0
A	60+60=120	10+12½=22½	7½	168¾	48¾	15+33¾
B	60+60=120	12+15 =27	7½	202½	82½	15+2×33¾
C	60+60=120	14+17½=31½	7½	236¼	116¼	15+3×33¾
D	60+60=120	16+20 =36	7½	270	150	15+4×33¾
E	60+60=120	18+22½=40½	7½	303¾	183¾	15+5×33¾
Total					581¼	5×15+15×33¾

These Tables lead to the following conclusions:

In the first place they show that the series of rents maintains the same proportions as the series of degrees of fertility, taking the rentless regulating soil as the zero point. Not the absolute yields, but only the differences in yield are the determining elements of rent. Whether the different kinds of soil produce 1, 2, 3, 4, 5 bushels, or whether they produce 11, 12, 13, 14, 15 bushels of yield per acre, the rents are in both cases seriatim 0, 1, 2, 3, 4, bushels, or money to that amount.

But the result of our analysis is far more important with respect to the total yields of rent with a repeated investment of capital upon the same soil.

In five cases out of the analysed thirteen the total amount of the rents is doubled with the duplication of the investment of capital; instead of 10 times 12 shillings it becomes 10 times 24 shillings, or 240 shillings. These cases are:

Case I, constant price, Variant No. 1, the increase of productivity remaining the same (Table XII).

Case II, falling price, Variant No. III: increasing expansion of production (Table XVIII).

Case III, increasing price, first eventuality, where soil A remains the regulator, in all three Variants (Tables XIX, XX, and XXI).

In four cases the rent increases by more than double, namely:

Case I, Variant No. III, constant price, increasing expansion of production (Table XV). The amount of the rent rises to 330 shillings.

Case III, second eventuality, where soil A produces a rent, in all three variants (Table XXII, rent 15 times 30 = 450 shillings; Table XXIII, rent 5 times 20 plus 10 times 28 = 380 shillings; Table XXIV, rent 5 times 15 plus 15 times $33\frac{1}{3} = 581\frac{1}{4}$ shillings).

In one case the rent rises, but not to double the amount of the rent produced by the first investment of capital:

Case I, constant price, Variant II: falling productivity of the second investment, under conditions, in which B does not wholly lose its rent (Table XIV, rent 4 times 6 plus 6 times 21 = 150 shillings).

Finally, it is only in three cases that the total rent, with a second investment upon all kinds of soil, remains at the same level as with the first investment (Table XI); these are the cases, in which the soil A is thrown out of competition and soil B becomes the regulator and pays no rent. In this case the rent of B is not only lost, but is also deducted from every succeeding link of the rent series. This is the basis of the above result. We mean the following cases:

Case I, Variant II, when the conditions are such that soil A is eliminated (Table XIII). The sum of the rent is six times twenty, or $10 \times 12 = 120$, as in Table XI.

Case II, Variants I and II. Here soil A is necessarily eliminated, according to the assumption (Tables XVI and XVII) and the sum of the rent is again $6 \times 20 = 10 \times 12 = 120$ shillings.

This is to say: In the great majority of all possible cases
the rent rises, both per acre of the rent paying soils and for
the total amount, as a result of an increased investment of
capital upon the land.   Only in three cases out of the thirteen
analysed cases the total amount of the rent remains unaltered.
These are the cases, in which the lowest quality of soil, which
hitherto paid no rent, drops out of competition and the next
higher one takes its place and loses its rent.   But even in
these cases do the rents upon the superior soils rise in comparison to the rents due to the first investment.   When the
rent of C falls from 24 to 20, then that of D and E rises from
36 and 48 respectively to 40 and 60 shillings.

A fall of the total rents below the level of the first investment of capital (Table XI) would be possible only in the
case that soil B as well as soil A would drop out of competition and soil C become regulating and rentless.

The more capital is applied to a certain soil, and the higher
the development of agriculture and of civilization in general
is in a certain country, the more do the rents rise per acre
and per total amount of rental, and the more immense becomes the tribute paid by society to the great land owners
in the form of surplus profits — so long as the different soils
taken under cultivation remain capable of competition.

This law explains the wonderful vitality of the class of
great landlords.   No social class lives so sumptuously, no
other claims like it a right to a traditional luxury in keeping
with its " estate," regardless of where the money for that
purpose may come from, no other class piles debt upon debt
as lightheartedly as it.   And yet it always lands on its feet —
thanks to the capital invested by other people in the soil,
whereby the landlord collects a rent, which stand in no proportion to the profits to be drawn out of the soil by the capitalist.

However, the same law also explains, why the vitality of
the great landlord is gradually exhausted.

When the English corn taxes were abolished in 1846, the
English manufacturers believed that they had transformed
the landowning aristocracy into paupers.   Instead of that they

became richer than ever. How did that happen? Very simple. In the first place, the renting capitalists were now compelled by contract to invest 12 pounds sterling annually instead of 8 pounds, as heretofore. And in the second place, the landlords, being strongly represented also in the Lower House, granted to themselves a heavy subsidy for the drainage and other permanent improvements of their lands. Since no total displacement of the worst soil took place, but at the worst a temporary employment of such soil for other purposes, the rents rose in proportion to the increased investment of capital, and the landed aristocracy were better off than ever before.

But everything is perishable. The transoceanic steamboats and the railroads of North and South America and India enabled very peculiar masses of land to enter into competition upon the European grain markets. There were on the one hand the North American prairies, the Argentine pampas, steppes, made fertile for the plow by nature itself, virgin soil, which offered rich harvest for years to come even with a primitive cultivation and without any fertilization. Then there were the lands of the Russian and Indian communes, that had to sell a portion of their product, and an increasing one at that, for the purpose of obtaining money for the taxes wrung from them by the pitiless despotism of the state, very often by means of torture. These products were sold without regard to their cost of production, sold at the price offered by the dealer, because the peasant had to have money under all circumstances when tax paying day came around. And against the competition of the virgin prairie soils and of the Russian and Indian peasants ground down by taxation, the European capitalist farmer and peasant could not stand up at the old rents. A portion of the soil of Europe fell definitely out of the competition for the raising of grain, the rents fell everywhere. Our second case Variant II (falling prices and falling productivity of the additional investment of capital) became the rule for Europe. This accounts for the woes of the landlords from Scotland to Italy, and from Southern France to Eastern Prussia. Fortunately all prairie lands have not been taken under cultivation. There are enough of them left to ruin all the great landlords of Europe and the small ones into the bargain.— F. E.]

The heads, under which rent is to be analyzed, are the following:

A. Differential rent.
    1) Meaning of differential rent. Illustration by water power. Transition to real agricultural rent.
    2) Differential rent No. I, arising from different fertilities of different pieces of land.
    3) Differential rent No. II, arising from successive investments of capital upon the same soil. Differential rent No. II is to be analysed
        a) with a stationary price of production.
        b) with a falling price of production.
        c) with a rising price of production.
And furthermore
        d) the transformation of surplus profit into rent.
    4) Influence of this rent upon the rate of profit.
B. Absolute rent.
C. The price of land.
D. Final Remarks concerning ground rent.

As the general result of our analysis of differential rent we come to the following conclusions:

1) The formation of surplus profits may take place in different ways. On the one hand it may come about by the help of differential rent No. I, that is, by an investment of the entire agricultural capital upon one soil area consisting of soils of different fertilities. Or, it may come about by means of differential rent No. II, that is by means of the varying differential productivity of successive investments of capital upon the same soil, which signifies here a greater productivity, say in wheat measured by quarters, than is secured with the same investment of capital upon the worst

rentless soil, which regulates the price of production. But no matter how these surplus profits may arise, their transformation into rents, their transfer from the capitalist farmer to the landlord, always presupposes that the various individual prices of production represented by the partial products of the individual capitals invested in succession (independently of the general price of production by which the market is regulated) have previously been reduced to an individual average price of production. The excess of the general regulating price of production of the product of one acre over its individual average price, forms and measures the rent per acre. In differential rent No. I the differential results may be distinguished by themselves, because they take place upon differentiated portions of land lying side by side, with an investment of capital and a degree of cultivation considered normal per acre. In differential rent No. II they must first be made distinguishable; they must in fact be reconverted into differential rent No. I, and this cannot take place in any other but the indicated way. Take for instance Table III, Chapter XLI, 3.

Soil B gives for the first investment of capital 2½ pounds sterling 2 quarters per acre, and for the second equally large one 1½ quarters; together 3½ quarters upon the same acre. These 3½ quarters do not show what part of them is a product of the investment of capital No. I and what part a product of capital No. II, for they are all grown upon the same soil. They are in fact the product of the total capital of 5 pounds sterling; and the actual condition of the matter is that a capital of 2½ pounds sterling produced 2 quarters, and a capital of 5 pounds sterling produced only 3½ quarters, not 4 quarters. The case would be just the same, if these 5 pounds sterling were producing 4 quarters, so that the proceeds of both investments of capital would be the same, or even 5 quarters, so that the second investment of capital would yield a surplus of 1 quarter. The price of production of the first 2 quarters is 1½ pounds sterling per quarter, and that of the second 1½ quarters is 2 pounds sterling per quarter. Consequently the 3½ quarters together cost 6 pounds sterling.

This is the individual price of production of the total product, and it makes an average of 1 pound and $14\frac{2}{7}$ shillings per quarter, in round figures $1\frac{3}{4}$ pounds sterling. With the average price of production regulated by soil A, namely 3 pounds sterling, this makes a surplus profit of $1\frac{1}{4}$ pounds sterling per quarter, and for the total $3\frac{1}{2}$ quarters a surplus profit of $4\frac{3}{8}$ pounds sterling. With the average price of production of B this is represented by about $1\frac{1}{2}$ quarters. In other words, the surplus profit of B is represented by an aliquot portion of the product of B, by these $1\frac{1}{2}$ quarters, which express the rent in terms of grain, and which under the prevailing price of production sell at $4\frac{1}{2}$ pounds sterling. But on the other hand, the surplus product of one acre of B compared to that of A is not without ceremony a formation of surplus profit, is not offhand a surplus product. According to our assumption one acre of B produces $3\frac{1}{2}$ quarters, whereas one acre of A produces only 1 quarter. The surplus of the product of B is, therefore, $2\frac{1}{2}$ quarters, but the surplus product is only $1\frac{1}{2}$ quarters; for the capital invested in B is twice that of A, and for this reason its cost of production is doubled. If soil A should also receive an investment of 5 pounds sterling, and the rate of productivity should remain the same, then the product would amount to 2 quarters instead of 1 quarter, and it would then be seen that the actual surplus product is found, not by a comparison of $3\frac{1}{2}$ with 1, but of $3\frac{1}{2}$ with 2, so that it would be only $1\frac{1}{2}$ quarter, not $2\frac{1}{2}$ quarters. Furthermore, if B should invest a third capital of $2\frac{1}{2}$ pounds sterling, which would produce only 1 quarter, so that this quarter would cost 3 pounds sterling, the same as that of A, then its selling price would cover only the cost of production, would yield only the average profit, but not a surplus profit, and would not offer anything that could be converted into rent. The product per acre of any kind of soil, compared with the product per acre of soil A, shows neither whether it is a product of the same or of a larger investment of capital, nor whether the additional product covers merely the price of production, nor whether it is due to a greater productivity of the additional capital.

2) With a decreasing rate of productivity of the additional investments of capital, whose limits, so far as the new formation of surplus profit is concerned, is that investment of capital which just covers the cost of production, in other words, which produces one quarter at the same expense as the same investment of capital in one acre of soil A, amounting to 3 pounds sterling according to our assumption, we come to the following conclusions on the basis of what has gone before: That the limit, where the total investment of capital in one acre of B would not yield any more rent, is reached when the individual average price of production of the product per acre of B would rise to the price of production per acre of A.

If B invests only such additional capital as pays just the price of production, but forms no surplus profit, no rent, then this raises only the individual average price of production per quarter, but does not affect the surplus profit, or eventually the rent, formed by previous investments of capital? For the average price of production always remains under that of A, and when the excess over the price per quarter decreases, then the number of quarters increases in the same ratio, so that the total excess over the price remains unaltered.

In the case assumed, the first two investments of capital of 5 pounds sterling produce $3\frac{1}{2}$ quarters upon B, which amounts to $1\frac{1}{2}$ quarters of rent, at $4\frac{1}{2}$ pounds sterling, according to our assumption. Now, if a third investment of capital of $2\frac{1}{2}$ pounds sterling is added, which produces only one additional quarter, then the total price of production (including a profit of 20%) of the $4\frac{1}{2}$ quarters is 9 pounds sterling, so that the average price per quarter is 2 pounds sterling. The average price of production per quarter upon B has then risen from $1\frac{5}{7}$ pounds sterling to 2 pounds sterling, so that the surplus profit per quarter, compared with the regulating price of A, has fallen from $1\frac{2}{7}$ pounds sterling to 1 pound sterling. But $1 \times 4\frac{1}{2} = 4\frac{1}{2}$ pounds sterling, just as formerly $1\frac{2}{7} \times 3\frac{1}{2} = 4\frac{1}{2}$ pounds sterling.

upon B, and that these investments produce one quarter only at its average price of production, then the total product per acre would be $6\frac{1}{2}$ quarters, and their cost of production 15 pounds sterling. The average price of production per quarter of B would have risen once more, from 1 pound sterling to $2\frac{4}{13}$ pound sterling, and the surplus profit per quarter, compared with the regulating price of production of A, would have dropped once more, from 1 pound sterling to $\frac{9}{13}$ pound sterling. But these $\frac{9}{13}$ would now have to be calculated upon $6\frac{1}{2}$ quarters instead of $4\frac{1}{2}$ quarters. And $\frac{9}{13} \times 6\frac{1}{2} = 1 \times 4\frac{1}{2} = 4\frac{1}{2}$ pounds sterling.

The inference from this is, in the first place, that no raising of the regulating price of production is necessary under these circumstances, in order to make possible additional investments of capital even to the point where the additional capital ceases wholly to produce any surplus profit and yields only the average profit. It follows furthermore that the sum of the surplus profit per acre remains the same here, no matter how much the surplus profit per quarter may decrease; this decrease is always balanced by a corresponding increase of the quarters produced per acre. In order that the average price of production may rise to the general price of production (in this case to 3 pounds sterling for soil B) it is necessary that additions should be made to the capital, which must have a product of a higher price of production than the regulating one of 3 pounds sterling. But we shall see that this does not suffice without further ado in order to raise the average price of production per quarter of B to the general price of production of 3 pounds sterling.

Let us assume that soil B produced.

1) $3\frac{1}{2}$ quarters as before at a price of production of 6 pounds sterling; this with two investments of capital of $2\frac{1}{2}$ pounds sterling each, which both form surplus profits, but of a decreasing amount.

2) 1 quarter at 3 pounds sterling; an investment of capital, in which the individual price of production shall be equal to the regulating price of production.

3) 1 quarter at 4 pounds sterling; an investment of capi-

tal, in which the individual price of production shall be higher by 25% than the regulating price.

We should then have $5\frac{1}{2}$ quarters per acre, at 13 pounds sterling, with an investment of a capital of 10 pounds sterling; this would be four times the original investment of capital, but not quite three times the product of the first investment of capital.

$5\frac{1}{2}$ quarters per acre at 13 pounds sterling make an average price of production of $2\frac{4}{11}$ pounds sterling, which would give a surplus of $\frac{7}{11}$ pound per quarter at the regulating price of production of 3 pounds sterling. This surplus may be converted into rent. $5\frac{1}{2}$ quarters sold at the regulating price of production of 3 pounds sterling make $16\frac{1}{2}$ pounds sterling. After deducting the cost of production of 13 pounds sterling a surplus, or rent of $3\frac{1}{2}$ pounds sterling remains, which, calculated at the present average price of production per quarter of B, that is, at $2\frac{4}{11}$ pounds per quarter, represent $1\frac{5}{72}$ quarters. The money rent would have fallen by 1 pound sterling, the grain rent by about $\frac{1}{2}$ quarter, but in spite of the fact that the fourth additional investment upon B does not produce a surplus profit, but even less than the average profit, a surplus profit and a rent still continue to exist. Let us assume that not only the investment of capital as illustrated in No. 3), but also that in No. 2), produce at a cost exceeding the regulating price of production, then the total production is $3\frac{1}{2}$ quarters at 6 pounds sterling plus 2 quarters at 8 pounds sterling, total $5\frac{1}{2}$ quarters at 14 pounds sterling cost of production. The average price of production per quarter would be $2\frac{6}{11}$ pounds sterling, and it would leave a surplus of $\frac{5}{11}$ pound sterling. The $5\frac{1}{2}$ quarters, sold at 3 pounds sterling, make $16\frac{1}{2}$ pounds sterling; subtract the 14 pounds sterling of cost of production, and $2\frac{1}{2}$ pounds sterling remain for rent. At the present average price of production upon B this would be equivalent to $\frac{55}{56}$ quarters. In other words, a rent would still remain, although less than before.

This shows at any rate, that upon the better soils with additional investments of capital, whose product costs more than the regulating price of production, the rent does not disappear, at least not within the bounds of admissible practice, although it must decrease, and will do so in proportion, on the one hand, to the aliquot part formed by this unproductive capital in the total investment of capital, on the other hand in proportion to the decrease of its fertility. The average price of its fertility would still stand below the regulating price and would still leave a surplus profit that could be converted into rent.

Let us now assume that the average price per quarter of B coincides with the general price of production, in consequence of four successive investments of capital ($2\frac{1}{2}$, $2\frac{1}{2}$, 5 and 5 pounds sterling) with a decreasing productivity.

Capital P. St.	Profit P. St.	Yield Qrs.	Cost of Production		Selling Price P. St.	Proceeds P. St.	Surplus for Rent	
			per Qr. P. St.	Together P. St.			Qrs.	P St.
(1) $2\frac{1}{2}$	$\frac{1}{2}$	2	$1\frac{1}{2}$	3	3	6	1	3
(2) $2\frac{1}{2}$	$\frac{1}{2}$	$1\frac{1}{2}$	2	3	3	$4\frac{1}{2}$	$\frac{1}{2}$	$1\frac{1}{2}$
(3) 5	1	$1\frac{1}{2}$	4	6	3	$4\frac{1}{2}$	$-\frac{1}{2}$	$-1\frac{1}{2}$
(4) 5	1	1	6	6	3	3	-1	-3
15	3	6		18		18	0	0

The capitalist renter in this case sells every quarter at its individual price of production, and consequently the total number of quarters at their average price of production per quarter, which coincides with the regulating price of 3 pounds sterling. Hence he still makes a profit of 20%, or 3 pounds sterling, upon his capital of 15 pounds sterling. But the rent is gone. What has become of the surplus in this compensation of individual prices of production per quarter with the general price of production?

The surplus profit on the first $2\frac{1}{2}$ pounds sterling was 3 pounds sterling; on the second $2\frac{1}{2}$ pounds sterling it was $1\frac{1}{2}$ pound sterling; total surplus profit on one-third of the invested capital, that is, on 5 pounds sterling, $4\frac{1}{2}$ pounds sterling, or 90%.

In the case of investment No. 3) the 5 pounds sterling do not only yield no surplus profit, but its product of $1\frac{1}{2}$ quarters, if sold at the general price of production, gives a minus of $1\frac{1}{2}$ pounds sterling. Finally, in the case of in-

3B

vestment No. 4), which amounts likewise to 5 pounds sterling,
its product of 1 quarter, if sold at the general price of production, gives a minus of 3 pounds sterling. Both investments of capital together give a minus of $4\frac{1}{2}$ pounds sterling,
equal to the surplus profit of $4\frac{1}{2}$ pounds sterling, which was
realized on investments Nos. 1) and 2).

The surplus profits and deficits balance one another.
Therefore the rent disappears. In fact this is possible only
because the elements of surplus-value, which form a surplus
profit, or rent, now pass into the formation of the average
profit. The capitalist renter makes this average profit of 3
pounds sterling on 15 pounds sterling, or of 20%, at the
expense of the rent.

The compensation of the individual average price of production of B to the general price of production of A, which
regulates the market, presupposes that the difference, by which
the individual price of the product of the first investment of
capital stands below the regulating price, is more and more
compensated and finally balanced by the difference, by which
the product of the subsequent investments of capital stands
above the regulating price. What appears as a surplus profit,
so long as the product of the first investment of capitals sold
by itself, becomes by degrees a part of their average price of
production, and thereby enters into the formation of the average profit, until it is finally absorbed in this way.

If only 5 pounds sterling are invested in B, instead of 15
pounds sterling, and if the additional $2\frac{1}{2}$ quarters of the last
Table are produced by taking $2\frac{1}{2}$ new acres of A under cultivation with an investment of $2\frac{1}{2}$ pounds sterling per acre,
then the invested additional capital would amount only to $6\frac{1}{4}$
pounds sterling, so that the total investment on A and B
for the production of these 6 quarters would be only $11\frac{1}{4}$
pounds sterling instead of 15 pounds sterling, and the total
cost of production of these including the profit of $13\frac{1}{2}$ pounds
sterling. The 6 quarters would still be sold at 18 pounds
sterling, but the investment of capital would have decreased
by $3\frac{3}{4}$ pounds sterling, and the rent upon B would be $4\frac{1}{2}$
pounds sterling per acre, as before. It would be different, **if**

the production of the additional $2\frac{1}{2}$ quarters would require that inferior soil than A, for instance A — 1, A — 2, should be taken under cultivation; so that the price of production per quarter, for $1\frac{1}{2}$ quarters on soil A — 1 would be 4 pounds sterling, and for the last quarter on soil A — 2 would be 6 pounds sterling. In this case these 6 pounds sterling would be the regulating price of production per quarter. The $3\frac{1}{2}$ quarters of B would then be sold at 21 pounds sterling instead of $10\frac{1}{2}$ pounds sterling, and this would leave a rent of 15 pounds sterling instead of $4\frac{1}{2}$ pounds sterling, or in grain a rent of $2\frac{1}{2}$ quarters instead of $1\frac{1}{2}$ quarter. In the same way the one quarter on A would now leave a rent of 3 pounds sterling, or of $\frac{1}{2}$ quarter.

Before we discuss this point any further, we will pause to make the following observation.

The average price of one quarter of B is compensated and coincides with the general price of production of 3 pounds sterling per quarter, regulated by A, as soon as that portion of the total capital, which produces the excess of $1\frac{1}{2}$ quarter, is balanced by that portion of the total capital, which produces a deficit of $1\frac{1}{2}$ quarter. How soon this compensation is effected, or how much capital with less than average productivity must be invested in B for that purpose, will depend, assuming the surplus productivity of the first investments of capital to be given, upon the relative underproductivity of the later invested capitals, compared with an investment of the same amount upon the worst regulating soil A, or upon the individual price of production of their product, compared with the regulating price.

———

We now come to the following conclusions from the foregoing:

1) So long as the additional capitals are invested in the same soil with a surplus productivity, even a decreasing one, the absolute rent in grain and money increases per acre, although it decreases relatively, in proportion to the advanced capital (in other words, the rate of surplus profit, or rent).

The limit is here formed by that additional capital, which yields only the average profit, or the price of production of whose product coincides with the general price of production. The price of production remains the same under these circumstances, unless the production upon the lesser soils becomes superfluous through an increased supply. Even with a falling price may these additional capitals still produce a surplus profit, though a smaller one, within certain limits.

2) The investment of additional capital, which produces only the average profit, whose surplus productivity is therefore zero, does not alter anything in the level of the existing surplus profit, and consequently of the rent. The individual average price per quarter increases thereby upon the superior soils; the surplus per quarter decreases, but the number of quarters, which carry this decreased surplus, increases, so that the product remains the same.

3) Additional investments of capital, whose product has an individual price of production exceeding the regulating price, whose surplus productivity is therefore not merely zero, but less than zero, that is, a minus lower than the productivity of the same investment of capital upon the regulating soil A, bring the individual average price of production of the total product of the superior soil closer to the general price of production, reduce more and more the difference between both, which forms the surplus profit, or rent. More and more of that which forms a surplus profit, or rent, passes over into the formation of the average profit. But nevertheless the total capital invested in one acre of B continues to yield a surplus profit, although a decreasing one in proportion as the capital with undernormal productivity and the degree of its underproductivity increase. The rent, with an increasing capital and increasing production, decreases in this case absolutely per acre, not merely relatively as compared to the increasing size of the invested capital, as in the second case.

The rent cannot disappear, unless the individual average price of production of the total product of the better soil B coincides with the regulating price, so that the entire surplus profit of the first more productive investment of capital is consumed in the formation of the average profit.

The minimum limit of the fall for the rent per acre is the point at which it disappears. But this point does not assert itself, as soon as the additional investments of capital work with an underproductivity, but rather as soon as the additional investment of the underproductive capitals becomes so great that their effect paralyzes the overproductivity of the first investments of capital, so that the productivity of the total capital becomes the same as that of A, and the individual average price of the quarter of B the same as that of the quarter of A.

In this case, likewise, the regulating price of production, 3 pounds sterling per quarter, remains the same, although the rent would have disappeared. Only after this point would have been passed, would the price of production have to rise in consequence of an increase of either the degree of under-productivity of the additional capital or of the magnitude of the additional capital of the same underproductivity. For instance, if in the above Table $2\frac{1}{2}$ quarters were produced instead of $1\frac{1}{2}$ quarters, at 4 pounds sterling per quarter, upon the same soil, then we should have altogether 7 quarters at 22 pounds sterling cost of production; the quarter would cost $3\frac{1}{7}$ pounds sterling; it would be $\frac{1}{7}$ above the general price of production which would have to rise.

For a long time, then, additional capital with underpro-ductivity, or even increasing underproductivity, might be in-vested, until the individual average price per quarter of the best soils would become equal to the general price of produc-tion, until the excess of the latter over the former, and with it the surplus profit and the rent, would entirely disappear.

And even in this case the disappearance of the rent from the better kinds of soil would only signify that the individual average price of their products would coincide with the general price of production, so that this last price would not have to rise.

In the above illustration, upon soil B, which is there the lowest of the better rent paying soils, $3\frac{1}{2}$ quarters were pro-

duced by a capital of 5 pounds sterling with a surplus productivity, and 2½ quarters by a capital of 10 pounds sterling
with underproductivity, together 6 quarters, of which $\frac{5}{12}$ are
produced by the capitals with underproductivity. . And only
at this point does the individual average price of production
of the 6 quarters rise to 3 pounds sterling and coincide with
the general price of production.

Under the law of landed property, however, the last 2½
quarters could not have been produced in this way at 3
pounds sterling per quarter, with the exception of the case, in
which they may be produced upon 2½ new acres of the soil A.
The case, in which the additional capital produces only at
the general price of production, would have been the limit.
Beyond it the additional investment of capital would have
to cease upon the same soil.

If the capitalist renter once pays 4½ pounds sterling of
rent for the first two investments of capital, he must continue
to pay them, and every investment of capital, which produces
one quarter below 3 pounds sterling, would cause him a deduction from his profit. The compensation of the individual
price of production, in the case of underproductivity, is
thereby prevented.

Let us take this case in the previous illustration, in which
the price of production of the soil A, at 3 pounds sterling per
quarter, regulates the price for B.

Capital P. St.	Profit P. St.	Cost of Production P. St.	Yield Qrs.	Cost of Production per Qr.	Selling Price per Qr. P. St.	Selling Price Together P. St.	Surplus Profit P. St	Loss P. St.
2½	1½	3	2	1½	3	6	3	—
2½	½	3	1½	2	3	4½	1½	—
5	1	6	1½	3	3	4½	—	1½
5	1	6	1	6	3	3	—	3
15	4	18		.		18	4½	4½

The cost of production of the 3½ quarters in the first two
investments is likewise 3 pounds sterling per quarter for the
capitalist renter, since he has to pay a rent of 4½ pounds
sterling, the difference between his individual price of production and the general price of production not flowing into his

pocket. In his case, then, the excess of the price of the first
two investments of capital cannot serve for the compensation
of the deficit incurred in the production of the third and fourth
investment of capital.

The $1\frac{1}{2}$ quarters in investment No. 3) cost the capitalist
renter, with profit included, 6 pounds sterling; but at the
regulating price of 3 pounds sterling per quarter he can sell
them only for $4\frac{1}{2}$ pounds sterling. In other words, he would
not only lose his whole profit, but also $\frac{1}{2}$ pound sterling, or
10% of his invested capital of 5 pounds sterling. The loss
of profit and capital in the case of investment No. 3) would
amount to $1\frac{1}{2}$ pound sterling, and in the case of investment
No. 4) 3 pounds sterling, together $4\frac{1}{2}$ pounds sterling, just
as much as the rent of the better investments amounts to,
whose individual price of production cannot take part in the
compensation of the individual average price of production of
the total product of B, because its surplus is paid as a rent to
some third person.

If the demand should require that the additional $1\frac{1}{2}$ quarters must be produced by a third investment of capital, then
the regulating market price would have to rise to 4 pounds
sterling per quarter. In consequence of this rise in the regulating market price the rent upon B would rise for the first
and second investment, and a rent would be formed upon A.

Although the differential rent is but a formal transformation of surplus profit into rent, since property in land enables
the owner in this case to draw the surplus profit of the capitalist renter into his own hands, we find nevertheless that
the successive investment of capital upon the same land, or,
what amounts to the same, the increase of the capital invested
in the same land, reaches its limit far more rapidly when the
rate of productivity of the capital decreases and the regulating price remains the same, so that in fact a more or less artificial barrier is erected as a consequence of the mere formal
transformation of surplus profit into ground rent,— which is
the result of private property in land. The rise of the
general price of production, which becomes necessary when
the limit is narrowed beyond the ordinary, is in this case not

merely the cause of a rise of the differential rent, but the existence of differential rent as rent is at the same time a reason for the earlier and more rapid rise of the general price of production, in order to insure by this means the supply of the needed larger product.

Furthermore we must make a note of the following facts:

By an addition of capital to soil B the regulating price could not, as above, rise to 4 pounds sterling, if soil A should supply the additional product below 4 pounds sterling by a second investment of capital, or if new and worse soil than A should come into competition, whose price of production would be higher than 3 but lower than 4 pounds sterling. We see, then, that differential rent No. I and differential rent No. II, while the first is the basis of the second, are at the same time mutual limits for one another, by which now a successive investment of capital upon the same soil, now an investment of capital side by side upon new soil, is brought about. In like manner they act as mutual boundaries in other cases, for instance, when better land is taken up.

CHAPTER XLIV.

DIFFERENTIAL RENT EVEN UPON THE WORST SOIL UNDER CULTIVATION.

LET us assume that the demand for grain is rising, and that the supply cannot be made to cover the demand, unless successive investments of capital with deficient productivity are made upon the rent-paying soils, or by an additional investment of capital, likewise with a decreasing productivity, upon soil A, or by the investment of capital in new lands of a lesser quality than A.

Let us take soil B as a representative of the rent paying soils.

The additional investment of capital demands a rising of the market price above the prevailing price of production of

3 pounds sterling per quarter, in order that the increased production of one quarter (which may here stand for one million
quarters, as may every acre for one million acres) upon B may
be possible. An increased production may also take place
upon soils C and D, etc., the soils paying the highest rent,
but only with a decreasing power to produce a surplus; but
it is assumed that the one quarter upon B must necessarily
be produced in order to cover the demand. If this one
quarter is more easily produced by investing more capital
in B than with the same addition of capital to A, or by
descending to soil A — 1, which may, perhaps, produce
one quarter only for 4 pounds sterling, whereas the additional capital upon A might do so at $3\frac{3}{4}$ pounds sterling per
quarter, then the additional capital upon B will regulate the
market price.

Let us also assume that A produces one quarter at 3 pounds
sterling, as it did heretofore. Let B likewise, as before, produce altogether $3\frac{1}{2}$ quarters at an individual price of production of 6 pounds sterling for its total output. Now, if an
addition of 4 pounds sterling becomes necessary upon B (including the profit) in order to produce an additional quarter,
whereas it might be produced upon A at $3\frac{3}{4}$ pounds sterling,
then it would naturally be produced upon A, not upon B. Let
us assume, then, that this additional quarter can be produced
upon B with an additional cost of production of $3\frac{1}{2}$ pounds
sterling. In this case $3\frac{1}{2}$ pounds sterling would become the
regulating price for the entire production. B would now
sell its product of $4\frac{1}{2}$ quarters at $15\frac{3}{4}$ pounds sterling. The
cost of production of the first $3\frac{1}{2}$ quarters, or 6 pounds sterling, would have to be deducted from this, also that of the last
quarter, or $3\frac{1}{2}$ pounds sterling, total $9\frac{1}{2}$ pounds sterling. This
leaves a surplus profit for rent of $6\frac{1}{4}$ pounds sterling, as
against the former $4\frac{1}{2}$ pounds sterling. In this case one acre
of A would also yield a rent of $\frac{1}{2}$ pound sterling; but not the
worst soil A, but the better soil B would regulate the price of
production with $3\frac{1}{2}$ pounds sterling. Of course we assume
here that new soil of the quality of A is not accessible in the
same favorable location as that hitherto cultivated, but that

either a second investment of capital upon the already cultivated soil A is required at a higher cost of production, or the cultivation of still inferior soil, such as A — 1. As soon as differential rent No. II comes into action by successive investments of capital, the limits of the rising price of production may be regulated by better soil, and the worst soil, the basis of differential rent No. I, may also carry a rent. Under these circumstances all cultivated lands would pay a rent under a mere differential rent system. We should then have the following two Tables, in which we mean by the term cost of production the sum of the invested capital plus 20% profit, in other words, on every $2\frac{1}{2}$ pounds sterling of capital $\frac{1}{2}$ pound sterling of profit, total 3 pounds sterling.

Class of Soil	Acres	Cost of Production P. St.	Product Qrs.	Selling Price P. St.	Proceeds in Money P. St	Grain Rent Qrs.	Money Rent P. St.
A	1	3	1	3	3	—	—
B	1	6	3 1/2	3	10 1/2	1 1/2	4 1/2
C	1	6	5 1/2	3	16 1/2	3 1/2	10 1/2
D	1	6	7 1/2	3	22 1/2	5 1/2	16 1/2
Total	4	21	17 1/2	—	52 1/2	10 1/2	31 1/2

This is the condition of affairs, before the new capital of $3\frac{1}{2}$ pounds sterling is invested in B, which supplies only one quarter. After this investment has been made, we have the following condition: ,

Class of Soil	Acres	Cost of Production P. St.	Product Qrs.	Selling Price P. St.	Proceeds in Money P. St.	Grain Rent Qrs.	Money Rent P. St.
A	1	3	1	3½	3½	1/7	½
B	1	9½	4½	3½	15¾	1 11/14	6¼
C	1	6	5½	3½	19¼	3 11/14	13¼
D	1	6	7½	3½	26¼	5 11/14	20¼
Totals	4	24½	18½		64¾	11½	40¼

[This, again, is not quite correctly calculated. The capitalist renter of B has to meet a cost of production of $9\frac{1}{2}$ pounds sterling for the $4\frac{1}{2}$ quarters and besides $4\frac{1}{2}$ pounds sterling in rent, a total of 14 pounds sterling; average per quarter $3\frac{1}{2}$ pounds sterling. This average price of his total production thus becomes the regulating market price. According to this the rent upon A would amount to $\frac{1}{9}$ pound sterling instead of $\frac{1}{2}$ pound sterling and that upon B would remain $4\frac{1}{2}$ pounds sterling, as heretofore. $4\frac{1}{2}$ quarters at $3\frac{1}{2}$ pounds sterling make 14 pounds sterling, and if we deduct $9\frac{1}{2}$ pounds sterling of cost of production we have $4\frac{1}{2}$ pounds sterling left for surplus profit. We see, then, that in spite of the required change in figures this illustration shows the way in which the better rent paying soil, by means of differential rent No. II, may regulate the price and thus transform all soil, even a hitherto rentless one, into rent paying soil.— F. E.]

The grain rent must rise, as soon as the regulating price of production of the grain rises, that is, as soon as the quarter of grain rises upon the regulating soil, or the regulating investment of capital upon one of the various kinds of soil. It is the same as though all kinds of soil had become less productive, and as though they were producing only 5-7 quarter instead of one quarter with a new investment of $2\frac{1}{2}$ pounds sterling. Whatever they produce more in grain with the same investment of capital, is converted into a surplus product, in which the surplus profit and with it the rent are incorporated. Assuming that the rate of profit remains the same, the capitalist renter will have to buy less grain with his profit. The rate of profit may remain the same, if the wages do not rise, either because they are depressed to the physical minimum, below the normal value of labor-power, or because the other things needed for consumption by the laborer and supplied by the manufacturer have become relatively cheaper; or because the working day has been prolonged or has become more intensive, so that the rate of profit in other than agricultural lines of production, which, however, regulates the agricultural profit, has remained the same or has risen; or, finally, because there may be more constant and less variable capital employed in agriculture, even though the total capital invested be the same.

Now we have considered the first condition in which rent may arise upon the worst soil A without taking still worse soil under cultivation; that is, in which rent may arise out of the difference between the old individual price of this land, which was hitherto the regulating price of production, and the new, higher, price of production, at which the last additional capital with less than normal productive power upon the better soil supplies the necessary additional product.

If the additional product had to be supplied by soil A — 1, which cannot produce one quarter at less than 4 pounds sterling, then the rent would have risen to one pound sterling upon A. But in this case the soil A — 1 would have taken the place of A as the worst cultivated soil, and A would have risen in the scale to the place of the lowest link in the series of rent paying soils. Differential rent No. I would have changed. This case, then, is outside of the consideration of differential rent II, which arises out of the different productivity of successive investments of capital upon the same piece of land.

But aside from this, differential rent may arise upon soil A in two other ways.

In the first place, it may arise so long as the price remains unchanged (any price, even a lower one compared to former ones), if the additional investment of capital creates a surplus product, which it must always do, on first sight, and up to a certain point, upon the worst soil.

In the second place, it may arise, if the productivity of the successive investments of capital upon soil A decreases.

The assumption in either case is that the increased production is required on account of the condition of the demand.

But from the point of view of differential rent, a peculiar difficulty arises here on account of the previously developed law, according to which it is always the individual average price of production per quarter in the total production (or the total investment of capital) which acts as the determining factor. In the case of soil A, however, it is not, as it is in the case of the better soils, a question of a price of production existing outside of it, which limits the equalization of the individual price of production and the general price of production, for new investments of capital. For the individual price of production of A is precisely the general price of production regulating the market price.

Let us assume:

1) When productive power of successive investments of capital is increasing, that one acre of A will produce 3 quarters instead of 2 quarters with an investment of 5 pounds sterling of capital, corresponding to 6 pounds sterling of cost of production. The first investment of $2\frac{1}{2}$ pounds sterling supplies one quarter, the second 2 quarters. In this case 6 pounds sterling of cost of production will correspond to a product of 3 quarters, so that the average price of one quarter will be 2 pounds sterling. If the 3 quarters are sold at 2 pounds sterling per quarter, then A does not produce any rent any more than it did before. Only the basis of differential rent No. II has been altered. The regulating price of production is now 2 pounds sterling instead of 3 pounds. A capital of $2\frac{1}{2}$ pounds sterling produces now an average of $1\frac{1}{2}$ quarters upon the worst soil instead of 1 quarter, and this is now the official productivity for all better soils with an investment of $2\frac{1}{2}$ pounds sterling. A portion of the ordinary surplus product now passes over into the formation of their necessary product, just as a portion of their surplus profit now passes over into the formation of the average profit.

But if the calculation is made as it is upon the better soils, where the average calculation does not alter anything in the absolute surplus, because the general price of production is the limit of the investment of capital, then one quarter of the first investment of capital costs 3 pounds sterling and the 2 quarters of the second investment costs only $1\frac{1}{2}$ pounds sterling. This would give rise to a grain rent of one quarter and a money rent of 3 pounds sterling upon A, but the 3 quarters would be sold at the old price of 9 pounds sterling all together. If a third investment of $2\frac{1}{2}$ pounds sterling of capital were made at the same productivity as the second investment, then the total production would be 5 quarters at 9 pounds sterling of cost of production. If the individual average price of A should remain the regulating price, then one quarter would be sold at $1\frac{4}{5}$ pound sterling. The average

price would have fallen once more, not through a new rise of
the productivity of the third investment of capital, but merely
through the addition of a new investment of capital with the
same additional productivity as the second one. Instead of
raising the rent upon the rent paying soils, the successive investments of capital of a higher, but sustained, fertility upon
the soil A would lower the price of production and with it
the differential rent upon all other soils in the same proportion, under conditions remaining the same. On the other
hand, if the first investment of capital, which produces one
quarter at 3 pounds sterling, should remain in force by itself,
then 5 quarters would be sold at 15 pounds sterling, and the
differential rent of the later investments of capital upon soil
A would amount to 6 pounds sterling. The additional capital per acre of soil A, whatever might be the manner of its
application, would be an improvement in this case, and it
would make the original portion of capital more productive.
It would be nonsense to say that $\frac{1}{3}$ of the capital had produced
one quarter and the other $\frac{2}{3}$ four quarters. For 9 pounds
sterling per acre would always produce 5 quarters, while 3
pounds sterling would produce only one quarter. Whether
a rent would arise here or not, whether a surplus profit would
be made or not, would depend wholly upon circumstances.
Normally the regulating price of production would fall. This
would be the case, if this improved, but more expensive cultivation of soil A should take place only for the reason that
it takes place upon all better soils, in other words, if a general
revolution in agriculture should occur. And the assumption
in that case would be that this soil is worked with 6 or 9
pounds sterling instead of 3 pounds. This would apply
particularly, if the greater part of the cultivated acres of soil
A, by which the bulk of the supply of this country is
furnished, should be handled by this new method. But if
the improvement should extend only to a small portion of the
area of A, then this better cultivated portion would yield a
surplus profit, which the landlord would be quick to transform
wholly or in part into rent and fix permanently in the form
of rent. In this way a rent might be gradually formed upon

all soil of the A quality, in proportion as more and more of the area of this soil is taken under cultivation by the new method, and the surplus productivity might be confiscated wholly or in part, according to market conditions. The equalization of the price of production of soil A to the average price of its product at an increased investment might thus be prevented by the fixation of the surplus profit of this increased investment of capital in the form of rent. If so, this would be once again an illustration of the way in which the transformation of surplus profit into ground-rent, in other words, the intervention of property in land, raises the price of production, as we have already noticed in the case of the better soils upon which the productivity of the additional capitals decreased, so that here the differential rent would not be a mere result of the difference between the individual and the general price of production. It would prevent, in the case of soil A, the identification of both prices in one, because it would interfere with the regulation of the price of production by the individual price of production of A. It would maintain a higher price of production than the necessary one and thus create a rent. Even if grain were freely imported from abroad, the same result could be brought about or perpetuated by compelling the tenants to use soil capable of competing in the raising of grain at the price of production regulated from abroad for other purposes, for instance for pastures, so that only rent paying soils could raise grain, that is, only soils whose individual average price of production per quarter would be below the price of production determined from abroad. On the whole it may be assumed that the price of production will fall, but not to the level of its average. Rather will it be higher than the average, but below the price of production of the worst cultivated soil A, so that the competition of new lands of the class A is held back.

2) When the productive power of the additional capitals is decreasing, let us assume that soil A — 1 can produce the additional quarter only at 4 pounds sterling, whereas soil A produces it at $3\frac{3}{4}$ pounds sterling, that is, more cheaply than the lesser soil, but still more dearly than the quarter produced

by the first investment of capital upon it. In this case the total price of the two quarters produced upon A would be $6\frac{3}{4}$ pounds sterling, and the average price per quarter $3\frac{3}{8}$ pounds sterling.   The price of production would rise, but only by $\frac{3}{8}$ pound sterling, whereas it would rise by another $\frac{3}{8}$, or to $3\frac{3}{4}$ pounds sterling, if the additional capital were invested upon new soil, which could produce at $3\frac{3}{4}$ pounds sterling and thus bring about a proportional raise of all other differential rents.

The price of production of $3\frac{3}{8}$ pounds sterling per quarter of A would thus be brought to the figure of its average price of production with an increased investment of capital, and would be the regulating price; it would not yield any rent, because it would not produce any surplus profit.

However, if this quarter, produced by the second investment of capital, were sold at $3\frac{3}{4}$ pounds sterling, then the soil A would yield a rent of $\frac{3}{4}$ pound sterling, and it would do so upon all acres of A, even those with no additional investment of capital, which would still produce one quarter at 3 pounds sterling.   So long as any uncultivated fields of A remain, the price could rise only temporarily to $3\frac{3}{4}$ pounds sterling.   The competition of new fields of A would hold the price of production at 3 pounds sterling, until all lands of the A class would be exhausted, whose favorable location would enable them to produce a quarter at less than $3\frac{3}{4}$ pounds sterling.   This would be a likely assumption, although the landlord will not let any tenant have any land free of rent, if one acre of A pays rent.

It would depend once more upon the greater or smaller generalization of the second investment of capital in the available soil A, whether the price of production shall be brought down to an average or whether the individual price of production of the second investment of capital shall be regulating at $3\frac{3}{4}$ pounds sterling.   This last case will take place only when the landlord gets time to fix the surplus profit, which would be made until the demand would be satisfied at the price of $3\frac{3}{4}$ pounds sterling, permanently in the form of rent.

Concerning the decreasing productivity of the soil with successive investments of capital, see Liebig. We have seen that the successive decrease of the surplus productive power of the investments of capital always increases the rent per acre, so long as the price of production remains the same, and this may take place even when the price of production is falling.

But in a general way the following remarks may be made.

From the point of view of the capitalist mode of production there is always a relative increase in the price of products, when a product cannot be secured unless an expense is incurred, a payment made, which did not have to be met formerly. For by a reproduction of the capital consumed in production we mean only the reproduction of values, which were represented by certain means of production. Natural elements passing into production as agencies, no matter what role they play in production, do not enter into the problem as parts of capital, but as free gifts of nature to capital, that is, as a free natural productivity of labor, which, however, appears as a productive power of capital, as do all other productive powers under the capitalist system. Therefore, if such a natural power, which originally does not cost anything, takes part in production, it does not count in the determination of prices, so long as the product supplied by its help suffices for the demand. But if a larger product is demanded than that which can be supplied by the help of this natural power, so that the additional product must be created without this power, or by assisting it with human labor power, then a new additional element enters into capital. A relatively larger investment of capital is required for the purpose of securing the same product. All other circumstances remaining the same, the price of the product is raised.

(From a manuscript " Started about the Middle of February, 1876.")

Differential Rent and Rent as a mere interest on capital invested in the soil.

3C

The so-called permanent improvements — which change the physical, and in part also the chemical, condition of the soil by means of operations requiring an expenditure of capital, and which may be regarded as an incorporation of capital in the soil — nearly all amount to giving to a certain piece of land in a certain limited locality such qualities as are possessed by some other piece of land at some other locality, sometimes quite near to the other one, by nature. One piece of land is by nature level, another has to be leveled; one possesses natural drainage, another has to be drained artificially; one has naturally a deep top soil, another must be artificially deepened; one clay soil is naturally mixed with a proper modicum of sand, another has to be treated for the purpose of making it so; one meadow is irrigated or moistened naturally, another requires labor to get it into this condition, or in the language of bourgeois economists, it requires capital.

It is indeed a very exhilarating theory, which calls rent by the name of interest in the case of one piece of land, whose comparative advantages have been acquired, whereas it does not do so in the case of a piece of land which has the same advantages naturally. (As a matter of fact, this is distorted in practice into saying that because rent really coincides in the one case with interest, it must falsely be called interest in cases where this is positively not the case.) However, the land yields a rent after the investment of capital, not because capital has been invested, but because the investment of capital makes this land more productive than it was formerly. Assuming that all land requires this investment, then every piece of land which has not received it must first pass through this stage, and the rent which the soil already endowed with capital yields (the interest which it may pay in a certain case), constitutes as much a differential rent as though it possessed this advantage by nature and the other land had to acquire it artificially.

This rent, which may be resolved into pure interest, becomes altogether a differential rent, as soon as the invested capital is sunk in the land. Otherwise the same capital would have to appear twice as capital.

It is one of the most amusing incidents, that all opponents of Ricardo, who combat the determination of value exclusively by labor, criticize in the case of differential rent arising from differences of soil the determination of value by nature instead of by labor. But at the same time they credit the location of the land with this determination, or perhaps, even more, the interest on capital sunk in the land during its cultivation. The same labor produces the same value in the product created during a certain time. But the magnitude, or the quantity, of this product, and consequently also that portion of value, which falls upon some aliquot part of this product, depends only upon the quantity of the product, so long as the quantity of labor is given, and the quantity of the product, in its turn, depends upon the productivity of the given quantity of labor, not upon the size of this quantity. It is immaterial, whether this productivity is due to nature or to society. Only in the case in which the productivity costs labor, and consequently capital, does it increase the cost of production by a new element, but this is not the case with nature alone.

CHAPTER XLV.

ABSOLUTE GROUND-RENT.

In the analysis of ground-rent we proceeded from the assumption, that the worst soil does not pay any ground-rent, or, to put it more generally, that only such land pays ground-rent as produces at an individual price of production which is below the price of production regulating the market, so that in this way a surplus profit arises which is transformed into rent. It should be remembered that the law of differential rent as such is entirely independent of the correctness or incorrectness of this assumption.

Let us call the general price of production, by which the market is regulated, P. Then P coincides for the product of the worst soil A with its individual price of production; that is to say, its price pays for the constant and variable capital consumed in its production plus the average profit (profits of enterprise plus interest).

The rent amounts to zero in this case. The individual price of production of the next better soil B is equal to P′, and P is larger than P′; that is P pays more than the actual price of production of the product of the soil B. Now let us assume that P minus P′ is d; in this case d, the excess of P over P′, is a surplus profit, which the tenant realises upon class B of soil. This d is converted into rent, which must be paid to the landlord. Let the actual price of production of the third class of soil, C, be P″, and P minus P″ equal to 2d; then this 2d is converted into rent; likewise let the individual price of production of the fourth class of soil, D, be P‴, and P minus P‴ equal to 3d, which is converted into ground-rent, etc. Now take it that the assumption of a rent upon soil A equal to zero and of a price of production equal to P plus zero is wrong. Rather let the class A of soil also pay a rent, equal to r. In that case we come to two conclusions.

First: The price of the product of the land of class A would not be regulated by its price of production, but by containing a surplus above it would come to P + r. For assuming the capitalist mode of production to be in a normal condition, that is, assuming that the surplus r, which the tenant pays to the landlord, is neither a deduction from wages nor from the average profit of capital, it can be paid only by selling the product above its price of production, so that a surplus profit arises, which the tenant might keep if he did not have to turn it over to the landlord as a rent. In that case the regulating market price of the total product of all soils existing on the market would not be the price of production, which capital generally makes in all spheres of production, which is a price equal to the cost of production plus the average profit, but it would be the price of production plus the rent, P + r, and not merely P. For the price of the product of soil A expresses generally the limit of the regulating general market price, at which the total product can be supplied, and to that extent it regulates the price of this total product.

Secondly: Nevertheless the law of differential rent would not be suspended in this case, although the general price of the products of the soil would be essentially modified. For if the price of the product of class A should be $P + r$, and this should be the general market price, then the price of class B would be likewise $P + r$, and so would be the price of classes C, D, etc. But since $P - P' = d$, in the case of class B, it is evident that $(P + r) - (P' + r)$ is also equal to d, and $P - P''$ in the case of class C would mean that $(P + r) - (P'' + r)$ is equal to 2d, and $P - P''$ in the case of class D would mean that the formula $(P + r) - (P'' + r)$ is equal to 3d, and so forth. In other words, the differential rent would still be regulated by the same law as before, although the rent would contain an element independent of this law and would show a general increase in the same way as would the price of the products of the soil. It follows, then, that no matter what may be the condition of the rent upon the least fertile lands, the law of differential rent is not only independent of it, but that also the only manner of viewing differential rent in keeping with its character, is to place the rent of class A at zero. Whether this is zero or larger than zero, is immaterial, so far as the differential rent is concerned, and is not considered in the calculation.

The law of differential rent, then, is independent of the results of the following investigations.

If we now go more deeply into the question, as to what is the sound basis of the assumption that the product of the worst soil A does not pay any rent, we necessarily get the answer: If the market price of the products of the land, say of grain, reaches such a level that an additional investment of capital in the class A of soils pays the ordinary price of production and yields the ordinary average profit to the capitalist, then this is sufficient incentive for investing additional capital in soil of class A. In other words, this condition satisfies the capitalist that new capital may be invested at the average profit and employed in the normal manner.

It should be noted here that in this case, likewise, the market price must be higher than the price of production of A. For as soon as the additional supply has been created, the relation between supply and demand has been altered. Formerly the supply was insufficient, now it is sufficient. So the price must fall. In order to fall, it must have been higher than the price of production of A. But the lesser fertility of the newly added soils of class A brings it about that the price does not fall quite as low as it was at the time when the price of production of the class B regulated the market. The price of production of A forms the limit, not for the temporary, but for the relatively permanent rise of the market price.

On the other hand, if the newly cultivated soil is more fertile than that of the hitherto regulating class A, yet only to the extent of satisfying the increased demand, then the market price remains unchanged. The inquiry as to whether the lowest class of land pays any rent, nevertheless coincides also in this case with our present inquiry, for here again the assumption that class A does not pay any rent must be explained out of the fact that the market price satisfies the capitalist tenant that this price will cover the invested capital plus the average profit, in brief, that the market price will cover the price of production of his commodities.

At any rate, the capitalist tenant can cultivate soil of class A under these conditions, in so far as he has any decision in this matter in his capacity as a capitalist. The prerequisite for a normal self-expansion of capital is now present upon soil A. But the fact that the average conditions of self-expansion would now enable the capitalist tenant to invest capital in soil of the class A if he did not have to pay any rent, does not imply that such land is at the disposal of the capitalist without any further ceremony. The circumstance that the capitalist tenant might invest his capital at the average profit, if he did not have to pay any rent, is no incentive for the landlord to lend his land to the tenant gratis and be so philanthropic as to grant free credit to this friend in business. To assume that this would be done would be to do away with private property in land, for its existence is precisely an obstacle to the investment of capital and to the liberal self-expansion of capital through land. This obstacle does not fall by any means before the simple reflection of the tenant that the condition of grain prices would enable him to get the average profit out of an invest- ·ment of capital in class A of soil, if he did not have to pay any rent, in other words, if he could proceed as though private property in land did not exist. But differential rent is based upon the fact that private property in land exists, that the land monopoly is an obstacle of capital, for without it the surplus profit would not be converted into ground-rent and would not fall into the hands of the landlord instead of those of the capitalist tenant. Private property in land remains as an obstacle, even where differential rent as such is not paid, that is, upon soils of the class A. If we observe the cases, in which capital may be invested in the land, in a country with capitalist production, without paying any rent, we shall find that they imply, all of them, a practical abolition of private property in land, even if not a legal abolition, a condition which is found only under very definite circumstances, which are in their very nature accidental.

First: This may take place when the landlord is himself a capitalist, or the capitalist himself a landlord. In this case he may himself exploit his land, as soon as the market price shall have risen sufficiently to enable him to get the price of production, that is, cost of production plus the average profit, out of what is now land of class A. But why? Because for himself private property in land is not an obstacle to the investment of his capital. He can treat his land simply as an element of nature, and can listen wholly to considerations of expediency concerning his capital, to capitalist considerations. Such cases occur in practice, but only as exceptions. Just as the capitalist cultivation of the land presupposes the separation of the active capital from property in land, so it excludes as a rule the self-management of property in land. It is evident, that·

the opposite is only an exception. If the increased demand after grain requires the cultivation of a larger area of land of the class A than is in the hands of self-managing proprietors, in other words, if a part of such land must be rented in order to be cultivated at all, then this hypothetical conception of the obstacle created by private property in land for capital and its investment at once collapses. It is an absurd contradiction to start out from the differentiation between capital and land, capitalist tenants and landlords, which corresponds to the capitalist system, and then to turn around and assume that the landlords, as a rule, exploit their own land in all cases and to the full extent, where capital would not get a rent out of the cultivation of the soil, if private property in land were not separate and distinct from it. (See the passage from Adam Smith concerning mining rent, quoted further along.) Such an abolition of private property in land is accidental. It may or may not occur.

Secondly: In the total area of some rented land there may be certain portions, which do not pay any rent under the existing condition of market prices, so that they are virtually loaned gratis, although the landlord does not look upon it in that light, because he does not consider the special rent of some particular patches in the total rental of his rented land. In such a case, so far as such patches are exempt from rent, private property as an obstacle to the investment of capital is obliterated for the capitalist tenant, and his contract with the landlord implies as much. But he does not pay any rent for such patches for the simple reason that he pays rent for the land to which they belong. The assumption in this case deals with a combination, in which the worse land of the class A is not an independent resort by which to supply the missing product, but rather an inseparable part of some better land. But the case to be investigated is precisely that in which certain pieces of land of class A are independently cultivated, and must be rented separately under the general conditions of capitalist production.

Thirdly: A capitalist tenant may invest additional cap-

ital upon the same rented land, although the additional product secured in this way nets him only the price of production at the prevailing market prices, so that he gets only the
average profit, but does not get any surplus profit with which
to pay rent. In that case he pays ground-rent with a portion of the capital invested in the land, but does not pay
any ground-rent with the remainder of his invested capital.
How little this assumption solves the problem in question, is
seen by the following considerations: If the market price
(and the fertility of the soil) enables him to obtain a larger
yield with his additional capital, so that this additional capital secures for him not merely the price of production, the
same as his old capital, but also a surplus profit, then he
pockets this surplus profit himself so long as his present
lease runs. But why? Because the obstacle of private
property has been eliminated for his capital during the time
of his lease. But the simple fact, that new and inferior soil
must be independently cleared and independently rented, in
order to secure this surplus profit for him, proves that the
investment of additional capital upon the old soil no longer
suffices to fill the required increased demand. One assumption excludes the other. It is true that one might say: The
rent of the worst soil A is itself a differential rent, compared
either to the land cultivated by the owner himself (which
is an accidental exception), or with the additional investment of capital upon the old leaseholds which do not produce any rent. However, this would be a differential rent,
which would not arise from the difference in fertility of the
various classes of soil, and which would, therefore, not be
based upon the assumption that class A of soil does not pay
any rent and sells its product at the price of production.
And furthermore, the question as to whether additional investments of capital upon the same leasehold produce any
rent or not is quite immaterial for the question, whether the
new soil of class A, which is about to be taken under cultivation, pays any rent or not, just as it is immaterial for the
organization of a new and independent manufacturing business whether another manufacturer of the same line of busi-

ness invests a portion of his capital in interest-bearing papers, because he cannot use all of it in his business; or whether he makes certain improvements, which do not secure the full profit for him, but at least more than interest. This is immaterial for him. The new establishments must produce the average profit and are built on this assumption. It is true that the additional investments upon the old leaseholds and the additional cultivation of new land of class A mutually restrict one another. The limit, up to which additional capital may be invested upon the same leasehold under less favorable conditions of production, is determined by the new competing investments upon soil of class A; on the other hand, the rent which may be produced by this class of soil is limited by the competing additional investments of capital upon the old leaseholds.

But all these false subterfuges do not solve the problem, which in simple language consists of this: Assuming the market price of grain (which shall be typical of all products of the soil in this inquiry) to be sufficient for the purpose of taking portions of soil of class A under cultivation and securing the price of production (cost of production plus average profit) by means of the capital invested in these new fields; in other words, assuming the conditions for the normal self-expansion of capital upon the soil A to be existent, is this sufficient cause for making the investment of such capital really possible? Or must the market price rise to a point where even the worst soil A will produce a rent? Does the monopoly of the land owner place an obstacle in the way of the capitalist who wants to invest, an obstacle which would not exist from the capitalist's point of view without that monopoly in land? The conditions, under which this question is put, show that the question as to whether capital may really be invested in soil of A class A, which would produce the average profit, but no rent. is not at all solved by the fact that, for instance, additional investments upon the old leaseholds may exist, which produce only the average profit but no rent at the prevailing market prices. The question still remains unanswered. The fact that the additional investments, which do not produce any rent, do not satisfy the demand is proved by the necessity of taking new land under cultivation out of class A. If the additional cultivation of land of class A takes place only to the extent that it produces a rent, that is, more than the price of production, then only two cases are possible. Either the market price must be such that even the last additional investments of capital upon the old leaseholds produce a surplus profit, which may be pocketed by the tenant or by the landlord. This raise in price and this surplus profit of the last additional investment of capital would then be a result of the fact that soil A cannot be cultivated without producing a rent. For if the price of production were sufficient to bring about a cultivation of land A, if the mere average profit were enough for that, then the price would not have risen to this point and the competition of new lands would have manifested itself as soon as they could produce just this price of production. The additional investments upon the old leaseholds, which do not produce any rent, would then have to compete with the investments upon soil A, which likewise do not produce any rent. Or, the last investments upon the old leaseholds may not produce any rent, but still the market price may have risen sufficiently to make the cultivation of soil A possible and to get a rent out of it. In this case, the additional investment of capital, which does not produce any rent, would be possible only for the reason that soil A could not be cultivated until the market price enabled it to produce a rent. Without this condition its cultivation would have begun when prices stood lower; and those later investments of capital upon the old leaseholds, which require a high market price in order to produce the ordinary profit without any rent, could not have taken place. For they produced only the average profit at the high market prices. At a lower market price, which would have become the regulating market price of production from the time that soil A would have been taken under cultivation, those later investments upon the old leaseholds could not have produced this average profit, and this means that the investments would not have been made under such conditions. In this way, the rent of soil A would indeed form a differential rent, compared to the investments upon the old leaseholds, which do not produce any rent. But the fact that the area of A forms such a differential rent is but a consequence of the condition that this area is not taken under cultivation at all, unless it produces a rent. The first condition in this case is that the necessity of this rent, which is not based upon any differences of soil, must exist and form a barrier to the possible investment of additional capitals upon the old leaseholds. In either case, the rent of soil A would not be a simple consequence of the rise in grain prices, but on the contrary, the fact that the worst soil must produce a rent in order to become available for cultivation would be the cause of a rise in the price of grain to the point at which this condition may be fulfilled.

The differential rent has this peculiarity, that the landlord merely catches the surplus profit which would otherwise go into the pocket of the tenant, and which the tenant may actually pocket under certain circumstances during the time of his lease. The property in land is here merely the cause of the transfer of a portion of the price of the product, which arises without any active participation of the landlord in production and resolves itself into surplus profit. This transfer of a portion of the price from one individual to another, from the capitalist to the landlord, is due to private property in land. But private ownership of land is not the cause which creates this portion of the price, or brings about the rise in the price, upon which it is conditioned. On the other hand, if the worst soil A cannot be cultivated — although its cultivation would yield the price of production — until it produces something in excess of the price of production, then private property in land is the creative cause of this rise in price. Private property in land itself has created rent. This fact is not altered, if, as in the second case mentioned, the rent now produced by soil A is a differential rent compared with the last additional investment of capital upon the old leaseholds, which pays only the price of production. For the circumstance, that soil A cannot be cultivated, until the regulating price of production has risen high enough to admit of a rent for soil A, is in this case the sole reason of the rise of the market price to that level, which enables the last investments upon the old leaseholds to secure the price of production, by means of which a rent is obtained from soil A. The fact that this soil has to pay any rent at all is in this case the cause which creates a differential rent between soil A and the last investment upon the old leaseholds.

Speaking in general of the fact that class A of soil, under the assumption that the price of grain is regulated by the price of production, does not pay any rent, we mean rent in the categorical sense of the word. If the tenant pays a rent, which is either a deduction from the normal wages of his laborers, or from his own normal average profit, then he does not pay a rent which is clearly distinguished from wages and profit in the price of his product. We have already indicated that this takes place continually in practice. To the extent that the wages of the agricultural laborers in a certain country are continually depressed below the normal level of wages, so that a part of the wages, being deducted from them, passes generally over into the rent, this is no exception for the tenant upon the worst kind of soil. In the same price of production, which makes the cultivation of the worst soil possible, these low wages already form a constituent element, and the sale of his product at the price of production does not enable the tenant upon this soil to pay any rent. The landlord might rent his land also to some laborer, who may be satisfied to pay all or a part of that in the form of rent which he may get in the selling price above the wages. In all these cases, however, no real rent is paid, but merely lease money. But wherever conditions correspond to the capitalist mode of production, rent and lease money must coincide. It is precisely this normal condition which must be analyzed here.

A reference to colonial conditions proves even less for our problem than do the above-mentioned cases, in which actual investments of capital under conditions of capitalist production may take place upon the land without producing any rent. What makes a colony of a colony — we have in mind only true agricultural colonies — is not merely the vast area of fertile lands in a natural state. It is rather the circumstance that these lands are not appropriated, are not brought under private ownership. It is this which makes the enormous difference between the old countries and the colonies, so far as the land is concerned, it is this nonexistence, legal or actual, of private property in land, as Wakefield remarks correctly;[128] and long before him the elder Maribeau, the physiocrat, and other older economists had discovered. It is quite immaterial here, whether the colonists take possession of the land without further ceremony, or whether they pay to the state a fee for a valid title to the land under the title of a nominal price of land. It is also immaterial, that already settled colonists may be legally the owners of land. In fact the land ownership is not an obstacle to the investment of capital here, nor to the employment of labor upon land without any capital. The settling of a part of the land by the established colonists does not prevent the newcomers from employing their capital or their labor upon new land. Therefore, if we are asked to investigate the influence of private ownership of land upon the prices of the products of land and upon the rent in places where such ownership is an obstacle to the investment of capital, it is very absurd to speak of free bourgeois colonies, in which neither the capitalist mode of production in agriculture, nor the form of private property belonging to it, exist, and in which the latter does not exist at all in fact. Ricardo is an illustration of this in his chapter on ground-rent. In the beginning he says that he is going to investigate the effect of the appropriation of land upon the value of the products of the soil, and immediately after that he takes for an illustration the colonies, assuming that real estate exists in a relatively elementary form and that its exploitation is not limited by the monopoly of private ownership in land.

The mere legal property in land does not create any ground-

[128] Wakefield, *England and America,* London, 1833. Compare also *Capitcl,* Volume I, Chapter XXVII.

rent for the landlord. But it gives him the power to with-draw his land from exploitation until the economic conditions permit him to utilize it in such a way that it will yield him a surplus, whenever the land is used either for agricul-ture proper or for other productive purposes, such as build-ings, etc. He cannot increase or decrease the absolute quan-tity of its field of employment, but he can do so with its mar-ketable quantity. For this reason, as Fourier has already remarked, a characteristic fact in all civilized countries is that a comparatively considerable portion of the land always remains uncultivated.

Assuming, then, that the demand requires the opening up of new lands, and that these lands are less fertile than those hitherto cultivated, will the landlord rent such lands for nothing, just because the market price of the products of the soil has risen high enough to pay to the tenant the price of production on his investment in this land and enable him to reap the average profit? By no means. The investment of capital must net him a rent. He does not rent his land un-til he can get lease money for it. Therefore the market price must have risen above price of production to the point P + r, so that a rent can be paid to the landlord. Since the real estate does not net any income, according to our assump-tion, until it is rented, so that it is economically valueless until then, a small rise of the market price above the price of production will suffice to bring the new land of the worst class upon the market.

The question is now: Does it follow from the ground-rent of the worst soil, which cannot be derived from any differ-ence of fertility, that the price of the products of the soil is necessarily a monopoly price in the ordinary meaning of the term, or a price, into which the rent enters like a tax, only with the distinction that the landlord levies the tax instead of the state? It is a matter of course that this tax has certain definite economic limits. It is limited by the additional in-vestments of capital upon the old leaseholds, by the competi-tion of the products of the soil of foreign countries, which are imported free of duty, by the competition of the landlords among themselves, and finally by the wants and the solvency of the consumers. But this is not the point. The point is whether the rent paid by the worst soil passes into the price of its products, which price regulates the general market price according to our assumption, and whether it enters into this price in the same way as a tax enters into the price of commodities which are dutiable, in other words, whether this rent enters into the price as an element independent of its value.

This does not necessarily follow by any means, and the contention that it does has been made only because the distinction between the value of commodities and their price of production had not been understood up to the present. We have seen that the price of production of a commodity is by no means identical with its value, although the prices of production of all commodities, considered as a whole, are regulated only by their total value, and although the movement of the prices of production of the various kinds of commodities, taking all other circumstances as equal, is controlled exclusively by the movement of their values. It has been demonstrated that the price of production of a commodity may stand above or below its value, and coincides but rarely with its value. Hence the fact that the products of the soil are sold above their prices of production does not prove by any means that they are sold above their values. Neither does the fact that the products of industry are, on an average sold at their prices of production, prove that they are sold at their values. It is possible that the products of agriculture are sold above their price of production and below their value, while many products of industry bring the price of production only because they are sold above their value.

The relation of the price of production of a certain commodity to its value is exclusively determined by the proportion, in which the variable part of the capital with which it is produced stands to its constant part, or by the organic composition of the capital producing it. If the composition of the capital in a certain sphere of production is lower than that of the social average capital, in other words, if its variable portion, which is used for wages, is relatively larger than its constant portion, which is invested in material require- ments of production, compared to the social average capital, then the value of its products must stand above their price of production. In other words, such a capital, employing more living labor, produces at the same rate of exploitation of labor more surplus-value, and therefore more profit, than an equally large aliquot portion of the social average capital. The value of its products stands, therefore, above their price of production, since this price of production is equal to the cost of production plus the average profit, and the average profit is lower than the profit produced in these commodities. The surplus-value produced by the social average capital is smaller than that produced by a capital of this lower composition. On the other hand, when the capital invested in a certain sphere of production is of higher than average composition, then the case is reversed. The value of the commodities pro- duced by it stands below their price of production, and this is generally the case with the products of the most highly developed industries.

If the capital in a certain sphere of production is of a lower composition than the social average capital, then this is primarily an expression of the fact that the productive power of the social labor in this particular sphere of produc- tion is below the average; for the prevailing degree of pro- ductive power shows itself in the relative preponderance of the constant over the variable capital, or in the continual decrease of the portion used in a certain capital for wages. On the other hand, if the capital in a certain sphere of pro- duction is of a higher composition, then it expresses a devel- opment of the productive power above the average.

Leaving aside the work of artists, which is naturally ex- cluded from our discussion, it is a matter of course that dif- ferent spheres of production require different proportions of constant and variable capital according to their technical pe- culiarities, and that living labor must occupy more room in some, less room in others. For instance, in the extractive industries, which must be clearly distinguished from agri-

3D

culture, raw material as an element of constant capital is wholly absent, and even the auxiliary material plays only rarely an important role in them. Nevertheless the progress of development may be measured also in them by the relative increase of the constant over the variable capital.

If the composition of the capital in agriculture proper is lower than that of the social average capital, then this would be on its face an expression of the fact that in countries with a developed production agriculture has not progressed as far as the industries which work up its products. This fact could be explained, aside from all other economic circumstances which are of paramount importance, from the earlier and more rapid development of mechanical sciences, and especially by their application, compared to the later and partly quite recent development of chemistry, geology and physiology, and particularly their application to agriculture. For the rest it is an indubitable and long known fact[129] that also the progress of agriculture expresses itself steadily in a relative increase of the constant over the variable capital. Whether in a certain country with capitalist production, for instance in England, the composition of the agricultural capital is lower than that of the social average capital, is a question which can be decided only by statistics, and which need not be discussed in detail for the purposes of this inquiry. So much is theoretically accepted that the value of the agricultural products cannot be higher than their price of production unless this condition obtains. In other words, a capital of a certain size in agriculture produces more surplus-value, or what amounts to the same, sets in motion and commands more surplus-labor (and with it employs more living labor) than a capital of the same size in industry of social average composition.

This assumption, then, suffices for that form of rent which we are analyzing here, and which can take place only so long as this assumption holds good. Wherever this assumption falls, the form of rent corresponding to it falls likewise.

However, the mere fact of an excess of the value of agri-

---

[129] See Dombasle and R. Jones.

cultural products over their price of production would not suffice in itself for the explanation of the existence of a ground-rent, which is independent of differences of fertility or of successive investments of capital upon the same land, a rent which is to be clearly differentiated from differential rent, and which we may therefore call absolute rent. Quite a number of manufactured products have the peculiarity that their value is higher than their price of production, and yet they do not produce any excess above the average profit, a surplus profit, which might be converted into rent. On the other hand, the existence and meaning of the price of production and of the average rate of profit which it implies rest upon the fact that the individual commodities are not sold at their value. The prices of production arise from an equalization of the values of commodities. This equalization after restoring their respective capital values to the various spheres of production, in which they were consumed, distributes the entire surplus-value, not in proportion as it has been produced in the individual spheres of production and incorporated in their commodities, but in proportion to the magnitude of the capital invested in them. Only in this way is an average profit brought about and with it the price of production, whose characteristic element this average profit is. It is the continual tendency of the capitals to bring about this equalization in the distribution of the surplus-value produced by the total capital by means of competition, and to overcome all obstacles to this equalization. This implies the tendency to permit only such surplus profits as arise under all circumstances, not from differences between the values and the prices of production of the commodities, but rather from the general prices of production, which regulates the market and from the individual prices of production, which differ from it. In other words, only such surplus profits are tolerated, which occur within a certain sphere of production and not such as occur between two different spheres of production, so that they do not touch the general prices of production of the different spheres, or their general rate of profit, but which rather have for their basis the conversion of values into prices of production and into an average rate of profit for the whole. This condition rests, however, as previously explained, upon the continually changing proportional distribution of the total social capital among the various spheres of production, upon the unremitting emigration and immigration of capitals, upon their transfer from one sphere to another, in short upon their free movement between the various spheres of production, which represent so many available fields of investment for the independent constituents of the total capital of society. And the other assumption in this case is that no barrier, or at least only a temporary and accidental barrier, interferes with the competition of the capitals, for instance in some sphere of production, in which the value of the commodities is higher than their prices of production, or where the produced surplus-value is larger than the average profit, so that nothing prevents the reduction of value to a price of production and the proportional distribution of the excess of surplus-value of this sphere of production among all spheres exploited by capital. But if the reverse happens, if capital meets some foreign power, which it cannot overcome, or which it can but partially overcome, and which limits its investment in certain spheres, admitting it only under conditions which wholly or partly exclude that general equalization of surplus-value to an average profit, then it is evident that the excess of the value of commodities in such spheres of production over their prices of production would give rise to a surplus profit, which could be converted into rent and made independent as such compared to profit. Such a foreign power is private ownership of land, when it builds obstacles against capital in its endeavor to invest in land, such a power is the landlord in his relation to the capitalist.

Private property in land is then the barrier which does not permit any new investment of capital upon hitherto uncultivated or unrented land without levying a tax, in other words, without demanding a rent, although the land to be taken under new cultivation may belong to a class which does not produce any differential rent, and which, were it not for the inter-

vention of private property in land, might have been cultivated at a small increase in the market price, so that the
regulating market price would have netted to the cultivator
of this worst soil nothing but his price of production. But
on account of the barrier raised by private property in land,
the market price must rise to a point, where the land can
pay a surplus over the price of production, in other words,
where it can pay a rent. Now, since the value of the commodities produced by agricultural capital is higher than their
price of production, as we have assumed, this rent (with the
exception of one case which we shall discuss immediately)
forms the excess of the value over the price of production,
or a part of it. Whether the rent consumes the entire difference between the value and the price of production, or
only a greater or smaller part of it, will depend wholly upon
the relation between supply and demand and upon the area
of the new land taken in cultivation. So long as the rent
is not equal to the excess of the value of agricultural products over their price of production, a portion of this excess
would always enter into the general equalization and proportional distribution of all surplus-value among the various
individual capitals. As soon as the rent is equal to the excess of the value over the price of production, this entire portion of the surplus-value over and above the average profit
would be withdrawn from the equalization. But whether
this absolute rent is equal to the whole surplus of value over
the price of production, or only equal to a part of it, the agricultural products would always be sold at a monopoly price,
not because their price would exceed their value, but because
their price would be equal to their value, or because
their price would be lower than their value but higher
than their price of production. Their monopoly would
consist in the fact that they are not, like other products of industry whose value is higher than the general price
of production, leveled to the plane of the price of production.
Since one portion of the value and of the price of production is an actually existing constant element, namely the cost
price, representing the capital k consumed in production, their

difference consists in the other, the variable, portion, the surplus-value, which amounts to p in the price of production, that is, to the profit which is equal to the total surplus-value calculated on the social capital and on every individual capital as an aliquot part of the social capital. This profit equals in the value of commodities the actual surplus-value created by this particular capital, and forms an integral part of the value of commodities created by this capital. If the value of commodities is higher than their price of production, then the price of production is k + p, the value k + p + d, so that p + d represents the surplus-value contained in it. The difference between the value and the price of production is, therefore, equal to d, the excess of the surplus-value created by this capital over the surplus-value assigned to it by the average rate of profit. It follows from this that the price of agricultural products may stand higher than their price of production, without reaching up to their value. It follows, furthermore, that up to a certain point a permanent increase in the price of agricultural products may take place, before their price reaches their value. It follows also that the excess in the value of agricultural products over their price of production can become a determining element of their general market price only because there is a monopoly in private ownership of land. It follows, finally, that in this case the increase in the price of the product is not the cause of the rent, but rather the rent is the cause of the increase in the price of the product. If the price of the product of the unit of the worst soil is equal to P + r, then all differential rents will rise by the corresponding multiples of r, since the assumption is that P + r becomes the regulating market price.

If the average composition of the non-agricultural capital were 85 c + 15 v, and the rate of surplus-value 100%, then the price of production would be 115. If the composition of the agricultural capital were 75 c + 25 v, and the rate of surplus-value the same, then the value of the agricultural product and the regulating market price would be 125. If the agricultural and the non-agricultural product should be leveled to the same average price (we assume for the sake of brevity that the total capital in both lines of production is equal), then the total surplus-value would be 40, or 20%, upon the 200 of capital. The product of the one as of the other would be sold at 120. In the equalization into the prices of production the average market prices of the non-agricultural capital would stand above, and those of the agricultural capital below their value. If the agricultural products were sold at their full value, they would stand higher by 5, and the industrial products lower by 5, than they do in the equalization. If the market conditions do not permit the sale of the agricultural products at their full value, at the full surplus above the price of production, then the result hangs between the two extremes; the industrial products would be sold a little above their value, and the agricultural products a little above their price of production.

Although the private ownership of land may drive the price of the products of the soil above their price of production, it does not depend upon this ownership, but upon the general condition of the market, to what extent the market price shall exceed the price of production and approach the value, and to what extent the surplus-value created in agriculture over and above the given average profit shall either be converted into rent or enter into the general equalization of the surplus-value to an average profit. At any rate this absolute rent, which arises out of the excess of value over the price of production, is but a portion of the agricultural surplus-value, a conversion of this surplus-value into rent, its appropriation by the landlord; so does the differential rent arise out of the conversion of surplus-profit into rent, its appropriation by the landlord, under an average price of production which acts as a regulator. These two forms of rent are the only normal ones. Outside of them the rent can rest only upon an actual monopoly price, which is determined neither by the price of production nor by the value of commodities, but by the needs and the solvency of the buyers. Its analysis belongs in the theory of competition, where the actual movement of market-prices is considered.

If all the land suitable for agriculture in a certain country were leased — assuming the capitalist mode of production and normal conditions to be general — then there would not be any soil that would not pay any rent; but there might be certain parts of some capitals invested in land that might not produce any rent. For as soon as the land has been rented, private property in land ceases to be an absolute barrier against the investment of the necessary capital. Still it continues to act as a relative barrier even after that, to the extent that the appropriation of the capital incorporated in the soil by the landlord draws very definite lines for the activity of the tenant. Only in this case would all rent be converted into a differential rent, although this would not be a differential rent determined by any differences in the fertility of the soil, but rather by differences between the surplus profits arising from the last investments of capital in a certain soil and the rent paid for the lease of the soil of the worst quality. Private property in land serves as an absolute barrier to the investment of capital only to the extent that it exacts a tribute for the permission of giving access to the land. As soon as this access has been gained, it can no longer set any absolute obstacles in the way of the size of any investment of capital in a certain soil. The building of houses meets a barrier in the private ownership of the land upon which the houses are to be built by people who do not own this land. But after this land has once been leased for the purpose of building houses on it, it depends upon the tenant whether he wants to build a large or a small house.

If the average composition of the agricultural capital were the same, or higher than that of social average capital, then absolute rent, in the sense in which we use this term, would disappear; that is, absolute rent which is different from differential rent as well as from the rent which rests upon an actual monopoly price. The value of agricultural capital would not stand above its price of production, in that case, and the agricultural capital would not set any more labor in motion, would not realize any more surplus labor, than the non-agricultural capital. The same would take place, if the composition of the agricultural capital would gradually become the same as that of the average social capital with the progress of civilization.

It looks at first glance like a contradiction, that we should assume that on the one hand the composition of the agricultural capital should become higher, in other words that its constant portion should increase faster than its variable one, and on the other hand that the price of the agricultural product should rise high enough to admit of the payment of a rent on the part of worse soil than that cultivated previously, a rent which in this case could come only from an excess of the market price over the value and the price of production, in short, a rent which could be due only to a monopoly price of the product.

It is necessary to make a clear distinction here.

In the first place, we saw in the discussion of the way, in which the rate of profit is formed, that capitals, which have the same composition, so far as their technological side is concerned, so that they set the same amount of labor in motion compared to machinery and raw materials, may nevertheless have different compositions owing to the different values of the constant portions of capital. The raw materials or the machinery may be dearer in one capital than in the other. In order to set the same quantity of labor in motion (and this would have to be the case, according to our assumption, in order that the same mass of raw materials might be worked up), a larger capital would have to be advanced in the one case than in the other, since I cannot set the same amount of labor in motion, if the raw material, which must be paid out of 100, costs 40 in one case and 20 in another. But it would become evident that these two capitals have the same technological composition, as soon as the price of the expensive raw material would fall to the level of the cheap. The proportions of value between constant and variable capital would become the same in that case, although no change would have taken place in the technical proportions between the living labor and the mass and nature of the material requirements of production employed by this capital. On the other hand, a capital of low organic composition might assume the appearance of being in the same class with one of a higher organic composition, as soon as the value of its constant parts would rise through changes in the composition of its values. For instance, one capital might be composed of 60 c + 40 v, because it employs much machinery and raw material compared to living labor, and another capital might be composed of 40 c + 60 v, because it employs 60% of living labor, 10% of machinery, and 30% of raw material. In this case a simple rise in the value of raw and auxiliary materials from 30 to 80 would wipe out the difference in composition, for then the second capital would be composed of 10 machinery, 80 raw materials, and 60 labor-power, or of 90 c + 60 v, which, in percentages, would also be equal to 60 c + 40 v, although no change would have taken place in the technical composition. In other words, capitals of the same organic composition may have a different value-composition, and capitals with the same percentages of value-composition may be at different levels of organic composition and thus express different steps in the development of labor's social productivity. The mere circumstance, then, that the agricultural capital might stand upon the general level, would not prove that the social productivity of labor is equally high-developed in it. Nothing would be shown thereby but that its own product, which itself forms one of the conditions of its own production, had become dearer, or that auxiliary materials, such as manure, which used to be close at hand, must now be brought from far distant places, etc.

But aside from this, the peculiar character of agriculture must be taken into consideration.

Even though labor saving machinery, chemical helps, etc., may occupy more space in agriculture, so that the constant capital increases not merely in value, but also in mass, as compared to the mass of the employed labor-power, the question in agriculture (as in mining) is not only one of the social, but also of the natural productivity of labor which depends upon natural conditions. It is possible that the increase of the social productivity in agriculture barely balances

or does not even make up for, the decrease in natural power
— and compensation through social productivity will always
be effective for a short time only — so that in spite of the
technical development there is no cheapening of the product,
and that at best a greater increase in its price is prevented.
It is also possible that the absolute mass of products decreases
with a rising price of cereals, while the relative surplus product increases. This could take place, if the constant capital,
consisting chiefly of machinery or animals, which require only
a reproduction of their wear and tear, would increase relatively, and if the variable capital invested in wages, which
must always be reproduced in full out of the product, should
decrease correspondingly.

On the other hand it is possible, that only a moderate rise
of the market price above the average is necessary, in order
to cultivate and draw a rent from soil, which would have required a greater rise of the market prices so long as the technical helps were less developed.

The fact that, say in cattle raising on a large scale, the
mass of the employed labor-power is very small compared
with the constant capital represented by the cattle, might be
considered as a refutation of the claim that the percentage
of labor-power set in motion by agricultural capital is larger
than that employed by the average social capital outside of
agriculture. But it should be noted here that we have taken
for our basis in the analysis of rent that portion of the agricultural capital, which produces the principal vegetable food,
which is the chief means of subsistence among civilized nations. Adam Smith — and this is one of his merits — has
already demonstrated that quite a different method of determining prices is observed in cattle raising, and for that matter generally in the production of agricultural capitals not
engaged in raising the principal means of subsistence, say
of cereals. For in this case the price of cattle is determined
by the fact that the price of the product of the soil used for
cattle raising, say as an artificial pasture, but which might
just as well be transformed into cereal fields of a certain quality, must rise high enough to produce the same rent as cereal

land of the same quality. In other words, the rent of cereal lands becomes a determining element in the price of cattle. For this reason Ramsay has justly remarked that the price of cattle is artificially raised by the rent, by the economic expression of private ownership of land, in short by the private ownership of land.

Adam Smith says in Book I, Chapter XI, Part I, of his *Wealth of Nations,* that in consequence of the extension of cultivation the uncultivated fallow land no longer suffices to supply the demand for cattle. A large portion of the cultivated lands must be used for breeding and fattening cattle, the price of which must be high enough to pay not merely for the labor spent upon them, but also for the rent which the landlord and the profit which the tenant might have drawn out of this land, had it been cultivated as a field. The cattle raised upon the least tilled peat bogs are sold according to their weight and quality in the same market and at the same price as those raised upon the best cultivated land. The owners of peat bogs profit thereby and raise the rent of their lands in proportion to the prices of cattle.

In this case, likewise, Smith represents the differential rent in favor of the worst soil as distinguished from grain rent.

The absolute rent explains some phenomena, which seem to make a mere monopoly price responsible for the rent, at first sight. Take, for instance, the owner of some forest, which exists without any human assistance, say in Norway. This will do to make a connection with Adam Smith's example. If this owner of the forest receives a rent from some capitalist, who has timber cut, perhaps on account of some demand from England, or if this owner has the timber cut in his own capacity as a capitalist, then a greater or smaller rent will accrue to him in the timber, aside from the profit on the invested capital. This looks like a pure increment from monopoly in the case of this product of nature. But as a matter of fact the capital consists here almost exclusively of variable elements invested in labor-power, and therefore it sets more surplus labor in motion than another capital of the same size. The value of the timber contains a greater surplus of unpaid labor, or of surplus-value, than that of a product of some capital of higher organic composition. For this reason the average profit can be drawn from this timber, and a considerable surplus in the form of rent can fall into the hands of the owner of the forest. On the other hand it may be assumed that, owing to the ease with which the felling of timber as a line of production may be extended, the demand must rise very considerably, in order that the price of timber should equal its value, so that the entire surplus of unpaid labor (over and above that portion which falls into the capitalist's hands as an average profit) may accrue to the landlord in the form of rent.

We have assumed that the newly cultivated soil is of a still lesser quality than the worst previously cultivated one. If it is better, it pays a differential rent. But here we are analyzing precisely that case, in which the rent does not appear as a differential rent. There are only two cases possible under these circumstances. Either the newly cultivated soil is inferior to the previously cultivated soil, or it is just as good. If it is inferior, then we have already analyzed the question. Nothing remains for us to analyze but the case in which it is just as good.

We have already stated in our analysis of differential rent, that the progress of cultivation may just as well take equally good, or even better soil under new treatment as worse soil.

First. In differential rent (or any rent, generally speaking, since even in the case of differential rent the question comes up, whether on the one hand the fertility of the soil in general, and on the other hand its location, admit of its cultivation at the regulating market price in such a way as to produce a profit and a rent) two conditions work in different directions, now paralyzing each other, now alternately exerting the determining influence. The rise of the market price — provided that the cost price of cultivation has not fallen, in other words, provided that no technical progress becomes a new impetus to further cultivation — may bring more fertile soil under cultivation, which was formerly excluded from competition by its location. Or it may, in the case of inferior soil, enhance the advantage of location to such an extent, that its lesser fertility is balanced thereby. Or, without any rise in the market price, the location may carry better soils into competition through the improvement of means of communication, as we have seen on a large scale in the prairie states of North America. The same takes place also in the older civilized countries, continually if not to the same extent as in the colonies, in which, as Wakefield correctly states, the location determines the case. To sum up, then, the contradictory effects of location and fertility, and the variableness of the factor of location, which is continually balanced and passes perpetually through progressive changes tending towards a balance, carry alternately better or worse classes of soil into new competition with the older ones under cultivation.

Second. With the development of natural history and agronomics the fertility of the soil is also changed, by changing the means through which the elements of the soil may be rendered immediately serviceable. In this way light kinds of soil in France and in the eastern counties of England, which were considered inferior at one time, have recently risen to first place. (See Passy.) On the other hand soil, which was considered inferior, not for the reason that its chemical composition was bad, but that it placed certain mechanical and physical obstacles in the way of cultivation, is turned into good land, as soon as the means for overcoming such obstacles have been discovered.

Third. In all old civilized countries old historical and traditional conditions, for instance in the form of government lands, community lands, etc., have accidentally withdrawn large tracts of land from cultivation, and these come back into it very gradually. The succession, in which they are taken under cultivation, depends neither upon their good quality nor upon their location, but upon wholly external circumstances. In following up the history of English communal lands, as they were successively turned into private property through the Enclosure Bills and cultivated, nothing would be more ridiculous than the phantastic assumption, that a modern agricultural chemist like Liebig had indicated the selection of land in this succession, had designated certain fields for cultivation on account of their chemical peculiarities and excluded others. What decided the point in this case was the opportunity which tempted the thieves, it was the more or less plausible pretenses offered by the great landlords to excuse their appropriation of such lands.

Fourth. Aside from the fact that the stage of development reached at any time by the increased population and capital sets a certain barrier to the extension of cultivation, even though it be an elastic barrier, and aside from the effects of accidents, which temporarily influence the market price, such as a series of good or bad seasons, the extension of agriculture over a larger area depends upon the entire condition of the market in capitals and upon the business condition of the whole country. In periods of stringency it will not be enough that uncultivated soil may produce the average profit for the tenant — no matter whether he pays any rent or not — in order that additional capital be invested in agriculture. On the other hand, in periods with a plethora of capital it will flow into agriculture, even without any rise in market prices, so long as only the other normal conditions are present. Better soil than that hitherto cultivated would be excluded from competition for the sole reason that its location would be unfavorable, or that it would present insurmountable obstacles to its employment for the time being, or that it was kept out by accident. For this reason we must occupy ourselves with soils which are just as good as those last cultivated. Now there is always the difference in the cost of clearing for cultivation between the new soil and the last cultivated one. And it depends upon the stand of market prices and of credit whether new land is cleared or not. As soon as this soil actually enters into competition, the market price falls once more to its former level, assuming other conditions to be equal, and the new soil will then produce the same rent as the corresponding soil formerly cultivated as the last. The theory that it does not produce any rent is proved by its champions by assuming what they are precisely called upon to prove, namely that the soil which used to be the last did not pay any rent. One might prove in the same way that the houses which were built last do not produce any rent except the house rent proper, although they are leased. In fact, however, they do produce a rent even before they yield any house rent, for they often stand vacant for a long time. Just as successive investments of capital in a certain piece of land may bring a proportional surplus and thereby the same rent as the first investment, so fields of the same quality as those last cultivated may bring the same yield at the same cost. Otherwise it would be altogether inexplicable, how fields of the same quality could ever be taken successively under cultivation, and not all of them at the same time, or rather not a single one of them in order to avoid their coming into competition at all. The landlord is always ready to draw a rent, in other words, to receive something for nothing. But capital requires certain conditions before it can comply with this wish of the landlord. The competition of the lands among themselves does not, therefore, depend upon the wish of the landlord that they should, but upon the opportunities offered to capital for competition with other capitals upon the new fields.

To the extent that the agricultural rent proper is purely a monopoly price, such a price can only be small, just as the absolute rent can only be small under normal conditions, whatever may be the surplus of the product's value over its price of production. The nature of absolute rent, therefore, consists in this: Equally large capitals in different spheres of production produce, according to their different average composition, so long as the rate of surplus-value, or the degree of labor exploitation, is the same, different amounts of surplus-value. In industry these different masses of surplus-value are leveled into an average profit and distributed among the individual capitals uniformly and as aliquot parts of the social capital. Private property in land prevents such an equalization among capitals invested in the soil, whenever production requires real estate, either for agriculture or for the extraction of raw materials, and catches a portion of the surplus value which would otherwise assist in the formation of the average rate of profits. The rent, then, forms a portion of the value, or more specifically of the surplus-value, of commodities and instead of falling into the hands of the capitalists, who extract it from their laborers, it is captured by the landlords, who extract it from the capitalists. The assumption is in this case that the agricultural capital sets more labor in motion than an equally large portion of the non-agricultural capital. How far the difference goes, or whether it exists at all, depends upon the relative development of agriculture as compared to industry. In the nature of the case this difference must decrease with the progress of agriculture, unless the proportion, in which the variable capital decreases as compared to the constant, is still greater in the industrial than in the agricultural capital.

This absolute rent plays an even more important role in the extractive industry, properly so-called, where one element of constant capital, the raw material, is wholly missing, and where, with the exception of those lines, in which the capital consisting of machinery and other fixed capital is very considerable, by far the lowest composition of capital exists. Precisely here, where the rent seems wholly due to a monopoly price, extraordinarily favorable market conditions are necessary in order that commodities may be sold at their value, or that rent may become equal to the entire excess of surplus-value in a commodity over its price of production. This applies, for instance, to rent in fishing waters, stone quarries, naturally grown forests, etc.[130]

CHAPTER XLVI.

BUILDING LOT RENT. MINING RENT. PRICE OF LAND.

DIFFERENTIAL rent appears every time and follows the same laws as the agricultural differential rent, wherever rent ex-

[130] Ricardo passes over this very superficially. See his remarks against Adam Smith on Forest rent in Norway, in *Principles,* chapter II, in the beginning.

ists at all. Wherever natural forces can be monopolized and thereby guarantee a surplus profit to the industrial capitalist using these forces, whether it be waterfalls, or rich mines, or waters teeming with fish, or a favorably located building lot, there the person who by his or her title to a portion of the globe has been privileged to own these things will capture a part of the surplus profit of the active capital by means of rent. Concerning mining lands, Adam Smith has explained that the basis of their rent, like that of all land not employed in agriculture, is regulated by the agricultural rent (Book I, Chapter, XI, 2 and 3). This form of rent is distinguished, first, by the overwhelming influence exerted by location upon differential rent (an influence which is very considerable in vineyards and in building lots of large cities) ; secondly, by the palpable passiveness of the owner, whose sole activity consists (especially in mines) in exploiting the progress of social development, toward which he contributes nothing and for which he risks nothing, unlike the industrial capitalist; and finally by the preponderance of the monopoly price in many cases, particularly by the most shameless exploitation of poverty (poverty is for house rent a more lucrative source than the mines of Potosi ever were for Spain [131] and by the tremendous power wielded by private property in land when united with industrial capital in the same hand and used for the purpose of practically excluding the laborers in their struggle for wages from the earth as a place of domicile.[132] One section of society thus exacts from another a tribute for the permission of inhabiting the earth. Private property in land implies the privilege of the landlord to exploit the body of the globe, the bowels of the earth, the air, and with them the conservation and development of life. Not only the increase of population, and with it the growing demand for shelter, but also the development of fixed capital, which is either incorporated in the soil or takes root in it and is based upon it, such as all industrial buildings, railroads, warehouses, factory buildings, docks, etc., necessarily increase the building

[131] Laing, Newman
[132] Crowlington Strike. Engels, *The Condition of the Working Class In England,* page 256, Swan Sonnenschein edition.

rent. A mistake between the house rent, to the extent that it is an interest and mortgage upon the capital invested in a house, and the rent for the mere land is not possible in this case, even with all the good will of a Carey, particularly when the landlord and the building speculator are different persons, as they are in England. Two elements should be considered here: On the one hand, the exploitation of the earth for the purpose of reproduction or extraction, on the other hand the space required as an element of all production and all human activity. Private property in land demands its tribute in both directions. The demand for building lots raises the value of the land as a building ground and foundation, and the simultaneous demand for elements of the terrestrial globe serving as building material grows with it.[133]

That it is the ground-rent, and not the house, which forms the actual object of building speculation in rapidly growing cities, especially when building is carried on as an industry, as it is in London, we have already shown in Volume II, Chapter XII, pages 266–267, of the present work, where we quoted from the testimony of a large London building speculator, Edward Capps, given before the Select Committee on Bank Acts. The same man said on that occasion, No. 5435: I believe that a man who wants to get on in the world can hardly expect to get along by sticking to a fair trade. . . . He must of necessity build also on speculation, and that on a large scale; for the contractor makes very little profit out of the buildings themselves, he makes his principal profits out of the rise of ground-rents. He takes up, for instance, a piece of land and pays 300 pounds sterling annually for it. If he erects the right class of houses upon it after a careful building plan, he may succeed in making 400 or 500 pounds sterling out of it, and his profit would consist much more of the increased ground-rent of 100 or 150 pounds sterling annually than of the profit from the buildings, which in many cases he does not consider at all.

And it should not be forgotten that after the lapse of the

---

[133] The paving of the London streets has enabled the proprietors of some naked rocks on the Scotch coast to draw a rent out of formerly absolutely useless stone soil. Adam Smith, Book I, Chapter XI, 2.

lease, at the end of 99 years, as a rule, the land with all the
buildings upon it and with the ground-rent, generally increased to twice or thrice its original amount, reverts from the
building speculator or from his legal successor to the original
landlord who was the last to rent it.

The mining rent, in its strict meaning, is determined in the
same way as the agricultural rent.

There are some mines, the product of which barely suffices
to pay for the labor and to reproduce the capital invested in
it together with the ordinary profit. They yield some profit
to the contractor, but no rent to the landlord. They can be
worked to advantage only by the landowner, who in his
capacity of a contractor makes the ordinary profit out of his
invested capital. Many coal mines in Scotland are operated
in this way, and cannot be operated in any other way. The
landowner does not permit anybody to work them without the
payment of rent, but no one can pay any rent for them.
(Adam Smith, Book I, Chapter XI, 2.)

It is necessary to distinguish, whether the rent flows from
a monopoly price, because a monopoly price of the product
or of the soil exists independently of it, or whether the products are sold at a monopoly price, because a rent exists. When
we speak of a monopoly price, we mean in a general way a
price which is determined only by the eagerness of the pur-
chasers to buy and by their solvency, independently of the
price which is determined by the general price of production
and by the value of the products. A vineyard producing wine
of very extraordinary quality, a wine which can be produced
only in a relatively small quantity, carries a monopoly price.
The winegrower would realize a considerable surplus profit
from this monopoly price, the excess of which over the value
of the product would be wholly determined by the wealth and
the fine appetite of the rich wine drinkers. This surplus
profit, which flows from a monopoly price, is converted into
rent and in this form falls into the hands of the landlord,
thanks to his title to this piece of the globe, which is endowed
with peculiar properties. Here, then, the monopoly price

creates the rent. On the other hand, the rent would create a monopoly price, if grain were sold not merely above its price of production, but also above its value, owing to the barrier erected by the private ownership of the land against the investment of capital upon uncultivated soil without the payment of rent. That it is only the title of a number of persons to the possession of the globe which enables them to appropriate a portion of the surplus labor of society to themselves, and to do so to an increasing extent with the development of production, is concealed by the fact that the capitalized rent, this capitalized tribute, appears as the price of the land, and that the land may be sold like any other article of commerce. The buyer, therefore, does not feel that his title to the rent is obtained gratis, and without the labor, the risk, and the spirit of enterprise of the capitalist, but rather that he has paid for it with an equivalent. To the buyer, as we have previously remarked, the rent appears merely as interest on the capital, with which he has bought the land and consequently his title to the rent. In the same way, the slave-holder considers a negro, whom he has bought, his property, not because slavery as such entitles him to that negro, but because he has acquired him just as he does any other commodity, by means of sale and purchase, but the title itself is only transferred, not created by sale. The title must exist, before it can be sold, and a series of sales cannot create this title by repetition any more than one single sale can. It was created in the first place by the conditions of production. As soon as these have arrived at a point, where they must shed their skin, the material source of the title, justified economically and historically and arising from the process which creates the material requirements of life, falls to the ground, and with it all transactions based upon it. From the point of view of a higher economic form of society, the private ownership of the globe on the part of some individuals will appear quite as absurd as the private ownership of one man by another. Even a whole society, a nation, or even all societies together, are not the *owners* of the globe. They are only its *possessors,* its users, and they have to hand it down to the coming generations in an improved condition, like good fathers of families.

In the following analysis of the price of land we leave out of consideration all fluctuations of competition, all land speculation, and small landed property, in which the land is the principal instrument of the producers and must, therefore, be bought by them at any price.

I. The price of land may rise, although the rent may not rise with it. This may take place,

1) by a mere fall of the rate of interest, which may cause the rent to be sold more dearly, so that the capitalized rent, the price of land rises;

2) because the interest of the capital incorporated in the land rises.

II. The price of land may rise, because the rent increases.

The rent may increase, because the price of the product of the land rises, in which case the rate of differential rent always rises, whether the rent upon the worst cultivated soil be large, small or nonexistent. But by the rate we mean the ratio of that portion of surplus-value, which is converted into rent, to the invested capital, which produces the product of the soil. This differs from the ratio of the surplus product to the total product, for the total product does not comprise the entire invested capital, namely not the fixed capital, which continues to exist by the side of the product. But it includes the fact that upon the soils carrying a differential rent an increasing portion of the product is converted into an overplus of a surplus product. Upon the worst soil the increase in the price of the product of the soil first creates a rent and consequently a price of land.

But the rent may also increase without a rise in the price of the product of the soil. This price may remain unaltered, or may even decrease.

If the price remains constant, the rent can grow only (aside from monopoly prices) because, on the one hand, the same amount of capital remains invested in the older lands, while new lands of a better quality are cultivated, which, however, suffice only to cover the increased demand, so that the regulating market price remains unchanged. In this case the price of the old lands does not rise, but the price of the newly cultivated lands rises above that of the older lands.

Or, on the other hand, the rent rises because the mass of the capital exploiting the land increases, while the relative productivity and the market price remain the same. Although the rent remains the same in this case, compared to the invested capital, still its mass, for instance, may be doubled, because the capital itself has doubled. Since no fall in the price has occurred, the second investment of capital yields a surplus profit as well as the first, and it likewise is converted into rent after the expiration of the lease. The mass of the rent rises here, because the mass of capital producing a rent increases. The contention that different investments of capital in succession upon the same piece of land can produce a rent only to the extent that their yield is unequal, so that a differential rent arises, amounts to the contention that when two capitals of 1,000 pounds sterling each are invested upon fields of equal productivity, only one of them can produce a rent, although these fields belong to the better class of soil, which produces a differential rent. (The mass of the rental, the total rent of a certain country, grows therefore with the mass of capital invested, although the price of the individual pieces of land, or the rate of rent, or the mass of rent upon the individual pieces of land, does not necessarily increase; the mass of the rental grows in this case with the extension of cultivation over a wider area. This may even be combined with a fall of the rent upon the individual holdings.) On the other hand, this contention would lead to another, to the effect that the investment of capital upon two different pieces of land side by side follows different laws than the successive investment of capital upon the same piece of land, whereas differential rent is precisely derived from the identity of the law in both cases, that is, from the increased productivity of investments of capital either upon the same field or upon different fields. The only modification which exists here and is overlooked is that successive investments of capital, when invested upon different pieces of land, meet the barrier of private ownership of land, which is not the case with successive investments of capital upon the same piece of land. This accounts for the opposite effects, by which these two forms of investments keep each other in check in practice. Whatever difference appears here is not due to capital. If the composition of the capital remains the same, and with it the rate of surplus-value, then the rate of profit remains unaltered, so that the mass of profits is doubled when the capital is doubled. In like manner the rate of rent remains the same under the conditions assumed by us. If a capital of 1,000 pounds sterling produces a rent of x, then a capital of 2,000 pounds sterling, under the assumed conditions, produces a rent of 2 x. But calculated with reference to the area of land, which has remained unaltered, since the doubled capital works upon the same field, according to our assumption, the level of the rent has risen together with its mass. The same acre, which brought a rent of 2 pounds sterling, now brings 4 pounds sterling.[134]

The relation of a portion of the surplus-value, of money rent — for money is the independent expression of value — to the land is in itself absurd and irrational. For the magnitudes, which are here measured by one another, are incommensurable, a certain use-value, a piece of land of so and so many square feet on the one hand, and of so much value, especially surplus-value, on the other. This expresses in fact

---

[134] It is one of the merits of Rodbertus whose important work on rent we shall discuss in volume IV (" *Theories of Surplus-Value,*" volume II, Part I), to have enlarged upon this point. He commits the mistake, however, to assume, in the first place, that in the case of capital the increase in profits is always expressed by an increase of capital, so that the ratio remains the same, when the mass of the profits increase. But this is an error, since the rate of profit may increase when the composition of the capital is changed, even if the exploitation of labor remains the same, just because the proportional value of the constant portion of capital, compared to its variable portion, may fall. In the second place he commits the mistake of dealing with the ratio of the money rent to a quantitatively limited piece of land, for instance to an acre, as though it had been the general assumption of classic economics in its analysis of the rise or fall of rent. This, again, is wrong. Classic economics always treats the rate of rent, so far as it considers rent in its natural form, with reference to the product, and so far as it considers rent as money rent, with reference to the advanced capital, because these are in fact its rational expressions.

nothing else but that, under the existing conditions, the ownership of so and so many square feet of land enables the landowner to catch a certain quantity of unpaid labor, which capital wallowing in square feet like a hog in potatoes has realized [The manuscript here has in brackets, but crossed out, the name " Liebig."]   But on first sight the expression is the same as though some one were to speak of the relation of a five-pound note to the diameter of the earth.   However, the reconciliation of the irrational forms, in which certain economic conditions appear and assert themselves in practice, does not concern the active agents of these relations in their every day life.   And as they are accustomed to moving about in them, they do not find anything strange about them.   A complete contradiction has not the least mystery for them, They are as much at home among the manifestations which, separated from their internal connections and isolated by themselves, seem absurd, as a fish in the water.   The same thing that Hegel says with reference to certain mathematical formulæ applies here.   The thing which seems irrational to ordinary common sense is rational, and what seems rational to it is irrational.

When considered in connection with the land area itself, a rise in the mass of the rent expresses itself in the same way that a rise in the rate of the rent does, and this accounts for the embarrassment caused to some thinkers when the conditions, which would explain the one case, are absent in the other.

Finally, the price of land may also rise, even when the price of the products of the soil decreases.

In this case, the differential rent and with it the price of land of the better classes may have risen, owing to further differentiations.   Or, if this should not be the case, the price of the products of the soil may have fallen through a greater productivity of labor, but in such a way that the increased productivity more than balances this.   Let us assume that one quarter cost 60 shillings.   Now, if the same acre, with the same capital, should produce two quarters instead of one, and the price of one quarter should fall to 40 shillings, then two quarters would cost 80 shillings, so that the value of the product of the same capital upon the same acre would have risen by one-third, although the price per quarter would have fallen by one-third. How this is possible without selling the product above its price of production or above its value, has been shown in the analysis of differential rent. As a matter of fact it is possible only in two ways. Either some bad soil is placed outside of competition, but the price of the better soil increases with the increase of differential rent, owing to the fact that the general improvement affects the various kinds of soil differently. Or, the same price of production (and the same value, in case absolute rent should be paid) expresses itself upon the worst soil through a larger mass of products, when the productivity of labor has become greater. The product represents the same value as before, but the price of its aliquot parts has fallen, while their number has increased. This is impossible, when the same capital has been employed; for in this case the same value always expresses itself through any portion of the product. It is possible, on the other hand, when additional capital has been used for gypsum, guano, etc., in short for improvements which extend their effects over several years. The premise is that the price of the individual quarter falls, but not to the same extent that the number of quarters increases.

III. These different conditions under which rent may rise and with it the price of land in general, or of particular kinds of land, may partly exist side by side and compete, or the one may exclude the other, so that they act alternately. But it follows from the foregoing that it will not do to conclude offhand that a rise in the price of land signifies also a rise of rent, or that a rise of rent, which always carries with it a rise in the price of land, also signifies a rise in the price of the products of the land.[135]

Instead of tracing to their source the natural causes which lead to an exhaustion of the soil, and which, by the way, were

[135] Concerning a fall in the price of land as a fact when the rent rises, see Passy.

unknown to all economists who have written anything on differential rent, owing to the condition of agricultural chemistry in their day, the shallow conception has been advanced, that any amount of capital cannot be invested in a limited space of land. For instance, the " *Westminister Review* " maintained against Richard Jones, that all England could not be fed by cultivating Soho Square. If this is considered a special disadvantage of agriculture, it is precisely the opposite which is true. It is possible to invest capital successively with good results, because the soil itself serves as a means of production, which is not the case with a factory, or is true of it only to a limited extent, since there the land serves only as a basis, as a space, as a foundation for operations upon a certain area. It is true that, compared to scattered handicrafts, great industries may concentrate large productive plants in a small space. But even so, a definite space is always required at any stage of development, and the building of high structures has its practical limits. Beyond these limits any expansion of production demands also an extension of the land area. The fixed capital invested in machinery, etc., does not improve through use, but on the contrary, it wears out. New inventions may, indeed permit some improvement in this respect, but with any given development of the productive power the machine will always deteriorate. If the productive power is rapidly developed, the entire old machinery must be replaced by a better one, so that the old is lost. But the soil, if properly treated, improves all the time. The advantage of the soil is that successive investments of capital may bring gains without losing the older ones, and this implies the possibility of differences in the yields of these successive investments of capital.

CHAPTER XLVII.

I. *Introductory Remarks.*

WE must be clear in our minds about the real difficulty in the analysis of ground-rent from the point of view of modern economics, to the extent that it is a theoretical expression of the capitalist mode of production. Even many of the more modern writers have not grasped this yet, as is shown by every renewed attempt to find a " new " explanation of ground-rent. The novelty consists almost always in a relapse into long outgrown conceptions. The difficulty is not to explain the surplus product and the surplus-value produced by agricultural capital. This question is solved by the general analysis of the surplus-value produced by all productive capital, no matter in what sphere it may be invested. The difficulty consists rather in demonstrating the source of the surplus over and above the general surplus-value paid by capital invested in the soil to the landlord in the form of rent after the general surplus-value has been distributed among the various capitals by means of the average profit, in other words, after the various capitals have shared in the total surplus-value produced by the social capital in all spheres of production in proportion to their relative size. Quite aside from the practical motives, which urged the modern economists as spokesmen of the industrial capitalists against the landlords to investigate this question, motives which we shall indicate more clearly in the chapter on the history of ground-rent, the question was of paramount interest for them as a theory. To admit that the rising of rent for capital invested in agriculture was due to some particular effect of the sphere of investment, to peculiar qualities of the land itself, was equivalent to giving up the conception of value as such,

equivalent to abandoning all attempts at a scientific understanding of this field. Merely the simple observation that
the rent is paid out of the price of the products of the soil, a
thing which takes place even where rent is paid in kind,
provided that the tenant is to get his price of production out
of the land, showed the absurdity of the attempt to explain
the excess of this price over the ordinary price of production,
in other words, to explain the relative dearness of the products of agriculture out of the excess of the natural productivity of agricultural industry over the productivity of the
other lines of industry. For the reverse is true. The more
productive labor is, the cheaper is every aliquot part of its
product, because the mass of use-values is so much greater,
in which the same quantity of labor and with it the same
value is incorporated.

The entire difficulty in the analysis of rent, therefore,
consists in the explanation of the excess of agricultural profit
over the average profit. It is not a question of surplus-value
as such, but of the peculiar surplus of surplus-value found
in this sphere of production, not a question of the "net
product," but of the excess of this net product over the net
product of the other lines of industry. The average profit
itself is a product, formed under very definite historical conditions of production by the movement of the process of social
life, a product which requires very far-reaching interrelations,
as we have seen. In order that we may be able to speak at
all of a surplus over the average profit, this average profit
itself must already exist as a standard and as a regulator
of production, such as it is under capitalist production. For
this reason there can be no such thing as a rent in the modern
sense, a rent consisting of a surplus over the average profit,
over and above the proportional share of each individual capital in the total surplus-value produced by the entire social capital, so long as capital does not perform the function of enforcing all surplus-labor and appropriating at first hand all surplus-
value, so long as capital has not yet brought under its control
the social labor, or has done so only sporadically. It shows
the naiveté of a man like Passy (see further along) that he

speaks of a rent, a surplus over the profit, in primitive society, a surplus over and above a historically defined form of surplus-value, which, according to Passy, might almost exist without any society.

For the older economists, who make the first beginning in an analysis of the capitalist mode of production, which was still undeveloped in their day, the analysis of rent either offers no difficulty, or a difficulty of another sort. Petty, Cantillon, and in general the writers who are closer to feudal times, assume that ground-rent is the normal form of surplus-value, whereas profit to them is still vaguely combined with wages, or at best looks to them like a portion of surplus-value filched by the capitalist from the landlord. These writers take their departure from a condition, in which the agricultural population still constitutes the overwhelming majority of the nation, and in which the landlord still appears as the individual, who appropriates at first hand the surplus labor of the direct producers through his land monopoly, in which land therefore still appears as the chief requisite of production. These writers could not yet face the question, which, contrary to them, seeks to investigate from the point of view of capitalist production, how it happens that private ownership in land manages to wrest from capital a portion of the surplus-value produced by it at first hand (that is, filched by it from the direct producers) and first appropriated by it.

The physiocrats are troubled by a difficulty of another kind. Being in fact the first systematic spokesman of capital, they try to analyze the nature of surplus-value in general. This analysis coincides for them with the analysis of rent, the only form of surplus-value that exists for them. Therefore the rent-paying, or agricultural capital, is to them the only capital which produces any surplus-value, and the agricultural labor set in motion by it the only labor which makes for surplus-value, which quite correctly is considered the only productive labor from a capitalist point of view. They are right in considering the production of surplus-value as the essential thing. Aside from other merits set forth by us in the volume dealing with "*Theories of Surplus-Value,*" they have the great merit of going back from the merchants' capital, which performs its functions wholly in the sphere of circulation, to the productive capital. In this they are opposed to the mercantile system, which, with its crude realism, constitutes the dominating vulgar economy of that time pushing the beginnings of scientific analysis by Petty and his successors into the background by means of its practical interests. By the way, in this critique of the mercantile system we aim only at its conceptions of capital and surplus-value. We have already indicated previously that the monetary system correctly proclaims production for the world market and the transformation of the product into commodities, and thus into money, as the prerequisite and condition of capitalist production. In the further development of this system into the mercantile system, it is no longer the transformation of the value of commodities into money, but the production of surplus-value, which decides the point, but merely from the meaningless point of view of the sphere of circulation and with the understanding that this surplus-value must present itself as surplus money in the surplus of the balance of trade. The characteristic mark of the interested merchants and manufacturers of that time, which is adequate to the period of capitalist development represented by them, is found in the fact that their principal aim in the transformation of the feudal and agricultural societies into industrial ones and in the corresponding industrial struggle of the nations upon the world market is a hastened development of capital, which is not supposed to take place in the so-called natural way, but by means of forced measures. It makes a tremendous difference, whether the national capital is gradually and slowly transformed into industrial capital, or whether the time of this development is hastened by means of a tax which they impose through protective duties mainly upon the real estate owners, the middle class and small farmers, and the handicraftsmen, by the accelerated expropriation of the independent direct producers, by a violently hastened accumulation and concentration of capitals, in short by a hastened introduction of the conditions of capitalist production.   It makes at the same time an enormous difference in the capitalist and industrial exploitation of the natural powers of national production.   Hence the national character of the mercantile system is not a mere phrase in the mouths of its spokesmen.   Under the pretense of occupying themselves merely with the wealth of the nation and the resources of the state, they practically proclaim the interests of the capitalist class and the gathering of riches to be the ultimate end of the state, and so they proclaim bourgeois society against the old supernatural state.   But at the same time they are conscious of the fact that the development of the interests of capital and of the capitalist class, of capitalist production, is the foundation of the national power and of the national preponderance in modern society.

The physiocrats are, furthermore, correct in stating that the production of surplus-value, and with it all development of capital, has for its natural basis the productivity of agricultural labor.   If human beings are not capable of producing by one day's labor more means of subsistence, which signifies in its strictest sense more products of agriculture, than every laborer needs for his own reproduction, if the daily expenditure of his entire labor-power suffices only to produce the means of subsistence indispensable for his own individual needs, then there can be no mention of any surplus product nor of any surplus-value.   A productivity of agricultural labor exceeding the individual requirements of the laborer is the basis of all societies, and is above all the basis of capitalist production, which separates a continually increasing portion of society from the production of the immediate requirements of life and transforms them into " free heads," as Steuart has it, making them available for exploitation in other spheres.

But what are we to say of more recent writers on economics, such as Daire, Passy, etc., who repeat the most primitive conceptions concerning the natural requirements of surplus labor and surplus-value in general, at a time when classic economy is in its declining years, or even on its deathbed, and who imagine that they are thus saying something new and convincing on ground-rent, after this ground-rent has long developed a peculiar form and has become a specific part of surplus-value?

It is precisely characteristic of vulgar economy that it repeats things which were new, original, deep and justified during a certain outgrown stage of development, at a time when they have become platitudinous, stale, false. In this way it confesses that it has not the slightest suspicion of the problems which used to occupy the attention of classic economy. It confounds them with questions that could be posed only on a low level in the development of bourgeois society. It is the same with its restless and self-complacent rumination of the physiocratic phrases concerning free trade. These phrases have long lost all theoretical interest, no matter how much they may engage the practical attention of this or that modern state.

In natural economy, properly so-called, when no part of the agricultural product, or but a very insignificant part of it, enters into the process of circulation, or even but a relatively small portion of that part of the product which represents the revenue of the landlord, as it did in many Roman latifundiæ, or upon the villae of Charlemagne, or more or less during the entire Middle Ages (see Vincard, *Histoire du Travail*), the product and the surplus product of the large estates consists by no means purely of the products of agricultural labor. Domestic handicrafts and manufacturing labor, as side issues to agriculture, which forms the basis, is the prerequisite of that mode of production upon which natural economy rests, in European antiquity and Middle Ages as well as in the Indian commune of the present day, in which the traditional organization has not yet been destroyed. The capitalist mode of production completely dissolves this connection. This process may be studied on a large scale during the last third of the 18th century, in England. Brains that had grown up in more or less semi-feudal societies, for instance Herrenschwand, still consider this separation of manufacture from agriculture as a foolhardy social

3F

adventure, as an unthinkably risky mode of existence, even as late as the close of the 18th century. And even in the agricultural societies of antiquity, which show the greatest analogy to capitalist agriculture, namely Carthage and Rome, the similiarity with plantation management is greater than with that form which really corresponds to the capitalist mode of exploitation.[136]

There existed at one time a formal analogy, which, however, appears as a deception in all essential points to a man familiar with the capitalist mode of production, and who does not, like Mr. Mommsen,[137] discover a capitalist mode of production in every monetary economy. This formal analogy did not exist at all in continental Italy during antiquity, but at best only in Sicily, because this island served as an agricultural tributary for Rome, so that its agriculture was chiefly aimed at export. It was there that tenants of the modern kind existed.

An incorrect conception of the nature of rent is based upon the fact that rent in a natural form, either as tithes to the church, or as a curiosity perpetuated by old contracts, has dragged itself into modern times out of the natural economy of feudal days, quite contrary to the conditions of the capitalist mode of production. This creates the impression that rent does not arise from the price of the agricultural product, but from its mass, not from social conditions, but from the soil. We have shown previously that a surplus product, representing a mere increase in the mass of products, does not constitute any surplus-value, although surplus-value represents itself in a surplus product. A surplus product may represent a minus in value. Otherwise the cotton industry of

[136] Adam Smith emphasizes the fact that at his time (and this applies also to the plantations in tropical and subtropical countries in our own time) rent and profit were not yet separated, for the landlord was at the same time a capitalist, just as Cato, for instance, was upon his estates. But this separation is precisely the premise of the capitalist mode of production. Moreover, the basis of slavery stands in contradiction with the nature of capitalist production.

[137] Mr. Mommsen, in his Roman history, does not use the term capitalist in the sense in which modern economics and modern society does, but rather in the way peculiar to popular conception, such as still continues to vegetate, not in England or America, but upon the European continent, as an ancient tradition of past conditions.

1860, compared to that of 1840, would represent an enormous surplus-value, whereas on the contrary the price of the yarn has fallen. The rent may increase enormously through a succession of crop failures, because the price of cereals rises, although this surplus-value is represented by an absolutely decreasing mass of dearer wheat. Vice versa, the rent may fall through a succession of fertile years, because the price falls, although the fallen rent is represented by a greater mass of cheaper wheat.

With regard to rent in kind it should be noted that it is a mere tradition dragged over from an outgrown mode of production and eking out an existence as a ruin. Its contradiction to the capitalist mode of production is shown by the fact that it disappeared from private contracts of its own accord, and that it was shaken off by force as an inconsistency in such instances as the church tithes in England, where legislation was able to step in. Furthermore, where rent in kind continued to exist on the basis of capitalist production, it was nothing else, and could be nothing else, but an expression of money rent in medieval garb. For instance, wheat is quoted at 40 shillings per quarter. One portion of this wheat has to reproduce the wages contained in it, and must be sold in order to be available for renewed expenditure. Another portion must be sold in order to pay its share of the taxes. Seeds and even a part of the manure enter as commodities into the process of reproduction, wherever the capitalist mode of production and division of labor are developed, and they must be bought for the purposes of reproduction. Therefore another portion of this quarter must be sold, in order to get money for these things. To the extent that they do not have to be bought as actual commodities, but are taken in their natural form out of the product, in order to enter once more as means of production into its reproduction — which is done, not only in agriculture, but in many other lines of production which create constant capital — they figure in the accounts as money of account and are thus deducted as component parts of the cost-price. The wear and tear of machinery, and of fixed capital in general, must be

made good in money. And finally comes the profit, which
is calculated on the basis of this sum of costs expressed either
in real or in accounting money. This profit is represented by
a definite portion of the gross product, which is determined
by its price. The portion which then remains is the rent.
If the rent in kind stipulated by contract is greater than
this remainder determined by the price, then it is not a rent,
but a deduction from the profit. On account of this possibility alone rent in kind is an old form, to the extent that
it does not follow the price of the product, but may amount
to more or less than the real rent, so that it may not only
contain a deduction from the profit, but also from elements
required for the reproduction of the capital. In fact, this
rent in kind, so far as it is a rent, not merely in name but in
essence, is exclusively determined by the excess of the price
of the product over its cost of production. Only it assumes
this variable magnitude to be a constant one. But it is such
a comforting reflection that the natural product should suffice, in the first place, to maintain the laborer, in the second
place, to leave for the capitalist tenant more food than he
needs, and finally, that the remainder should form a natural
rent. The same fancy is indulged in when a manufacturer
of cotton goods produces 200,000 yards of them. These yards
are supposed to suffice for the purpose of clothing his laborers, his wife and all his offspring, together with himself
abundantly, to leave over some cotton for sale, and besides
to pay an enormous rent with cotton goods. The matter is
so simple! Deduct the cost of production from 200,000
yards of cotton goods, and a surplus must remain for rent.
But it is indeed a naïve conception, to deduct the cost of production of, say, 10,000 pounds sterling from 200,000 yards
of cotton, without knowing the selling price, to deduct money
from cotton goods, to deduct from a natural use-value an exchange-value, and thus to determine the surplus of yards of
cotton goods over pounds of sterling. It is worse than the
squaring of the circle, which is at least based upon the conception that there is a boundary at which straight lines and
curves flow imperceptibly into each other. But such is the

recipe of Mr. Passy. Deduct money from cotton goods, before the cotton goods have been converted into money, either in your head or in reality! What remains is the rent, which, however, is to be grasped tangibly (see for instance, Karl Arnd) and not by deviltries of sophistry. The entire restoration of rent in kind amounts really to this foolishness, to this deduction of the price of production from so and so many bushels of wheat, the subtraction of a sum of money from a cubic measure.

II. *Labor Rent.*

If we observe ground-rent in its simplest form, that of labor rent, which means that the direct producer cultivates during a part of the week, with instruments of labor (plow, cattle, etc.), actually or legally belonging to him, the soil owned by him in fact, and works during the remaining days upon the estate of the feudal lord, without any compensation from the feudal lord, the proposition is quite clear, for in this case rent and surplus-value are identical. The rent, not the profit, is here the form through which the unpaid surplus labor expresses itself. To what extent the laborer, the self-sustaining serf, can here secure for himself a surplus above his indispensable necessities of life, a surplus above the thing which we would call wages under the capitalist mode of production, depends, other circumstances remaining unchanged, upon the proportion, in which his labor time is divided into labor time for himself and forced labor time for his feudal lord. This surplus above the indispensable requirements of life, the germ of that which appears as profit under the capitalist mode of production, is therefore wholly determined by the size of the ground-rent, which in this case not only is unpaid surplus labor, but also appears as such. It is unpaid surplus labor for the " owner " of the means of production, which here coincide with the land, and so far as they differ from it, are mere accessories to it. That the product of the laboring serf must suffice to reproduce both his subsistence and his requirements of production, is a fact which remains the same under all modes of production. For it is not a result of its specific form, but a natural requisite of all continuous and reproductive labor, of any continued production, which is always a reproduction, including the reproduction of its own labor conditions. It is furthermore evident that in all forms, in which the direct laborer remains the " possessor " of the means of production and labor conditions of his own means of subsistence, the property relation must at the same time assert itself as a direct relation between rulers and servants, so that the direct producer is not free. This is a lack of freedom which may be modified from serfdom with forced labor to the point of a mere tributary relation. The direct producer, according to our assumption, is here in possession of his own means of production, of the material labor conditions required for the realization of his labor and the production of his means of subsistence. He carries on his agriculture and the rural house industries connected with it as an independent producer. This independence is not abolished by the fact that these small farmers may form among themselves a more or less natural commune in production, as they do in India, since it is here merely a question of independence from the nominal lord of the soil. Under such conditions the surplus labor for the nominal owner of the land cannot be filched from them by any economic measures, but must be forced from them by other measures, whatever may be the form assumed by them.[138]

This is different from slave or plantation economy, in that the slave works with conditions of labor belonging to another. He does not work as an independent producer. This requires conditions of personal dependence, a lack of personal freedom, no matter to what extent, a bondage to the soil as its accessory, a serfdom in the strict meaning of the word. If the direct producers are not under the sovereignty of a private landlord, but rather under that of a state which stands over them as their direct landlord and sovereign, then rent and taxes coincide, or rather, there is no tax which differs

[138] After a country had been conquered, the next step for the conquerer was always to take possession of the human beings also. Compare Linguet. See also Möser.

from this form of ground-rent. Under these circumstances the subject need not be politically or economically under any harder pressure than that common to all subjection to that state. The state is then the supreme landlord. The sovereignty consists here in the ownership of land concentrated on a national scale. But, on the other hand, no private ownership of land exists, although there is both private and common possession and use of land.

The specific economic form, in which unpaid surplus labor is pumped out of the direct producers, determines the relation of rulers and ruled, as it grows immediately out of production itself and reacts upon it as a determining element. Upon this is founded the entire formation of the economic community which grows up out of the conditions of production itself, and this also determines its specific political shape. It is always the direct relation of the owners of the conditions of production to the direct producers, which reveals the innermost secret, the hidden foundation of the entire social construction, and with it of the political form of the relations between sovereignty and dependence, in short, of the corresponding form of the state. The form of this relation between rulers and ruled naturally corresponds always with a definite stage in the development of the methods of labor and of its productive social power. This does not prevent the same economic basis from showing infinite variations and gradations in its appearance, even though its principal conditions are everywhere the same. This is due to innumerable outside circumstances, natural environment, race peculiarities, outside historical influences, and so forth, all of which must be ascertained by careful analysis.

So much is evident in the case of labor rent, the simplest and most primitive form of rent: The rent is here the original form of surplus-value and coincides with it. Furthermore, the identity of surplus-value with unpaid labor of others does not need to be demonstrated by any analysis in this case, because it still exists in its visible, palpable form, for the labor of the direct producer for himself is still separated by space and time from his labor for the landlord, and this last labor appears clearly in the brutal form of forced labor for another. In the same way the " quality " of the soil to produce a rent is here reduced to a tangibly open secret, for the nature which here furnishes the rent also includes the human labor-power bound to the soil, and the property relation which compels the owner of labor-power to exert this quality and to keep it busy beyond the measure required for the satisfaction of his own material needs. The rent consists directly in the appropriation, by the landlord, of this surplus expenditure of labor-power. For the direct producer pays no other rent. Here, where surplus-value and rent are not only identical, but where surplus-value obviously has the form of surplus labor, the natural conditions, or limits, of rent lie on the surface, because those of surplus-value do. The direct producer must, 1), possess enough labor-power, and 2), the natural conditions of his labor, which means in the first place the soil cultivated by him, must be productive enough, in one word, the natural productivity of his labor must be so great that the possibility of some surplus labor over and above that required for the satisfaction of his own needs shall remain. It is not this possibility which creates the rent. The rent is not created until compulsion makes a reality of this possibility. But the possibility itself is conditioned upon subjective and objective facts of nature. And there is nothing mysterious about it. If the labor-power is small, and the natural conditions of labor poor, then the surplus labor is small, but so are in that case the wants of the producers on one side and the relative numbers of the exploiters of surplus labor on the other, and so is finally the surplus product, by which this little productive surplus labor is represented for those few exploiting land owners.

Finally, labor rent implies in itself that, all other circumstances remaining equal, it will depend wholly upon the relative amount of surplus labor, or forced labor, to what extent the direct producer shall be enabled to improve his own condition, to acquire wealth, to produce a surplus over and above his indispensable means of subsistence, or, if we wish to anticipate the capitalist mode of expression, whether he shall be able to produce a profit for himself, and how much of a profit, meaning a surplus over the wages produced by himself. The rent is here the normal, all absorbing, one might say legitimate, form of surplus labor. So far from being a surplus over the profit, which means in this case in excess of any other surplus over the wages, it is rather the amount of profit, and even its very existence, which depends, other circumstances being equal, upon the amount of rent, or upon the forced surplus labor to be surrendered to the landlord.

Some historians have expressed astonishment that it should be possible for the forced laborers, or serfs, to acquire any independent property, or relatively speaking, wealth, under such circumstances, since the direct producer is not an owner, but only a possessor, and since all his surplus labor belongs legally to the landlord. However, it is evident that tradition must play a very powerful role in the primitive and undeveloped circumstances, upon which this relation in social production and the corresponding mode of production are based. It is furthermore clear that here as everywhere else it is in the interest of the ruling section of society to sanction the existing order as a law and to perpetuate its habitually and traditionally fixed limits as legal ones. Aside from all other matters, this comes about of itself in proportion as the continuous reproduction of the foundation of the existing order and of the relations corresponding to it gradually assume a regulated and orderly form. And such regulation and order are themselves indispensable elements of any mode of production, provided that it is to assume social firmness and an independence from mere accident and arbitrariness. It is just through them that society is rendered more firm and emancipated relatively from mere arbitrariness and mere accident. Society assumes this form by the repeated reproduction of the same mode of production, where the process of production stagnates and with it the corresponding social relations. If this continues for some time, this order fortifies itself by custom and tradition and is finally sanctioned as an expressed law. Since the form of this surplus labor, of forced labor, rests upon the imperfect development of all pro-

ductive powers of society, and upon the crudeness of the methods of labor itself, it will naturally absorb a much smaller
portion, relatively, of the total labor of the direct producers
than under developed modes of production, particularly under the capitalist mode of production.   Take it, for instance,
that the forced labor for the landlord originally amounted to
two days per week.   These two days of forced labor are fixed,
are a constant magnitude, legally regulated by laws of usage
or written laws.   But the productivity of the remaining days
of the week, over which the direct producer has independent
control, is a variable magnitude, which must develop in the
course of his experience, together with the new wants he acquires, together with the expansion of the market for his product, together with the increasing security which guarantees
independence for this portion of his labor-power.   These
things will spur him on to a greater exertion of his labor-
power, and it must not be forgotten that the employment of
his labor-power is by no means confined to agriculture, but
includes rural house industry.   The possibility of a certain
economic development, depending, of course, upon the favor
of circumstances, upon inborn race characteristics, etc., is
open in this case.

III.   *Rent in Kind.*

The transformation of labor rent into rent in kind does
not change anything in the nature of rent, economically speaking.   This nature, in the forms of rent considered here, is
such that rent is the sole prevailing and normal form of surplus labor, or surplus-value.   This, again, expresses the fact
that rent is the only surplus labor, or the only surplus product
which the direct producer, being in possession of the labor
conditions needed for his own reproduction, must give up to
the owner of the land, which under this state of things is the
one condition of labor embracing everything.   And furthermore it expresses the fact that land is the only labor condition, which stands opposed to the direct producer as a property independent of him and held in the hands of another,

being personified by the landlord. To the extent that rent
in kind is the prevailing and dominant form of ground-rent,
it is always more or less in the company of survivals of the
preceding form, that is of rent paid directly by labor, forced
labor, no matter whether the landlord be a private person or
the state. Rent in kind requires a higher state of civilization for the direct producer, a higher stage of development
of his labor and of society in general. And it is distinguished
from the preceding form by the fact that the surplus labor is
no longer performed naturally, is no longer performed under
the direct supervision and compulsion of the landlord or of
his representatives. The direct producer is rather driven
by the force of circumstances than by direct coercion, rather
by legal enactment than by the whip, to perform surplus labor on his own responsibility. Surplus production, in the
sense of a production beyond the indispensable needs of the
direct producer, and within the field of production actually
in his own possession, upon the soil exploited by himself and
no longer upon the lord's estate outside of his own land, has
become a matter of fact rule here. In this relation the direct producer is more or less master of the employment of his
whole labor time, although a part of this labor time, at first
practically the entire surplus portion of it, belongs to the landlord without any compensation. Only, the landlord does not
get this surplus labor any more in its natural form, but rather
in the natural form of the product in which it is realized.
The burdensome interruption by the labor for the landlord
(see Volume I, chapter X, 2, *Manufacturer and Boyard*),
which disturbs the reproduction of the serf more or less, according to the way in which forced labor is regulated, disappears, wherever rent in kind has its pure form, or at least
it is reduced to a few short intervals during the year, which
demand a continuation of rent by forced labor by the side
of rent in kind. The labor of the producer for himself and
his labor for the landlord are no longer palpably separated
by time and space. This rent in kind, in its pure form, while
it may drag itself along sporadically into more highly developed modes of production and conditions of production, nev-

ertheless requires for its existence a natural economy, that is
an economy in which the conditions of production are either
wholly or for the overwhelming part produced by the system
itself in such a way that they are reproduced directly out of
its gross product. It furthermore requires the combination
of domestic rural industry with agriculture. The surplus
product, which forms the rent, is the product of this combined
agricultural and industrial family labor, no matter whether
rent in kind contains more or less of the industrial product,
as it often does in the middle ages, or whether it is paid only
in the form of actual products of the soil. In this form of
rent it is by no means necessary that rent in kind, which represents the surplus labor, should fully exhaust the entire surplus labor of the rural family. Compared to labor rent, the
producer rather has more elbow room to gain time for some
surplus labor whose product shall belong to himself, as does
that of the labor which produces his indispensable means of
subsistence. This form will also give rise to greater differences in the economic situation of the individual direct producers. At least the possibility for such a differentiation exists, and so does the possibility that the direct producer may
have acquired the means to exploit other laborers for himself,
but this does not concern us here, since we are dealing with
rent in its pure form. Neither can be pay any heed to the
endless variety of combinations, by which the various forms of
rent may be united, adulterated and amalgamated.

Owing to the peculiar form of rent in kind, by which it is
bound to a definite kind of products and of production, owing
furthermore to the indispensable combination of agriculture
and domestic industry attached to it, also to the almost complete selfsufficiency in which the peasant family supports itself and to its independence from markets and from the movement of production and history in the social spheres outside
of it, in short owing to the character of natural economy in
general this form is quite suitable for becoming the basis of
stationary conditions of society, such as we see in Asia. Here,
as previously in the form of labor rent, ground-rent is the
normal form of surplus-value, and thus of surplus labor, that

is of the entire surplus labor performed without any equivalent by the direct producer for the benefit of the owner of his essential means of production, the land, a labor which is still performed under compulsion, although no longer in the old brutal form. The profit, if, falsely anticipating, we may so call that portion of the direct producer's labor which exceeds his necessary labor and which he keeps for himself, has so little to do with determining the rent in kind, that this profit rather grows up behind the back of the rent and finds its natural limit in the size of the rent in kind. This rent may assume dimensions which seriously threaten the reproduction of the conditions of labor, of the means of production. It may render an expansion of production more or less impossible, and grind the direct producers down to the physical minimum of means of subsistence. This is particularly the case, when this form is met and exploited by a conquering industrial nation, as India is by the English.

IV. *Money Rent.*

By money 'rent we mean here — for the sake of distinction from the industrial and commercial ground-rent resting upon the capitalist mode of production, which is but a surplus over the average profit — that ground-rent which arises from a mere change of form of rent in kind, just as this rent in kind, in its turn, is but a modification of labor rent. Under money rent, the direct producer no longer turns over the product, but its price, to the landlord (who may be either the state or a private individual). A surplus of products in their natural form is no longer sufficient; it must be converted from its natural form into money. Although the direct producer still continues to produce at least the greater part of his means of subsistence himself, a certain portion of this product must now be converted into commodities, must be produced as commodities. The character of the entire mode of production is thus more or less changed. It loses its independence, it remains no longer detached from the social connections. The proportion of the cost of production, which now is more and more complicated with the expenditure of money, now becomes a determining factor. At any rate, the excess of that portion of the gross product, which must be converted into money, over that portion, which has to serve either as means of reproduction or as means of direct subsistence, assumes a determining role. However, the basis of this rent remains the same as that of the rent in kind, from which it starts, although money rent likewise approaches its dissolution. The direct producer still is the possessor of the land, either by inheritance or by some other traditional right, and he has to perform for his landlord, who is the owner of the land, of his most essential instrument of production, forced surplus labor, that is, unpaid labor for which no equivalent is returned, and this forced surplus labor is now paid in money obtained by the sale of the surplus product. The property in requirements of labor separate from the land, such as agricultural implements and other movable things, is transformed into the property of the direct producer even under the preceding form of rent, first in fact, then legally, and this is the condition even more under money rent. The transformation of rent in kind into money rent, taking place first sporadically, then on a more or less national scale, requires a considerable development of commerce, of city industries, of the production of commodities in general, and with them of the circulation of money. It furthermore requires that products should have a market price, and that they are sold more or less approximately at their values, which need not necessarily be the case under the preceding forms. In the East of Europe we may still see in a certain measure this transformation with our own eyes. How little it can be carried through without a certain development of the social productivity of labor, is proved by various unsuccessful attempts to carry it through under the Roman emperors, and by relapses into rent in kind after the attempt had been made to convert at least that portion of rent in kind into a money rent which had to be paid as a state tax. The same difficulties of transition are shown, for instance, by the prerevolutionary time in France, when money rent was combined and adulterated by survivals of the forms preceding it.

Money rent, as a converted form of rent in kind and as an antagonist of rent in kind, is the last form, and the dissolving form, of that form of ground-rent, which we have considered so far, namely of ground-rent as the normal form of surplus-value and of the unpaid surplus labor to be performed for the owner of the means of production. In its pure form, this rent, like labor rent and rent in kind, does not represent any surplus above the profit. It absorbs the profit, as it is understood. To the extent that profit arises in fact as a separate portion of the surplus labor by the side of the rent, money rent as well as rent in its preceding forms still is the normal barrier of such embryonic profit, which can only develop in proportion as the possibility of exploitation grows, whether it be the producer's own surplus labor or the surplus labor of another, which remains after the surplus represented by money rent has been paid. If any profit actually arises along with this rent, this profit is not a barrier of rent, but the rent is rather a barrier of this profit. However, we repeat that money rent is at the same time the disappearing form of the rent which we have considered so far, of that rent which is identical with surplus-value and surplus labor, of ground-rent as the normal and prevailing form of surplus-value.

In its further development money rent must lead — aside from all intermediate forms, such as that of the small peasant who is a tenant — either to the transformation of land into independent peasants' property, or into the form corresponding to the capitalist mode of production, that is, to rent paid by the capitalist tenant.

With the coming of money rent the traditional and customary relation between the landlord and the subject tillers of the soil, who possess and cultivate a part of the land, is turned into a pure money relation fixed by the rules of positive law. The cultivating possessor thus becomes virtually a mere tenant. This transformation serves on the one hand, provided that other general conditions of production permit

such a thing, to expropriate gradually the old peasant possessors and to put in their place capitalist tenants. On the
other hand it leads to a release of the old possessors from
their tributary relation by buying themselves free from their
landlord, so that they become independent farmers and free
owners of the land tilled by them. The transformation of
rent in kind into money rent is not only necessarily accompanied, but even anticipated by the formation of a class of prop-
ertyless day laborers, who hire themselves out for wages.
During the period of their rise, when this new class appears
but sporadically, the custom necessarily develops among the
better situated tributary farmers of exploiting agricultural
laborers for their own account, just as the wealthier serfs in
feudal times used to employ serfs for their own benefit. In
this way they gradually acquire the ability to accumulate a
certain amount of wealth and to transform themselves even
into future capitalists. The old selfemploying possessors of
the land thus give rise among themselves to a nursery for capitalist tenants, whose development is conditioned upon the
general development of capitalist production outside of the
rural districts. This class grows very rapidly, when particularly favorable circumstances come to its aid, as they did in
England in the 16th century, where the progressive depreciation of money made them rich, under the customary long
leases, at the expense of the landlords.

Furthermore: As soon as rent assumes the form of money
rent, and with it the relation between rent paying peasants
and landlords becomes a relation fixed by contract —
a development which is not possible unless the world market, commerce and manufacture have reached a relatively
high level — the leasing of land to capitalists necessarily also puts in its appearance. These men, having stood
outside of the rural barrier so far, now transfer to the country and to agriculture some capital acquired in the cities and
with it the capitalist mode of production as developed in those
cities, which implies the creation of the product in the form
of a mere commodity and as a mere means of appropriating
surplus-value. This form can become the general rule only

in those countries, which dominate the world market in the
period of transition from the feudal to the capitalist mode of
production. When the capitalist tenant steps between the
landlord and the actually working tiller of the soil, all conditions have been dissolved, which arose from the old rural
mode of production. The capitalist tenant becomes the actual commander of these agricultural laborers and the actual
exploiter of their surplus labor, whereas the landlord has any
direct relations only with this capitalist tenant, the relation
being a mere money relation fixed by contract. This transforms also the nature of the rent, not merely in fact and accidentally, as it did sometimes even under the preceding forms,
but normally, by transforming its acknowledged and prevailing mode. Instead of continuing as the normal form of surplus-value and surplus labor, it becomes a mere surplus of
this surplus labor over that portion of it, which is appropriated by the exploiting capitalist in the form of profit. And
now the total surplus labor, both profit and surplus above the
profit, are extracted by him directly, appropriated in the form
of the surplus product, and turned into money. It is only
the surplus portion of the surplus-value extracted by him from
the agricultural laborer by direct exploitation, by means of
his capital, which he turns over to the landlord as rent. How
much or how little he gives away to him depends, as a rule,
upon the limits set by the average profit which is realized by
the capital in the non-agricultural spheres of production, and
by the non-agricultural prices of production regulated by this
average profit. From a normal form of surplus-value and
surplus labor the rent has now transformed itself into a surplus peculiar to the agricultural sphere of production, exceeding that portion of the surplus labor, which is claimed
at first hand by capital as its legitimate and normal share.
Profit, instead of rent, has now become the normal form of
surplus-value, and rent exists only as a form, not of surplus-
value in general, but of one of its offshoots, called surplus
profit, which assumes an independent existence only under
very peculiar circumstances. It is not necessary to dwell any
further upon the way in which this transformation is accom-
3G

panied by a gradual transformation of the mode of production itself. This is shown by the mere fact that it is the
normal thing for the capitalist tenant to produce the products of the soil as commodities, and that, while formerly only
the surplus over his means of subsistence was converted into
commodities, now but a relatively small part of these commodities is directly used as means of subsistence for him.   It
is no longer the land, but the capital, which has now brought
under its direct sway and under its own productivity the labor of the agriculturalist.

The average profit and the price of production regulated by
it are formed outside of the conditions of the rural country
within the circles of city commerce and manufacture.   The
profit of the rent-paying farmers does not enter into it as a
balancing element, for their relation to the landlord is not
a capitalist one.   To the extent that he makes profits, that is,
realizes a surplus above his necessary means of subsistence,
either by his own labor or by the exploitation of other people's labor, it is done behind the back of the normal relationship.   Other circumstances being equal, the size of this profit
does not determine the rent, but on the contrary, it is determined by the limits set by the rent.   The high rate of profit
in the Middle Ages is not entirely due to the low composition
of the capital, in which the variable capital, invested in
wages, predominates.   It is due also to the robbery commit-
ted against the land, the appropriation of a portion of the
landlord's rent and of the income of his vassals.   While the
country exploits the town politically in the Middle Ages,
wherever feudalism has not been broken down by an exceptional development of the towns, the town, on the other hand,
everywhere and without exception exploits the land economically by its monopoly prices, its system of taxation, its guild
organizations, its direct mercantile fraud and its usury.

One might imagine that the mere advent of the capitalist
tenant in agricultural production would prove that the price
of those products of the soil, which had always paid a rent in
one form or another, must stand above the prices of production of manufacture, at least at the time of this advent.   And

this for the reason that the price of such products of the soil had reached the level of a monopoly price or that it had risen as high as the value of the products of the soil, and that this value actually stood above the price of production regulated by the average profit. Unless this were so, the capitalist tenant could not very well realize first the average profit out of the price of these products, at the existing prices of the products of the soil, and then pay out of this same price a surplus above his profit in the form of rent. One might conclude from this that the average rate of profit, which guides the capitalist tenant in his contract with the landlord, had been formed without including the rent, and that as soon as this average rate of profit assumes a regulating part in agricultural production it finds this surplus ready at hand and turns it over to the landlord. It is in this traditional manner that, for instance, Rodbertus explains this matter.

But several points must be considered here.

1) This advent of capital as an independent and leading power in agriculture does not take place generally all at once, but gradually and separately in various lines of production. It seizes at first, not agriculture proper, but such lines of production as cattle raising, especially sheep raising, whose principal product, wool, offers a steady surplus of the market price over the price of production during the rise of industry, and this is not balanced until later. This was the case in England during the 16th century.

2) Since this capitalist production appears at first but sporadically, nothing can be argued against the assumption, that it takes hold in the beginning only of such groups of land as are able, through their particular fertility, or their exceptionally favorable location, to pay a differential rent in the long run.

3) Even assuming that at the time of the advent of this mode of production, which indeed requires an increasing preponderance of the demand in the towns, the prices of the products of the soil stood higher than the price of production, as was doubtless the case during the last third of the 17th century in England, nevertheless, as soon as this mode

of production will have worked its way somewhat out of the
mere subordination of agriculture to capital, and as soon as
the improvement of agriculture and the reduction of its cost
of production, which accompany its development, will have
taken place, the balance will be restored by a reaction, a fall
in the price of the products of the soil, as happened in the
first half of the 18th century in England.

In this traditional way, then, rent as a surplus above the
average profit cannot be explained. Whatever may be the
historical circumstances of the time in which rent appears
at first, once that it has taken root it cannot exist under any
other modern conditions than those previously explained.

Finally, it should be noted in the transformation of rent
in kind into money rent, that with it capitalized rent, or the
price of land, and its salableness and sale become essential
elements, and that with them not only the formerly rent-paying tenant may be transformed into an independent peasant
proprietor, but also urban and other moneyed people may buy
real estate, in order to lease them either to peasants or to capitalists and thus to enjoy rent in the form of interest on capital
so invested; that, therefore, this likewise assists in the
transformation of the former mode of exploitation, of the relation between the owner and the actual tiller of the land, and
of the rent itself.

V. *Share Farming (Metairie System) and Small Peasants' Property.*

We have now arrived at the end of our line of development
of ground-rent.

In all these forms of ground-rent, whether labor rent, rent
in kind, or money rent (as a mere change of form of rent in
kind), the rent-paying party is always supposed to be the actual tiller and possessor of the land, whose unpaid surplus labor passes directly into the hands of the landlord. Even in
the last form, money rent — to the extent that it is " pure,"
in other words, a mere change of form of rent in kind — this
is not only possible, but actually takes place.

As a form of transition from the original form of rent to capitalist rent, we may consider the metairie system, or share farming, under which the manager (tenant) furnishes not only labor (his own or that of others), but also a portion of the first capital, and the landlord furnishes, aside from the land, another portion of the first capital (for instance cáttle), and the product is divided between the tenant and the landlord according to definite shares, which differ in various countries. In this case, the tenant lacks the capital required for a thorough capitalist operation of agriculture. On the other hand, the share thus appropriated by the landlord has not the pure form of rent. It may actually include interest on the capital advanced by him and a surplus rent. It may also absorb practically all the surplus labor of the tenant, or leave to him a greater or smaller portion of this surplus labor. But the essential point is that rent no longer appears here as the normal form of surplus-value in general. On the one hand, the tenant, whether he employ his own labor or another's, is supposed to have a claim upon a portion of the product, not in his capacity as a laborer, but as a possessor of a part of the instruments of labor, as his own capitalist. On the other hand, the landlord claims his share not exclusively in his capacity as the owner of the land, but also as a lender of capital.[139]

A remainder of the old community in land, which had been preserved after the transition to independent peasant economy, for instance in Poland and Roumania, served there as a subterfuge for accomplishing a transition to the lower forms of ground-rent. A portion of the land belongs to the individual farmers and is tilled independently by them. Another portion is tilled collectively and creates a surplus product, which serves either for the payment of community expenses, or as a reserve in case of crop failures, etc. These last two parts of the surplus product, and finally the whole surplus product together with the land, upon which it has been grown, are gradually usurped by state officials and private individuals, and by this means the originally free peas-

[139] Compare Buret, Tocqueville, Sismondi.

ant proprietors, whose obligation to till this land collectively
is maintained, are transformed into vassals, who are compelled
to perform forced labor or pay rent in kind, while the usurp-
ers are transformed into owners, not only of the stolen community lands, but of the lands of the peasants themselves.

We need not dwell upon actual slave economy (which likewise passes through a development from the patriarchal system, working pre-eminently for home use, to the plantation
system, working for the world market) nor upon that management of estates, under which the landlords carry on agriculture for their own account, own all the instruments of
production, and exploit the labor of free or unfree servants,
who are paid in kind or in money. In this case, the landlord and the owner of the instruments of production, and
thus the direct exploiter of the laborers counted among these
instruments of production, are one and the same person.
Rent and profit likewise coincide then, there being no separation of the different forms of surplus-value. The entire
surplus labor of the workers, which is here represented by
the surplus product, is extracted from them directly by the
owner of all the instruments of production, to which the land
and, under the original form of slavery, the producers themselves, belong. Where capitalist conceptions predominate, as
they did upon the American plantations, this entire surplus-
value is regarded as profit. In places where the capitalist
mode of production does not exist, nor the conceptions corresponding to it have been transferred from capitalist countries, it appears as rent. At any rate, this form does not
present any difficulties. The income of the landlord, whatever may be the name given to it, the available surplus product appropriated by him, is here the normal and predomi-
nating form, under which the entire unpaid labor is directly
appropriated, and the property in land forms the basis of this
appropriation.

There is, furthermore, the small peasants' property. Here
the farmer is the free owner of his land, which appears as
his principal instrument of production, the indispensable field
of employment for his labor and his capital. No lease money

is paid under this form. Rent, therefore, does not appear as a separate form of surplus-value here, although in countries, in which capitalist industry in other lines is developed, it appears as a surplus profit by comparison with other lines of production. But it is a surplus profit which, like all the rest of the product of his labor, falls into the hands of the farmer himself.

This form of property in land requires that, as was the case under the earlier forms, the rural population should have a great preponderance over the city population, so that, while capitalist production may generally prevail, it is nevertheless but relatively little developed, concentration of capitals moves in narrow circles in the other lines of production, and dissipation of capitals predominates. Under these conditions, the greater part of the rural product will have to be consumed, as a direct means of subsistence, by the producers, the farmers themselves, and only the surplus above that will pass as commodities into the commerce with the cities. Whatever may be the manner, in which the average market price of the products of the soil is regulated in this case, the differential rent, a surplus portion of the price of commodities from the superior or more favorably located lands, must evidently exist in this case just as it does under the capitalist mode of production. This differential rent would exist, even if this form should appear under social conditions, in which no general market price has as yet been developed. It appears then in the spare surplus product. Only it flows into the pocket of the farmer, whose labor realises itself under favorable natural conditions. It is precisely under this form that the assumption is correct, as a rule, that no absolute rent exists, so that the worst soil does not pay any rent. For under this form the price of land enters as an element into the actual cost of production for the farmer, since in the course of the further development of this form the price of land may have been figured, for instance in the case of a division of an estate, at a certain money value, or, in view of the continuous change in the ownership of the whole property, or of its parts, the land may have been bought by the tiller himself, largely by taking up money on a mortgage. In this way the price of land, which is nothing else but a capitalized rent, is a pre-existing condition and rent seems to exist independently of any differentiation in the fertility and location of the land. Absolute rent is conditioned either upon the realized surplus of the value of the product above its price of production, or a monopoly price exceeding the value of the product. But since agriculture is carried on here largely as an agriculture for direct subsistence, so that the land is an indispensable field of employment for the labor and capital of the majority of the population, the regulating market price of the product will come up to its value only under extraordinary circumstances. But its value will, as a rule, stand higher than its price of production on account of the predominance of the element of living labor, although this excess of its value over its price of production will be in its turn limited by the low composition of the capital, even of that of the industries outside of agriculture, in countries with a predominance of small farmers' property. For the small farmer the limit of exploitation is not set by the average profit of the capital, if he is a small capitalist, nor by the necessity of making a rent, if he is a landowner. Nothing appears as an absolute limit for him, as a small capitalist, but the wages which he pays to himself, after deducting his actual costs. So long as the price of the product covers these wages, he will cultivate his land, and will do so often down to the physical minimum of his wages. As for his capacity as a landlord, the barrier of property is eliminated in his case, since it can exert its influence only against a capital (including labor) separated from it, by erecting an obstacle against its investment. It is true that interest on the price of land, which generally has to be paid to another, the holder of the mortgage, also forms a barrier. But this interest can be paid out of that portion of the surplus labor, which would form the profit under capitalist conditions. The rent anticipated in the price of land, and in the interest paid for it, cannot be anything else but a portion of the capitalized surplus labor of the farmer, performed by him beyond the labor indispensable for his subsistence, without realising this surplus labor in a part of the value of commodities equal to the entire average profit, and still less in a surplus profit, which would constitute a surplus above the surplus labor realised in the average profit. The rent may be a deduction from the average profit, or even the only portion of it which is realised. In order that the small farmer may cultivate his land, or may buy land for cultivation, it is therefore not necessary, as it is under a normal capitalist production, that the market price of his products should rise high enough to allow him the average profit, and still less a surplus above this average profit fixed in the form of a rent. Therefore it is not necessary that the market price should rise, either as high as the value or as high as the price of production of his product. This is one of the causes which keeps the price of cereals lower in countries with a predominance of small farmers than in countries with a capitalist mode of production. One portion of the surplus labor of the farmers, who work under the least favorable conditions, is given to society without an equivalent and does not pass over into the regulation of the price of production or into the formation of values in general. This lower price is also a result of the poverty of the producers and by no means of the productivity of their labor.

This form of free farmers' property managing their own affairs, as the prevailing, normal, form constitutes on the one hand the economic foundation of society during the best times of classical antiquity, on the other hand it is found among modern nations, as one of the forms arising from the dissolution of feudal landlordism. In this way we meet the yeomanry in England, the peasantry in Sweden, the farmers in France and Western Germany. We do not mention the colonies here, since the independent farmer there develops under different conditions.

The free ownership of the selfemploying farmer is evidently the most normal form of landed property for small scale production, that is, for a mode of production, in which the possession of the land is a prerequisite for the ownership of the product of his own labor by the laborer, and in which the agriculturist, whether he be a free owner or a vassal, always has to produce his own means of subsistence independently, as a single laborer with his family. The ownership of the soil is as necessary for the complete development of this mode of production as the ownership of the instrument is for the free development of handicraft production. This ownership forms here the basis for the development of personal independence. It is a necessary stage of transition for the development of agriculture itself. The causes which bring about its downfall show its limitations. These causes are: Destruction of rural house industries, which form its normal supplement, as a result of the development of great industries; a gradual deterioration and exhaustion of the soil subjected to this cultivation; usurpation, on the part of the great landlords, of the community lands, which form everywhere the second supplement of small peasants' property and alone enable them to keep cattle; competition, either of plantation systems or of great agricultural enterprises carried out on a capitalist scale. Improvements of agriculture, which on the one hand bring about a fall in the prices of the products of the soil, and on the other require greater investments and more diversified material conditions of production, also contribute towards this end, as they did in England during the first half of the 18th century.

Small peasants' property excludes by its very nature the development of the social powers of production of labor, the social forms of labor, the social concentration of capitals, cattle raising on a large scale, and a progressive application of science.

Usury and a system of taxation must impoverish it everywhere. The expenditure of capital in the price of the land withdraws this capital from cultivation. An infinite dissipation of means of production and an isolation of the producers themselves go with it. Also an enormous waste of human energy. A progressive deterioration of the conditions of production and a raising of the price of means of production is a necessary law of small peasants' property. Fertile seasons are a misfortune for this mode of production.[140]

One of the specific evils of small scale agriculture, when combined with the free ownership of the land, arises from the fact that the agriculturist invests a capital in the purchase of the land. (The same applies also to the form of transition, in which the great landlord invests capital, first, for the purpose of buying land, and secondly, for the purpose of managing it as his own tenant). Owing to the changeable nature, which the land here assumes as a mere commodity, the changes of ownership increase,[141] so that the land, from the point of view of the farmer, passes again into the calculation as a new investment of capital with every new generation, every division of estates, in other words, that it becomes land bought by him. The price of land here forms an overwhelming element of the individual false cost of production, or of the cost price of the product for the individual producer.

The price of land is nothing but the capitalized, and therefore anticipated, rent. If agriculture is carried on by capitalist methods, so that the landlord receives only the rent, and the tenant pays nothing for the land except his annual rent, then it is evident that the capital invested by the owner of the land himself in the purchase of the land constitutes an interest-bearing investment of capital for him, but that it has nothing to do with the capital invested in agriculture itself. It forms neither a part of the fixed nor of the circulating capital employed here;[142] it merely secures for the buyer a title to the annual rent, but has nothing to do with the production

---

[140] See the speech of the king of France in Tooke.

[141] See Mounier and Rubichon.

[142] Dr. H. Maron (*Extensive or Intensive?*) [No further information given about this pamphlet]. He starts from the false assumption of those whom he combats. He assumes that the capital invested in the purchase of land is "first capital," and engages in a controversy about first capital and running capital that is, fixed and circulating capital. His wholly amateurish conceptions of capital, which may be excused in one who is not an economist in view of the condition of German political economy, conceal from him the fact that this capital is neither first nor running capital, any more than the capital, which some one may invest at the Stock Exchange in the purchase of consols or state bonds, and which represents a personal investment of capital for him, is "invested" in any productive line of industry.

of the rent itself. For the buyer of land pays his capital out to the one who sells the land, and the seller relinquishes his ownership of the land for this consideration. This capital does not exist any more as the capital of the buyer after that. He has not got it any longer. Therefore it does not belong to the capital, which he can invest in any way in the land itself. Whether he bought the land at a high or a low price, or whether he received it for nothing, does not alter anything in the capital invested by the tenant in his establishment, and does not make any change in the rent, but merely changes the question, whether it appears to him as interest or not as interest, or as a high or a low interest.

Take, for instance, the slavery system. The price paid for a slave is nothing but the anticipated and capitalized surplus-value or profit, which is to be ground out of him. But the capital paid for the purchase of a slave does not belong to the capital, by which profit, surplus labor, is extracted from him. On the contrary. It is capital, which the slave holder gives away, it is a deduction from the capital, which he has available for actual production. It has ceased to exist for him, just as the capital invested in the purchase of land has ceased to exist for agriculture. The best proof of this is the fact, that it does not come back into existence for the slave holder or the land owner, until he sells the slave or the land once more. Then the same condition of things holds good for the buyer. The fact that he has bought the slave does not enable him to exploit the slave without further ceremony. He is not able to do so until he invests some other capital in production by means of the slave.

The same capital does not exist twice. It does not exist one time in the hands of the seller, and a second time in the hands of the buyer of the land. It passes from the hands of the buyer to those of the seller, and that settles the matter. The buyer has then no longer any capital, but in its stead he has a piece of land. The fact that the rent produced by a real investment of capital in this land is figured by the new owner of the land as interest on a capital, which he did not invest in the soil, but gave away as a purchase price for the

land, does not alter the economic nature of the factor land
in the least, any more than the fact that some one may have
paid 1,000 pounds sterling for 3% consols has anything to do
with the capital, out of whose revenue the interest on the national debt is paid.

In fact, the money expended in the purchase of land, like
that spent for the purchase of national bonds, is merely capital in itself, just as any amount of values is capital in itself
on the basis of capitalist production. It is potential capital.
The thing paid for the land, like that paid for national bonds
or any other purchased commodity, is a sum of money. This is
capital in itself, because it may be converted into capital. It
depends upon the use to which the seller puts it, whether the
money obtained by him really becomes capital or not. For
the buyer it can never again perform the functions of capital,
any more than any other money which he has finally spent.
It figures in his calculations as interest-bearing capital, because he considers the income, which he receives as rent from
his land or as interest on his bonds, as interest on the money,
which he paid for his title to this revenue. He cannot realise
it as capital unless he sells his title again. If he does, then
the new buyer assumes the same relationship in which the
old one was, and the money spent in this transaction cannot
transform itself into actual capital by any change of hands.

In the case of small property in land the illusion, that the
land itself has value and may, therefore, pass as a capital into
the price of production of the product, like a machine or raw
materials, fortifies itself still more. But we have seen that
the rent, and with it capitalised rent, or the price of land, can
pass over into the price of the products of the soil in two
cases only. The first case is that, in which the value of the
products of the soil stands higher than their price of production and the market conditions enable the landlord to realise
this difference; this condition of values and prices of production obtains, when the composition of the agricultural capital
raises the value above the price of production. This agricultural capital has nothing to do with the capital invested in
the purchase of the land. The second case is that in which

a monopoly price exists. And both cases occur less under small peasants' property and small land ownership than under any other form, because production largely satisfies the producers' own wants in their case and is carried on independently of the regulation by the average rate of profit. Even where small peasants' economy is carried on upon leased land, the lease money comprises more than under any other conditions a portion of the profit and even a deduction from the wages; this money is then only a nominal rent, not a rent representing an independent category as compared to wages and profit.

The expenditure of money-capital for the purchase of land, then, is not an investment of agricultural capital. It is a proportionate deduction from the capital, which the small farmers can employ in their own sphere of production. It reduces to that extent the size of their means of production and thereby narrows the economic basis of their reproduction. It subjects the small farmer to the money lender's extortion, since credit, in the strict meaning of the term, occurs but rarely in this sphere. It is an obstacle to agriculture, even where such a purchase takes place in the case of large estates. In fact, it contradicts the capitalist mode of production, which is on the whole indifferent to the question whether the landowner is in debt, no matter whether he inherited or bought his estate. The management of the leased estate itself is not altered in its nature, whether the landowner pockets the rent himself or whether he has to pay it over to the holder of his mortgage.

We have seen that the price of land is regulated by the rate of interest, if the ground-rent is a given magnitude. If the rate of interest is low, then the price of land is high, and vice versa. Normally, then, a high price of land and a low rate of interest would have to go hand in hand, so that if the farmer paid a high price for the land in consequence of a low rate of interest, the same low rate of interest should also secure for him his running capital on easy terms of credit. But in reality, things turn out differently under small peasants' property, as the prevailing form. In the first place, the general laws of credit do not apply to the farmer, since these laws rest upon the capitalist as a producer. In the second place, where small peasants' property predominates — we are not speaking of colonies here — and the small peasant forms the foundation of the nation, the formation of capital, that is social reproduction, is relatively weak, and the formation of loanable money-capital, in the sense in which we have previously analyzed this term, is still weaker. For this is conditioned upon concentration and the existence of a class of rich and idle capitalists (Massie). In the third place, where the ownership of the land is a necessary condition for the existence of the greater part of the producers, as it is here, and an indispensable field of investment for their capital, the price of land is raised independently of the rate of interest, and often in an inverse ratio to it, by the preponderance of the demand for land over its supply. If sold in small lots, the land in this case brings a far higher price than it does by its sale in large estates, because the number of small buyers is large and that of the large buyers small (*Bandes Noires, Rubichon;* Newman). For all these reasons the price of land rises here while the rate of interest is relatively high. The relatively low interest, which the farmer here derives from the capital invested in the purchase of land (Mounier), corresponds on the other hand to the high rate of interest exacted by usury, which he himself has to pay to his mortgage creditors. The Irish system shows the same thing, only in another form.

This price of land, an element foreign in itself to production, may here rise to such a point that it makes production impossible (Dombasle).

The fact that the price of land plays such a role, that the sale and purchase of land, the circulation of land as a commodity, develops to this degree, is a practical result of capitalist development, since a commodity is here the form generally assumed by all products and all instruments of production. On the other hand, this development takes place only wherever capitalist production develops but to a limited extent and does not bring forth all its peculiarities. For this condition rests precisely upon the fact that agriculture is no longer, or not yet, subject to the capitalist mode of production, but rather to a mode handed down from obsolete forms of society. The disadvantages of the capitalist mode of production, which makes the producers dependent upon the money price of their products, coincide here with the disadvantages due to the imperfect development of capitalist production. The farmer becomes a merchant and an industrial without the conditions which would enable him to produce his goods as commodities.

The conflict between the price of land, as an element in the cost price of the producers, but not an element in the price of production of the product (even though the rent should pass as a determining element into the price of the products of the soil, the capitalized rent, which is advanced for 20 years or more, does not pass into their price in this way), is but one of the forms through which the antagonism between private ownership of the land and between a rational agriculture, a normal social utilization of the soil, expresses itself. But on the other hand, the private ownership of the land, and with it the expropriation of the direct producers from the land — the private property of some, which implies lack of private property on the part of others — is the basis of the capitalist mode of production.

Here, in agriculture on a small scale, the price of the land a form and result of private ownership of the land, appears as a barrier of production itself. In agriculture on a large scale, and in the case of large estates resting upon a capitalist mode of production, private ownership likewise acts as a barrier, because it limits the tenant in his investment of productive capital, which in the last analysis benefits, not him, but the landlord. In both forms the exploitation and devastation of the powers of the soil takes the place of a consciously rational treatment of the soil in its role of an eternal social property, of an indispensable condition of existence and reproduction for successive generations of human beings. And besides, this exploitation is made dependent, not upon the attained degree of social development, but upon the accidental and unequal situations of individual producers. In the case of small property this happens from lack of means and science, by which the social productivity of labor-power might be utilized. In the case of large property, it is done by the exploitation of such means for the purpose of the most rapid accumulation of wealth for the tenant and proprietor. The dependence of both of them upon the market price is instrumental in accomplishing this result.

All critique of small property resolves itself in the last resort into a critique of private ownership as a barrier and obstacle of agriculture. And so does all counter-critique of large property. In either case, we leave aside, of course, all minor considerations of politics. This barrier and this obstacle, which are set up by all private property of land against agricultural production and against a rational treatment, conservation and improvement of the soil itself, develop on both sides merely in different forms. In the controversy over these specific forms of the evil its ultimate cause is forgotten.

Small property in land is conditioned upon the premise that the overwhelming majority of the population is rural, and that not the social, but the isolated labor predominates; that, therefore, in view of such conditions, the wealth and development of reproduction, both in its material and intellectual sides, are out of the question and with them the prerequisites of a rational culture. On the other hand, large landed property reduces the agricultural population to a continually decreasing minimum, and induces on the other side a continual increase of the industrial population crowded together in large cities. In this way it creates conditions, which cause an incurable break in the interconnections of the social circulation of matter prescribed by the natural laws of life. As a result the strength of the soil is wasted, and this prodigality is carried far beyond the boundaries of a certain country by commerce (Liebig).

While small property in land creates a class of barbarians standing half way outside of society, a class suffering all the tortures and all miseries of civilized countries in addition to

3H

the crudeness of primitive forms of society, large property in land undermines labor-power in the last region, in which its primal energy seeks refuge, and in it which stores up its strength as a reserve fund for the regeneration of the vital power of nations, the land itself. Large industry and large agriculture on an industrial scale work together. Originally distinguished by the fact, that large industry lays waste and destroys principally the labor-power, the natural power, of human beings, whereas large agriculture industrially managed destroys and wastes mainly the natural powers of the soil, both of them join hands in the further course of development, so that the industrial system weakens also the laborers of the country districts, and industry and commerce supply agriculture with the means by which the soil may be exhausted.

PART VII.

THE REVENUES AND THEIR SOURCES.

CHAPTER XLVIII.

THE TRINITARIAN FORMULA.

I.[143]

CAPITAL — Profit (Profit of Enterprise plus Interest), Land — Ground-Rent, Labor — Wages, this is the trinitarian formula which comprises all the secrets of the social process of production.

Furthermore, since interest, as previously demonstrated, appear as the characteristic product of capital, and profit of enterprise distinguishes itself from interest by appearing as wages independent of capital, the above trinitarian formula reduces itself more specifically to the following: Capital — Interest, Land — Ground-Rent, Labor — Wages. Here profit, the specific mark characterizing the form of surplus-value belonging to the capitalist mode of production, is happily eliminated.

Now, if we look more closely at this economic trinity, we observe:

1) The alleged sources of the annually available wealth belong to widely dissimilar spheres and have not the least analogy with one another. They have about the same relation to each other as lawyer's fees, carrots, and music.

Capital, Land, Labor! But capital is not a thing. It is a

[143] The following three fragments were found in different places of the manuscript for Part VI.— F. E.

947

definite interrelation in social production belonging to a definite historical formation of society. This interrelation expresses itself through a certain thing and gives to this thing a specific social character. Capital is not the sum of the material and produced means of production. Capital means rather the means of production converted into capital, and means of production by themselves are no more capital than gold or silver are money in themselves. Capital signifies the means of production monopolized by a certain part of society, the products and material requirements of labor made independent of labor-power in living human beings and antagonistic to them, and personified in capital by this antagonism. Capital means not merely the products of the laborers made independent of them and turned into social powers, the products turned into rulers and buyers of their own producers, but also the social powers and the future . . . (illegible) form of labor, which antagonize the producers in the shape of qualities of their products. Here, then, we have a definite and, at first sight, very mystical, social form of one of the factors in a historically produced process of social production.

By the side of this factor we have the land, the unorganic nature as such, a crude and uncouth mass, in its whole primal wildness. Value is labor. Therefore surplus-value cannot be land. The absolute fertility of the soil accomplishes no more than that a certain quantity of labor produces a certain product conditioned upon the natural fertility of the soil. The difference in the fertility of the soil brings it about that the same quantities of labor and capital, hence the same value, express themselves in different quantities of agricultural products, so that these products have different individual values. The equalization of these individual values into market-values is responsible for the fact that the " advantages of fertile over inferior soil . . . are transferred from the cultivator or consumer to the landlord." (Ricardo, *Principles,* p. 6.)

And finally, the third party in this conspiracy is a mere ghost, " Labor," a mere abstraction, and which does not exist when taken by itself, or, if we take . . . (illegible), the productive activity of human beings in general, by which they promote the circulation of matter between themselves and nature, divested not only of every definiteness of social form and character, but even of its mere natural existence, independent of society, lifted above all societies, being the common attribute of unsocial man as well as of man with any form of society and a general expression and assertion of life.

II.

Capital — Interest; Private Land, Private Ownership of the Earth, in modern form and corresponding to the capitalist mode of production — Rent; Wage Labor — Wages. This is supposed to be the connection between the sources of revenue. Wage Labor and Private Land, like Capital, are historically determined social forms; one a social form of labor, the other a social form of the monopolized terrestrial globe, and both forms belong to the same economic formation of society corresponding to capital.

The first remarkable thing about this formula is that Land and Labor are placed indiscriminately by the side of Capital. The one, Capital, is a definite form of an element of production belonging to a definite mode of production having a definite cast. It is an element of production combined with and represented by a definite social form. The other two, Land on the one hand and Labor on the other, are two elements of the real labor process. In their material form they are common to all modes of production, they are the material elements of all processes of production, and have nothing to do with the social form of productive processes.

Secondly. In this formula (Capital — Interest, Land — Ground-Rent, Labor — Wages of Labor), capital, land and labor respectively appear as sources of interest (instead of profit), ground-rent and wages, and these things appear as their fruits; capital, land and labor appear as the cause, interest, ground-rent and wages as the effect; and this is done in such a way that each individual source is combined with the thing which it puts forth and produces. All three revenues, interest (instead of profit), rent, wages, are three parts of the value of the product; generally speaking they are parts of value, or, expressed in money, they are certain parts of money, certain parts of price. The formula " Capital — Interest " has indeed the least meaning of any formula of capital; still it is one of its formulæ. But how is land supposed to create value, that is, a socially defined quantity of labor, or even that particular portion of the value of its own products which forms the rent? For instance, land takes part as an agent of production, in the creation of a use-value, of a material product, of wheat. But it has nothing to do with the production of the value of wheat. To the extent that value is represented by wheat, we consider wheat merely as a definite quantity of materialized social labor, regardless of the particular substance, in which this labor is materialized, or of the particular use-value of this substance.

This is not in contradiction with the fact that, in the first place, other circumstances being equal, the cheapness or dearness of the wheat depends upon the productivity of the soil. The productivity of agricultural labor is conditioned upon natural circumstances, and the same quantity of labor is represented by many or by few products, use-values, according to the productivity of such labor. How large the quantity of labor may be, which is materialized in one bushel of wheat, depends upon the number of bushels produced by the same quantity of labor. It depends, in this case, upon the productivity of the soil, in what proportions of product value shall be materialized. But this value is given, independently of such a distribution. Value is represented by use-value; and use-value is a prerequisite for the creation of exchange-value; but it is folly to construe an antagonism by placing upon one side a use-value, like land, and upon the other side an exchange-value, and at that some particular portion of exchange-value. In the second place . . . [here the manuscript stops short].

III.

Vulgar economy really does nothing else but to interpret, in doctrinaire fashion, the ideas of persons entrapped in capitalist conditions of production and performing the function of agents in such production, to systematize and to defend these ideas. We need not wonder, then, that vulgar economy feels particularly at home in the estranged form of manifestation, in which economic conditions are absurd and complete contradictions, and that these conditions appear so much more self-explanatory to it, the more their internal connection is concealed. So long as the ordinary brain accepts these conceptions, vulgar economy is satisfied. But all science would be superfluous, if the appearance, the form, and the nature of things were wholly identical. Vulgar economy has not the slightest inkling of the fact that the trinity from which it takes its departure, namely Land — Rent, Capital — Interest, Labor — Wages of Labor (or Price of Labor), are on their very face three incompatible propositions. First we have the use-value Land, which has no value, and the exchange-value Rent. Here a social relation is conceived as a thing and proportioned to nature. Two incommensurable magnitudes are supposed to be proportional to each other. Then we have Capital — Interest. If capital is conceived as a certain sum of values independently represented by money, then it is manifestly nonsense to say that a certain value shall be valued higher than its value. It is precisely in the formula Capital — Interest that all intermediate links are eliminated, and capital is reduced to its most general formula, which for this reason is inexplicable by itself and absurd. It is also for this reason that the vulgar economist prefers the formula Capital — Interest, with its occult faculty of making a value unequal to itself, to the formula of Capital — Profit, which approaches more nearly to the actual capitalist relations. Then again, driven by the restless thought that four is not five and that 100 dollars cannot be 110 dollars, he flees from Capital as an exchange-value to the material substance of capital, to its use-value as a material requirement of labor, as machinery, raw materials, etc. By this means he succeeds in putting into the place of the first incomprehensible relation, which makes four equal to five, a wholly incommensurable one between a use-value, a thing, upon the one hand, and a definite relation of social production, surplus-value, upon the other, as he does also in the case of private property in land. As soon as the vulgar economist has arrived at this incommensurable magnitude, everything becomes clear to him, and he no longer feels the need of thinking any further. For he has arrived at what is " rational " in bourgeois conception. Finally we have Labor — Wages of Labor, or Price of Labor. This last expression, as we have shown in Volume I, contradicts on its very face the conception of value as well as of price. Price, generally speaking, is but a definite expression of value. And " Price of Labor " is just as irrational as a yellow leogarithm. But here the vulgar economist is all the more satisfied, because it brings him to the deep understanding of the bourgeois, that he pays for labor with money, and because the fact that this formula contradicts the conception of value relieves him from all obligation to understand value.

We [144] have seen that the capitalist process of production is a historically determined form of the social process of production in general. This process is on the one hand the process by which the material requirements of life are produced, and on the other hand a process which takes place under specific historical and economic conditions of production and which produces and reproduces these conditions of production themselves, and with them the human agents of this process, their material conditions of existence and their mutual relations, that is, their particular economic form of society. For the aggregate of these relations, in which the agents of this production live with regard to nature and to themselves, and in which they produce, is precisely their society, considered from the point of view of its economic structure. Like all its predecessors, the capitalist process of

[144] Beginning of Chapter XLVIII according to the manuscript.

production takes place under definite material conditions, which are at the same time the bearers of definite social relations maintained towards one another by the individuals in the process of producing their life's requirements. These conditions and these relations are on the one hand preriquisites, on the other hand results and creations of the capitalist process of production. They are produced and reproduced by it. We have also seen that capital (the capitalist is merely capital personified and functions in the process of production as the agent of capital), in the social process of production corresponding to it, pumps a certain quantity of surplus labor out of the direct producer, or laborer. It extorts this surplus without returning an equivalent. This surplus labor always remains forced labor in essence, no matter how much it may seem to be the result of free contract. This surplus labor is represented by a surplus-value, and this surplus-value is materialized in a surplus product. It must always remain surplus labor in the sense that it is labor performed above the normal requirements of the producer. In the capitalist system as well as in the slave system, etc., it merely assumes an antagonistic form and is supplemented by the complete idleness of a portion of society. A certain quantity of surplus labor is required for the purpose of discounting accidents, and by the necessary and progressive expansion of the process of reproduction in keeping with the development of the needs and the advance of population, called accumulation from the point of view of the capitalist. It is one of the civilizing sides of capital that it enforces this surplus labor in a manner and under conditions which promote the development of the productive forces, of social conditions, and the creation of the elements for a new and higher formation better than did the preceding forms of slavery, serfdom, etc. Thus it leads on the one hand to a stage, in which the coercion and the monopolization of the social development (including its material and intellectual advantages) by a portion of society at the expense of the other portion are eliminated; on the other hand it creates the material requirements and the germ of conditions, which make it possible to combine this surplus labor in a higher form of society with a greater reduction of the time devoted to material labor. For, according to the development of the productive power of labor, surplus labor may be large in a small total labor day, and relatively small in a large total labor day. If the necessary labor time equals three, and the surplus labor three, then the total working day is equal to six, and the rate of surplus labor 100%. If the necessary labor is equal to nine, and the surplus labor three, then the total working day is twelve and the rate of surplus labor only $33\frac{1}{3}\%$. Furthermore, it depends upon the productivity of labor, how much use-value shall be produced in a definite time, hence also in a definite surplus labor time. The actual wealth of society, and the possibility of a continual expansion of its process of reproduction, do not depend upon the duration of the surplus labor, but upon its productivity and upon the more or less fertile conditions of production, under which it is performed. In fact, the realm of freedom does not commence until the point is passed where labor under the compulsion of necessity and of external utility is required. In the very nature of things it lies beyond the sphere of material production in the strict meaning of the term. Just as the savage must wrestle with nature, in order to satisfy his wants, in order to maintain his life and reproduce it, so civilized man has to do it, and he must do it in all forms of society and under all possible modes of production. With his development the realm of natural necessity expands, because his wants increase; but at the same time the forces of production increase, by which these wants are satisfied. The freedom in this field cannot consist of anything else but of the fact that socialized man, the associated producers, regulate their interchange with nature rationally, bring it under their common control, instead of being ruled by it as by some blind power; that they accomplish their task with the least expenditure of energy and under conditions most adequate to their human nature and most worthy of it. But it always remains a realm of necessity. Beyond it begins that development of human power, which is its own end, the true realm of freedom, which, however, can flourish only upon that realm of necessity as its basis. The shortening of the working day is its fundamental premise.

In a capitalist society, this surplus-value, or this surplus product (leaving aside accidental fluctuations in its distribution and considering only the regulating law of these fluctuations), is divided among the capitalists as a dividend in proportion to the percentage of the total social capital held by each. In this shape the surplus-value appears as the average profit, which falls to the share of the capital, an average profit, which in its turn is separated into profits of enterprise and interest, and which in this way may fall into the hands of different kinds of capitalists. This appropriation and distribution of the surplus-value, or surplus product, by the capital however, has its barrier in private ownership of land. Just as the active capitalist pumps surplus labor, and with it surplus-value and surplus products in the form of profit out of the laborer, so the landlord in his turn pumps a portion of this surplus-value, or surplus product, out of the capitalist, in the shape of rent, according to the laws previously demonstrated by us.

Hence, when speaking of profit as that portion of surplus-value, which falls to the share of capital, we mean average profit (profits of enterprise plus interest), which has already been limited by deducting the rent from the aggregate profits (identical in mass with the aggregate surplus-value). That rent has been deducted in the premise here. Profits of capital (profits of enterprise plus interest) and ground-rent are merely particular constituents of surplus-value, categories, by which surplus-value is distinguished according to whether it falls into the hands of capital or of private land. This classification does not alter its nature in any way. If added together, these parts form the sum of the social surplus-value. Capital pumps the surplus labor, which is represented by surplus-value and surplus product, directly out of the laborers. To this extent it may be regarded as the producer of surplus-value. Private Land has nothing to do with the actual process of production. Its role is confined to carrying a portion of the produced surplus-value from the pockets of capital to its own. However, the landlord plays a role in the capitalist process of production, not merely by the pressure, which he exerts upon capital, nor by the fact that large property in land is a prerequisite and condition of capitalist production, seeing that it separates the laborer from the means of production, but particularly because the landlord appears as the personification of one of the most essential requirements of production.

Finally, the laborer, in his capacity as the owner and seller of his individual labor-power, receives a portion of his product under the name of wages, in which that portion of his labor is materialized, which we call necessary labor, that is, the labor required for the conservation and reproduction of his labor-power, regardless of whether the conditions of this conservation and reproduction are scanty or bountiful, favorable or unfavorable.

Whatever may be the disparity of these conditions in other respects, they all have this in common: Capital yields year after year a profit to the capitalist, land a ground-rent to the landlord, and labor-power, under normal conditions and so long as it remains a useful labor-power, a wage to the laborer. These three parts of the total value produced annually, and the corresponding parts of the annually created total product, may be annually consumed by their respective owners, without draining the source of their reproduction (leaving aside for the present any consideration of accumulation). They are like the annually consumable fruits of a perennial tree, or rather of three trees. They form the annual revenue of three classes, the capitalist, the landlord and the laborer. They are revenues distributed at large by the active capitalist in his capacity as the direct exploiter of surplus labor and employer of labor in general. In this way the capital appears to the capitalist, the land to the landlord, and the labor-power or rather the labor itself, to the laborer (since he sells labor-power only to the extent that it is actively employed, and since the price of his labor-power, as previously shown, necessarily appears as the price of his labor under the capital-

ist system) as three different sources of their respective revenues, of profit, ground-rent and wages. They are so in
fact in the sense that capital is for the capitalist a perennial pumping machine of surplus labor, the land for the landlord a perennial magnet attracting a portion of the surplus-
value pumped out by capital, and finally, labor the continually self-renewing condition and the ever self-renewing means
of acquiring a portion of the value created by the laborer and
with it a part of the social product measured by this portion
of value, the necessities of life, under the title of wages.
They are so, furthermore, in the sense that capital fixes a
portion of the value, and thus of the product, of annual labor
in the form of profit, the private land fixes another portion
in the form of rent, and wage labor fixes a third portion in
the form of wages, and converts them by this transformation
into revenues of the capitalist, the landlord, and the laborer,
without, however, creating the substance itself, which is transformed into these different categories.

Their distribution rather presupposes the existence of this
substance, namely the total value of the annual product,
which is nothing but materialized social labor. But this is
not the form, in which the matter appears to the human
agents in production, to the human bearers of the various
functions in the process of production. It rather appears
to them reversed. We shall point out in the further course
of our analysis, why this happens. Capital, ground-rent and
labor appear to those human agents in production as three
different, independent sources, from which arise three different constituents of the annually produced value, and of the
product, in which it exists. They fancy that not merely the
different forms of this value as revenues falling to the share
of particular agents in the social process of production, but
this value itself arises from these sources, and with it the
substance of these forms of revenue.

[Here one folio sheet of the manuscript is missing.]

. . . Differential rent is bound up with the relative
fertility of the soil, in other words, with qualities, which
arise from the soil as such. But in the first place, to the

extent that it rests upon the different individual values of
the products of different kinds of soil, it is determined only
in the manner just mentioned; in the second place, to the
extent that it rests upon the regulating general market value,
which differs from the individual value, it is a social law
carried through by means of competition, and this law has
nothing to do either with the soil or with the different degrees of its fertility.

It might seem that a rational relation was expressed at
least in the term " Labor — Wages of Labor." But this is
no more the case than it is in the term " Land — Ground-
Rent." To the extent that labor creates value, and materializes itself in the value of commodities, it has nothing to do
with the distribution of this value among the different categories. And so far as it has the specifically social character of wage labor, it does not create any value. We have
already shown that wages of labor, or price of labor, is but
an irrational expression for the value, or price, of labor-
power; and the definite social conditions, under which this
labor-power is sold, have nothing to do with labor as a general agent in production. Labor is also materialized in that
portion of the value of a commodity, which forms the price
of labor-power in the shape of wages; it creates this portion
just as it does the other portions of the product; but it does
not materialize itself in this portion to any other extent, or
in any other way, than it does in the portions representing
rent or profit. Besides, if we regard labor as a faculty creating value, we do not look upon its concrete form as a means
of production, but upon its social relation, which differs from
that of wage labor.

Even the term " Capital — Profit " is not correct here. If
capital is viewed in the only relation, in which it produces
surplus-value, namely in its relation to the laborer, in which
it extorts surplus labor by compulsion exerted upon the wage
laborer and his labor-power, then this surplus-value comprises
not merely profit (profit of enterprise plus interest), but also
rent, in short, the entire undivided surplus-value. Here, on
the other hand, as a source of revenue, it is considered only

in relation with that portion, which falls into the hands of
the capitalist. This is not the surplus-value which it extracts, all together, but only that portion, which it extracts
for the capitalist. Still more is all connection lost, as soon as
the formula is transformed into " Capital — Interest."

Now, having first considered the disparity of the above
three sources, we must note, in the second place, that their
products, their offspring, the revenues, all belong to the same
sphere, namely that of value. However, this relation, not
only between incommensurable magnitudes, but also between
wholly unlike, mutually unrelated, and incomparable things,
·is accounted for by the fact that capital, like land and labor,
is indeed taken only in its meaning as a material substance,
that is, simply as a produced means of production, and in
so doing both its relation to the laborer and its value are ig-
nored.

In the third place, if understood in this way, the formula
Capital — Interest (Profit), Land — Rent, Labor — Wages
of Labor, presents a uniform and symmetrical inconsistency.
In fact, when wage labor does not appear as a socially determined form of labor, but rather all labor is considered naturally as wage labor (because it appears in this light to people who are biased by capitalist conditions of production),
then the particular, specific, social forms observed by the material requirements of labor (the produced means of production and the land) towards wage labor (which is in its turn
a prerequisite of those conditions), easily coincide with the
material existence of these requirements of labor, or with
the form possessed by them generally in the actual labor
process, divested of all historically determined social forms,
or even of any social form. The changed form of the requirements of labor, divested of labor and facing it as an independent element, which is assumed by the produced means
of production when they become capital, and by the land
when it becomes monopolized land, private property, this
form belonging to a definite period of history then coincides
with the existence and the function of the produced means
of production and of the earth, in the general process of pro-

duction. Those means of production are then capital in
themselves, by nature; capital is merely an "economic
name" for those means of production; and in the same way
land is then naturally the earth monopolized by a certain
number of landlords. Just as the products become an independent power opposed to the producer when they become
capital and capitalists (for capitalists are but the personification of capital), so the land becomes personified in the landlord and likewise rises on its feet to demand, as an independent power, its share of the product created by its assistance.
Thus it is not the land, which receives its due portion of its
product for the reproduction and improvement of its productivity, but the landlord, who takes a share of this product
and sells or wastes it. It is evident that capital is conditioned upon labor in the capacity of wage labor. But it is
likewise evident that if wage labor is taken as a point of departure for labor, so that the identity of any labor with wage
labor appears to be a matter of course, then capital and monopolized land must also appear as the natural form of the
material requirements of production as distinguished from
labor. It then appears natural for the material prerequisites of labor to be capital, and this looks like their general
character necessarily arising from their function in the labor
process. Capital and produced means of production thus become identical terms. In like manner land and land monopolized by private owners become identical terms. In this
way the requirements of production in their assumed natural
capacity of capital are considered as the source of profit, and
so does the land assume the guise of the source of rent.

Labor as such, in its simple capacity as a useful productive activity, refers to the means of production, not as concerns their form due to social conditions, but rather as concerns their material substance, their capacity as material and
means of labor. And they are distinguished merely as use-
values, the land as an unproduced, the others as produced
means of production. If, then, labor is identical with wage
labor, so is the particular social form assumed by the requirements of labor in their opposition to labor identical with

their material existence. The requirements of labor are then natural capital, and the land is natural private property. The formal separation of these requirements of labor from labor, the peculiar form of their independence as compared to labor, thus becomes a necessary attribute, an inherent character, inseparable from the material conditions of production. The social character given to them in the process of capitalist production by a definite epoch of history becomes a natural character belonging to them, as it were, from time immemorial, as elements in the process of production. So it is that the respective part played by the earth as the original field of activity of labor, as the realm of natural forces, as the pre-existing armory of all objects of labor, and the other respective part played by the produced means of production (instruments, raw materials, etc.) in the general process of production, must seem to be expressed in the respective shares claimed by them as capital and private land, in other words, which are pocketed by their social representatives in the form of profit (interest) and rent, just as the laborer seems to receive in his wages that share which is due to his labor in the process of production. Rent, profit and wages thus seem to grow out of the role played by the land, the produced means of production, and the labor in the simple labor process, even when we look upon this labor process as one passing merely between man and nature, without regard to any historical determination.

It is merely the same thing in another form, when it is argued that the product, in which the labor of the wage laborer materializes itself for himself, as his income, his revenue, is just his wages, is just that portion of value (and of the social product measured by this value), which represents his wages. If wage labor is identical with any labor, then so is the wage and the product of labor, and so is the portion of value representing wages and the value created by any labor. But in this way the other portions of value, profit and rent, also become independent and separated from wages, and must seem to arise from sources of their own, which differ from that of wages and are independent of it.

31

They must seem to arise out of the participating elements of production, by the owners of which they are claimed, so that profit seems to come from the means of production, the material elements of capital, and rent from the earth, or nature, represented by the landlord (Roscher).

Private land, capital and wage labor are thus transformed into actual sources of revenue. It is thought that rent, profit and wages and the respective portions of the product representing these parts of value, in which they exist and for which they may be exchanged, arise from these sources directly, and that the value of the product itself arises in the last analysis from them.[145] They are not considered as sources of revenue in the sense that capital assigns to the capitalist, in the form of profit, a portion of the surplus-value extracted by him from labor, that monopoly in land attracts for the landlord another portion in the form of rent, and that labor gives to the laborer the remaining portion of value in the form of wages. They are not conceived as sources, by which one portion of value is transformed into profit, another into rent, a third into wages.

In the case of the simplest categories of the capitalist mode of production, and even of the production of commodities, in the case of commodities and money, we have already pointed out the mystifying character, which transforms the social conditions that use the material elements of wealth as bearers of production into qualities of these things themselves (commodities) and still more pronouncedly transforms the interrelations of production themselves into a thing (money). All forms of society, to the extent that they reach the stage in which commodities are produced and money circulated, take part in this perversion. But under the capitalist mode of production and in the case of capital, which forms its ruling category, its determining relationship in production, this enchanted and perverted world develops still more. If we consider capital in the actual process of production, as a

---

[145] Wages, profit, and rent are the three original sources of all revenue, as well as of all exchangeable value (A. Smith).— In this way the causes of material production are at the same time the sources of the existing primitive revenues. (Storch, I., p. 259.)

means of extracting surplus-value, then this relationship is still very simple. The actual connection impresses itself upon the bearers of this process, the capitalists, and they are conscious of it. The violent struggle about the limits of the working day shows this clearly. But even within this undisguised sphere, the sphere of the direct process between labor and capital, matters do not rest in this simplicity. With the development of relative surplus-value in the typical, specifically capitalist mode of production, by which the social powers of production of labor are developed, these powers of production and the social interrelations of labor in the actual labor process seem transferred from labor to capital. This endows capital with a very mystic nature, since all of labor's social powers of production appear to be due to capital, not to labor as such, and seem to sprout from the womb of capital itself. Then the process of circulation intervenes, with its changes of substance and form, to which all parts of the capital, even of agricultural capital, must submit to the extent that the specifically capitalist mode of production develops. This is a sphere, in which the conditions under which value is originally produced are pushed completely into the background. Even in the direct process of production the capitalist acts at the same time in the capacity of a producer of commodities, of a manager in the production of commodities. Hence this process of production appears to him by no means as a simple process by which surplus-value is produced. But whatever may be the surplus-value extorted by capital in the actual process of production and offered in the shape of commodities, the value and surplus-value contained in the commodities must first be realized in the process of circulation. And both the restitution of the values advanced in production and, particularly, the surplus-value contained in the commodities do not seem to be merely realized in the circulation, but actually to rise from it. This appearance of things is strengthened by two circumstances. In the first place, it is strengthened by the profit made through cheating, cunning, inside knowledge, ability and a thousand market constellations in the selling of commodities. In the second place, it is enhanced by the circumstance that a second determining element, the time of circulation, is here added to the labor time. It is true that the time of circulation asserts itself as a negative barrier against the formation of value and surplus-value, but it has the appearance of being quite as positive a cause as labor itself and of carrying into the problem a determining element independent of labor and due to the nature of capital itself.

In Volume II we had of course, to present merely the forms created and determined by this sphere of circulation, to demonstrate the further development of the form of capital, which takes place in it. But in reality this sphere is the sphere of competition, which, considered in each individual case, is dominated by accident. In other words, the internal law, which enforces itself in these accidents and regulates them, does not become visible until large numbers of these accidents are grouped together. It remains invisible and unintelligible to the individual agents in production. Furthermore: The actual process of production, considered as the unison of the strict process of production and the process of circulation, gives rise to new formations, in which the vein of the internal connections is lost, the conditions of production become separate identities, and the component parts of value become ossified into forms independent of one another.

We have seen that the conversion of surplus-value into profit is determined as much by the process of circulation as it is by the process of production. The surplus-value, in the form of profit, is no longer referred back to that portion of capital, which is invested in labor and from which it arises, but to the total capital. The rate of profit is regulated by laws of its own, which admit, or even require, a change in it while the rate of surplus-value remains unaltered. All this obscures more and more the true nature of surplus-value and thus the actual running gear of capital. Still more is this done by the transformation of profit into average profit and of the values into prices of production, into the regulating averages of the market prices. Here a

complicated social process intervenes, the process by which
the capitals are equalized, and which separates the relative
average prices of the commodities from their values, as it
separates also the average profits of the various spheres of
production (quite aside from the individual investments of
capital in each particular sphere of production) from the
actual exploitation of labor by the different capitals. No
longer does the average price of the commodities merely seem
to differ from their value, but it actually does differ, it actually is not the same as the labor realised in them, and the
average profit of some particular capital differs from the
surplus-value, which this capital has extracted from the laborers employed by it. The value of the commodities appears no longer directly down to their very last boundaries,
but remains visible only in the influence of the fluctuating
productivity of labor upon the rise and fall of the prices of
production. The profit seems to be determined only inci-
dentally by the direct exploitation of labor, namely to the
extent that this exploitation permits the capitalist to realize
a profit differing from the average profit at the regulating
market prices, which appear to be independent of such exploitation. The normal average profits themselves seem
immanent in capital and independent of exploitation.
The abnormal exploitation, or even the average exploitation under exceptionally favorable conditions, seems to
determine only the deviations from the average profit, not
this profit itself. The division of profit into profit of enterprise and interest (not to mention the intervention of commercial profit and financial profit founded upon the circulation and seemingly arising wholly from it and not at all
from the process of production itself) completes the selfde-
pendence of the form of surplus-value, the ossification of its
form as compared to its substance. One portion of the profit,
as compared to the other, separates itself wholly from the
relationship of capital as such and pretends to be an offspring not of the process by which wage labor is exploited,
but of the wage labor of the capitalist himself. On the other
hand, interest then seems to be independent both of the wage

labor of the laborer and of that of the capitalist, and to arise from no other source but capital itself. Capital, appearing originally, on the surface of circulation, as a capitalist fetish, as a self-expanding value, now assumes in the form of interest-bearing capital, its most estranged and peculiar shape. For this reason the formula " Capital — Interest," as the third link in " Land — Rent " and " Labor — Wages of Labor," appears much more consistent than " Capital — Profit," since in " Profit " there still remains a recollection of its origin, which is not only extinguished in " Interest," but also placed in opposition to this origin and fixed in this antagonistic form.

Capital, as an independent source of surplus-value, is finally joined by private land, which acts as a barrier against average profit and transfers a portion of the surplus-value to a class that neither does any work of its own, nor directly exploits labor, nor can find moral consolation, like interest-bearing capital, in devotional subterfuges such as the alleged risk and sacrifice of lending money to others. Since a part of the surplus-value seems here bound up directly, not with a social relation, but with a natural element, the land, the form of the mutual estrangement and ossification of the various parts of surplus-value is completed, their internal connection completely disrupted, and its source entirely buried, because the relations of production have been made selfdependent in spite of the fact that they are bound up with the different material elements of the process of production.

In Capital — Profit, or better Capital — Interest, Land — Rent, Labor — Wages of Labor, in this economic trinity expressing professedly the connection of value and of wealth in general with their sources, we have the complete mystification of the capitalist mode of production, the transformation of social conditions into things, the indiscriminate amalgamation of the material conditions of production with their historical and social forms. It is an enchanted, perverted, topsy-turvy world, in which Mister Capital and Mistress Land carry on their goblin tricks as social characters and at the same time as mere things. It is the great merit of classic economy to have dissolved this false appearance and illusion, this self-isolation and ossification of the different social elements of wealth by themselves, this personification of things and conversion of conditions of production into entities, this religion of everyday life. It did so by reducing interest to a portion of profit, and rent to the surplus above the average profit, so that both of them meet in surplus-value. It represented the process of circulation as a mere metamorphosis of forms, and finally reduced value and surplus-value of commodities to labor in the actual process of production. Nevertheless even the best spokesmen of classic economy remained more or less the prisoners of the world of illusion which they had dissolved critically, and this could not well be otherwise from a bourgeois point of view. Consequently all of them fall more or less into inconsistencies, half-way statements, and unsolved contradictions. On the other hand, it is equally natural that the actual agents of production felt completely at home in these estranged and irrational forms of Capital — Interest, Land — Rent, Labor — Wages of Labor, for these are the forms of the illusion, in which they move about and in which they find their daily occupation. It is also quite natural that vulgar economy, which is nothing but a didactic, more or less dogmatic, translation of the ordinary conceptions of the agents of production and which arranges them in a certain intelligent order, should see in this trinity, which is devoid of all internal connection, the natural and indubitiable basis of its shallow assumption of importance. This formula corresponds at the same time to the interests of the ruling classes, by proclaiming the natural necessity and eternal justification of their sources of revenue and raising them to the position of a dogma.

In our description of the way, in which the conditions of production are converted into entities and into independent things as compared to the agents of production, we do not enter into a discussion of the manner, in which the interrelations of the world market, its constellations, the movements of market prices, the periods of credit, the cycles of industry and commerce, the changes from prosperity to crises, appear to these agents as overwhelming natural laws that rule them irresistibly and enforce their rule over them as blind necessities. We do not enter into such a discussion, because the actual movements of competition belong outside of our plan, and because we have to present only the internal organization of the capitalist mode of production, as it were, in its ideal average.

In preceding forms of society this economic mystification arises principally in the case of money and of interest-bearing capital. In the nature of the case it is out of the question where, in the first place, production is mainly for use, for the satisfaction of immediate wants, and where, in the second place, slavery or serfdom form the broad foundation of social production, as they did in antiquity and during the Middle Ages. The rule of the conditions of production over the producers in those systems is concealed by the relation between masters and servants, which appear and are visible as the direct motive powers of the process of production. In the primitive societies, in which natural communism prevails, and even in the ancient urban communes, it is this community itself which appears as the basis of production, and its reproduction appears as its ultimate purpose. Even in the medieval guild system neither capital nor labor appear untrammeled. Their relations are rather defined by the corporate rules, by the conditions connected with them, and by the conceptions of professional duties, mastership, etc., which accompany them. Only when the capitalist mode of production . . .

CHAPTER XLIX.

A CONTRIBUTION TO THE ANALYSIS OF THE PROCESS OF PRODUCTION.

For the purposes of the following analysis we may leave out of consideration the distinction between the price of production and the value, since this distinction falls altogether to the ground, when, as is the case here, the value of the total annual product of labor is under discussion, in other words, the value of the product of the total social capital.

Profit (profit of enterprise plus interest) and rent are nothing but peculiar forms assumed by particular parts of the surplus-value of commodities. The magnitude of the surplus-value is the limit of the sum of parts, into which it may be divided. The average profit plus the rent are, therefore, equal to the surplus-value. It is possible that a part of the surplus labor contained in the commodities, and thus of the surplus-value, does not take part directly in the equalization tending toward an average rate of profit, so that a part of the value of commodities is not expressed at all in their price. But in the first place, this is balanced either by the fact that the rate of profit increases, when the commodities sold below their value form an element of the constant capital, or by the fact that profit and rent are represented by a larger product, when the commodities sold below their value pass over into that portion of the value which is consumed as revenue in the shape of articles for individual consumption. In the second place, the average movement strikes the balance. At any rate, even if a portion of the surplus-value is not expressed in the price and is lost so far as the formation of prices is concerned, the sum of average profit plus rent in their normal form can never be larger than the total surplus-value, although it may be smaller. Their normal form is conditioned upon wages corresponding to the value of labor-power. Even monopoly rent, to the extent that it is not a deduction from wages, and does not constitute a special category, must be indirectly always a part of the surplus-value. If it is not a part of the surplus price above the cost of production of the commodity itself, of which it is a constituent part, as in the case of differential rent, or a spare portion of the surplus-value of the commodity itself, of which it is a constituent part, above that portion of its own surplus-value which is measured by the average profit (as in the case of absolute rent), it is at least a part of the surplus-value of other commodities, that is, of commodities which are exchanged for this commodity, which has a monopoly price.

The sum of average profit plus ground-rent can never be greater than the magnitude of which they are the parts and which exists before they are so partitioned. It is, therefore, immaterial for our discussion, whether the entire surplus-value of the commodities, that is, all the surplus labor materialized in the commodities, is realized in their price or not. The surplus labor is not entirely realized for the simple reason that, owing to the continual change in the amount of socially necessary labor for the production of a certain commodity, a change arising out of the continual change in the productive power of labor, one portion of the commodities is always produced under abnormal conditions and must, therefore, be sold below its individual value. At any rate, profit plus rent equal the total realized surplus-value (surplus-labor), and for the purposes of the present discussion the realized surplus-value may be assumed as equal to all surplus-value; for profit and rent are realized surplus-value, or generally speaking the surplus-value which passes into the prices of commodities, which is practically all the surplus-value forming a constituent part of this price.

On the other hand, the wages, which are the third significant form of revenue, are always equal to the variable portion of capital, which is the portion invested, not in means of production, but in the purchase of living labor-power, in the payment of laborers. (The labor paid in the expenditure of revenue is itself paid in wages, profit, or rent, and therefore does not form any portion of the value of commodities by which it is paid. Hence it is not considered in the analysis of the value of commodities and of the component parts into which it is divided.) Wages are the materialization of that portion of the total working day of the laborer, in which the value of the variable capital and thus the price of labor is reproduced. It is that portion of the value of commodities, in which the laborer reproduces the value of his own labor-power, or the price of his labor. The total working day of the laborer is divided into two parts. One portion is that in which he performs the amount of labor necessary to reproduce the value of his own means of subsistence. It is the paid portion of his total labor, that portion which is necessary for his own maintenance and reproduction. The entire remaining portion of the working day, the entire surplus quantity of labor performed above the value of the labor realized in his wages, is surplus labor, unpaid labor, represented by the surplus-value of his entire product in commodities (and thus by a surplus quantity of commodities), surplus-value, which in its turn is divided into differently named parts, into profit (profit of enterprise plus interest) and rent.

The entire portion of the value of commodities, then, in which the total labor of the laborers added during one day, or one year, is realized, is divided into the value of wages, into profit and into rent. For this total labor is divided into necessary labor, by which the laborer creates that portion of the value of his product, with which he is himself paid, that is, his wages, and into unpaid surplus labor, by which he creates that portion of the value of the product, which represents surplus-value and which is later divided into profit and rent. Aside from this labor the laborer does not perform any labor, and he does not create any value outside of the total value of the product, which assumes the forms of wages, profit and rent. The value of the annual product, in which the new labor added by the laborer during the year is incorporated, is equal to the wages, or the value of the variable capital, plus the surplus-value, which in its turn is divided into profit and rent.

The entire portion of the value of the annual product, then, which the laborer creates in the course of the year, is expressed in the annual sum of the values of the three revenues, the values of wages, profit, and rent. Evidently, therefore, the value of the constant portion of capital is not reproduced in the value of the annually created product, for the wages are only equal to the value of the variable portion of capital advanced in production, and rent and profit are only equal to the surplus-value, the produced excess of value above the total

value of the advanced capital, which is equal to the value of
the constant plus the value of the variable capital.

It is immaterial for the difficulty to be solved here that a
portion of the surplus-value converted into the form of profit
and rent is not consumed as revenue, but is accumulated.
That portion, which is saved up as a fund for accumulation,
serves for the formation of new, additional, capital, but not
for the reproduction of the old capital, neither of that portion
of the old capital which is invested in wages nor of that which
is invested in means of production. We may, therefore, assume here for the sake of simplicity that the revenues pass
wholly into individual consumption. The difficulty has a
twofold aspect. On the one hand, the value of the annual
product, in which these revenues, wages, profit and rent, are
consumed, contains a portion of value, which is equal to the
portion of value of the constant part of capital used up in it.
It contains this portion of value in addition to the other portion, which resolves itself into wages and that which resolves
itself into profit and rent. Its value is therefore equal to
wages plus profit plus rent plus C (its constant portion of
value). How can an annually produced value, which equals
only wages plus profit plus rent, buy a product which has a
value of wages plus profit plus rent plus C?

How can the annually produced value buy a product, which
has a higher value than its own?

On the other hand, if we leave aside that portion of the
constant capital which did not pass over into the product, and
which, therefore, continues to exist after the annual production of commodities as it did before it; in other words, if we
leave aside the employed, but not consumed fixed capital, we
find that the constant portion of the advanced capital has been
wholly transferred to the new product in the shape of raw
and auxiliary materials, whereas a part of the instruments of
labor has been wholly consumed and another part of them only
partially, so that only a part of its value has been consumed
in production. This entire portion of the constant capital,
which has been consumed in production, must be reproduced

in its natural form. Assuming all other circumstances, particularly the productive power of labor, to remain unchanged, this portion requires for its reproduction the same amount of labor as before, that is, it must be replaced by its equivalent in value. If it is not, then reproduction itself cannot take place on the old scale. But who is going to perform this labor, and who performs it?

In the first question, to-wit, Who is going to pay for the constant portion of value, and with what? it is assumed that the value of the constant capital consumed in production reappears as a part of the value of the product. This does not contradict the assumptions of the second difficulty. For we have demonstrated already in Volume I, Chapter VII (The Labor Process and the Process of Producing Surplus-Value), that the mere addition of new labor, although it does not reproduce the old value, but creates merely an addition to it, creates only additional value, still preserves at the same time the old value in the product; that this is done, however, by labor, not to the extent that it is a labor producing value, labor in general, but in its function as a definite productive labor. Therefore no additional labor was necessary for the purpose of preserving the value of the constant portion in the product, in which the revenue, that is, the entire value created during the year, is expended. On the other hand, it requires new additional labor to replace the value and use-value of the constant capital consumed during the past year, for unless this is replaced no reproduction is possible at all.

All newly added labor is represented in the value newly created during the year, and this is divided into the three revenues, that is, into wages, profit and rent. On the one hand, then, no spare social labor remains for the reproduction of the consumed constant capital, which must partially be replaced in its natural form and its value, and partially merely in its value (for the mere wear and tear of fixed capital). On the other hand, the value annually created by labor, divided into wages, profit and rent, and to be spent in these forms, does not suffice to pay for, or buy, the constant portion of capital, which must be contained in the annual product outside of itself.

We see, then, that the problem presented here has already been solved in the discussion of the reproduction of the total social capital, Volume II, Part III. We return to it here, in the first place, for the reason that the surplus-value had not been developed in that volume into its revenue forms, profit (profit of enterprise plus interest) and rent and, therefore, could not be treated in these forms; in the second place, because the formula of wages, profit and rent is connected with an incredible aberration of the analysis, which pervades the entire political economy since Adam Smith.

In Volume II we divided all capital into two great classes: Class I, producing means of production, and Class II, producing articles of individual consumption. The fact that certain products may serve as well for personal consumption as for means of production (a horse, cereals, etc.), does not invalidate the absolute correctness of this division in any way. It is, in fact, no hypothesis, but merely the expression of a fact.

Take the annual product of a certain country. One portion of the product, whatever may be its ability to serve as means of production, passes over into individual consumption. It is the product for which wages, profit and rent are spent. This product is the product of a definite section of the social capital. It is possible that this same capital may also produce products belonging to Class I. To the extent that it does that, it is not the portion of capital consumed in the shape of the product of Class II, a product belonging actually to individual consumption, which supplies the productively consumed products passing into Class I. This entire product II, which passes into individual consumption, and for which the revenue is spent, is the material form of the capital consumed in it plus the produced surplus. It is also the product of a capital invested in the mere production of articles of consumption. And in the same way section I of the annual product, which serves as means of reproduction and consists of raw materials and instruments of labor, is the product of a capital invested in the mere production of means of production. By far the greater part of the products forming the constant capital exists also materially in a form, in which it cannot pass into individual consumption. To the extent that it might be so used, for instance, to the extent that a farmer might eat his seed corn, butcher his teaming cattle, etc., the economic barrier puts him into the same position in which he would be if this portion did not have a consumable form.

We have already said that we leave out of consideration, in both classes, the fixed part of the constant capital, which continues to exist so far as its material substance and value are concerned, independently of the annual product of both classes.

In Class II, consisting of products for which wages, profit and rent are spent and the revenues thus consumed, the product consists of three parts, so far as its value is concerned. One part is equal to the value of the constant portion of capital consumed in production; a second part is equal to the value of the variable capital invested in wages; finally, a third part is equal to the value of the produced surplus-value, that is, equal to profit plus rent. The first part of the product of Class II, the value of the constant portion of capital, cannot be consumed either by the capitalists of Class II, or by the laborers of this class, or by the landlords. It does not form any part of their revenues, but must be replaced in its natural form, and must be sold in order that this may be done. On the other hand, the other two parts of this product are equal to the value of the revenues created in this class, equal to wages plus profit plus rent.

In Class I the product consists of the same parts, so far as its form is concerned. But that part, which here forms revenue, wages plus profit plus rent, in short, the variable portion of capital plus the surplus-value, is not consumed here in the natural form of the products of this Class I, but in products of the Class II. The value of the revenues of Class I must, therefore, be consumed in the shape of that portion of the products of Class II, which forms the constant capital of II, that must be reproduced. That portion of the product of Class II, which must reproduce its constant capital, is consumed in its natural form by the laborers, the capitalists and the landlords of Class I. They spend their revenues for this product of II. On the other hand, the product of I, to the extent that it represents a revenue of Class I, is productively consumed in its natural form by Class II, whose constant capital it replaces in its natural form. Finally, the consumed constant portion of the capital of Class I is replaced out of the products of this class itself, which consist of instruments of labor, raw and auxiliary materials, either by an exchange of the capitalists of I among themselves, or in such a way that a portion of these capitalists can use their own product once more as means of production.

Let us take the diagram used in Volume II, Chapter XX, II, for simple reproduction:

$$\text{I.} \quad 4000\ c + 1000\ v + 1000\ s = 6000$$
$$\text{II.} \quad 2000\ c + 500\ v + 500\ s = 3000, \text{ Total } 9000.$$

According to this, the producers and landlords of II consume $500\ v + 500\ s = 1,000$ as revenue; $2,000\ c$ remain to be reproduced. This is consumed by the laborers, capitalists and rent owners of I, whose income is $1,000\ v + 1,000\ s = 2,000$. The consumed product of II is consumed as a revenue by I, and that portion of the revenue of I, which represents an unconsumable product, is consumed as a constant capital by II. It remains to account for the 4,000 c of I. This is replaced out of the product of I itself, which is 6,000, or rather 6,000 minus 2,000, for these last 2,000 have already been converted into constant capital of II. It should be noted that these numbers have been chosen at random, and so the proportion between the value of the revenues of I and the value of the constant capital of II also appears arbitrary. But it is evident that so far as the process of reproduction is normal and takes place under otherwise unchanged circumstances, leaving aside the question of accumulation, the sum of the values of wages, profit and rent in Class I must be equal to the value of the constant portion of the capital of

Class II. Otherwise Class II will not be able to reproduce its constant capital, or Class I will not be able to convert its revenue from unconsumable into consumable articles.

The value of the annual product in commodities, just like the value of the commodities produced by some particular investment of capital, and like the value of any individual commodity, resolves itself into two parts: Part A, which replaces the value of the advanced constant capital, and Part B, which presents itself in the form of wages, profit and rent. This last part of value, B, stands in opposition to the Part A to the extent that this Part A, under otherwise equal circumstances, in the first place never assumes the form of revenue, and in the second place always flows back in the form of capital, and of constant capital at that. The other portion, B, however, carries within itself an antagonism. Profit and rent have this in common with wages that all three of them are forms of revenue. Nevertheless they differ essentially from each other in that profit and rent are surplus-value, unpaid labor, whereas wages are paid labor. That portion of the value of the product, which represents spent wages and reproduces wages, and must be reconverted into wages under the conditions assumed by us, flows back first in the shape of variable capital, as a portion of the capital that once more must be advanced for the purposes of reproduction. This portion has a double function. It exists first in the form of capital and is exchanged as such for labor-power. In the hands of the laborer it is converted into revenue, which he draws out of the sale of his labor-power, and as revenue it is spent for means of subsistence and consumed. This double process is revealed through the intervention of money circulation. The variable capital is advanced in money, paid out as wages. This is its first function as capital. It is converted into labor-power and transformed into the expression of labor-power, into labor. This is the capitalist's side of the process. In the second place, the laborers buy with this money a part of the commodities produced by them, which part is measured by this money, and is consumed by them as revenue. If we imagine the circulation

3J

of money to be eliminated, then a part of the product of the laborer is in the hands of the capitalist in the form of existing capital. He advances this part as capital, hands it over to the laborer for new labor-power, while the laborer consumes it directly or indirectly by means of exchange for other commodities, as his revenue. That portion of the value of the product, then, which is destined in the course of reproduction to be converted into wages, into revenue for the laborers, flows back at first into the hands of the capitalist in the form of capital, more accurately of variable capital. That it should flow back in this form is an essential requirement, in order that labor as wage labor, the means of production as capital, and the process of production itself as a capitalist process may always be reproduced.

In order to avoid useless difficulties, it is necessary to distinguish the gross output and the net output from the gross income and the net income.

The gross output, or the gross product, is the total reproduced product. With the exception of the employed but not consumed portion of the fixed capital, the value of the gross output, or of the gross product, is equal to the value of the capital advanced and consumed in production, that is, the constant and variable capital plus the surplus-value, which resolves itself into profit and rent. Or, if we consider the product of the total social capital instead of that of some individual capital, the gross output is equal to the material elements forming the constant plus variable capital, plus the material elements of the surplus product, in which profit and rent are materialized.

The gross income is that portion of value and that portion of the gross product measured by it, which remains after deducting that portion of value and that portion of the total product measured by it, which replaces the constant capital advanced and consumed in production. The gross income, then, is equal to the wages (or to that portion of the product which is to become once more the income of the laborer) plus the profit plus the rent. On the other hand, the net income is the surplus-value, and thus the surplus product, which remains after the deduction of the wages, and which, in fact, represents the surplus-value realized by capital and to be divided with the landlords, and the surplus product measured by it.

Now we have seen that the value of each individual commodity and the value of the total commodities produced by each individual capital is divided into two parts, one of which replaces only constant capital, and the other of which, although a part of it flows back as variable capital, that is, also in the form of capital, nevertheless is destined to be wholly transformed into a gross income, and to assume the form of wages, profit and rent, the sum of which makes up the gross income. We have also seen that the same is true of the value of the annual total product of a certain society. There is only this difference between the product of the individual capitalist and that of society: From the point of view of the individual capitalist the net income differs from the gross income, for this last includes the wages, whereas the first excludes them. Viewing the income of the whole society, the national income consists of wages plus profit plus rent, that is, of the gross income. But even this is an abstraction to the extent that the entire society, on the basis of capitalist production, places itself upon the capitalist standpoint and considers only the income divided into profit and rent as the net income.

On the other hand, the dream of men like Say, to the effect that the entire output, the entire gross output, resolves itself into the net income of the nation and cannot be distinguished from it, so that this distinction disappears from the national point of view, is but the necessary and ultimate expression of the absurd dogma pervading political economy since Adam Smith, that the value of commodities resolves itself in the last analysis into an income, into wages, profit and rent.[146]

[146] Ricardo makes the following very apt comment on thoughtless Say: " Of net produce and gross produce, Mr. Say speaks as follows: ' The whole value produced is the gross produce; this value, after deducting from it the cost of production, is the net produce. (Vol. II, p. 491.) There can, then, be no net produce, because the cost of production, according to Mr. Say consists of rent,

Of course, it is very easy to understand, in the case of each individual capitalist, that a portion of his product must be reconverted into capital (even aside from an expansion of reproduction, or accumulation), not only into variable capital, which is destined to become in its turn an income for the laborers, a form of revenue, but also into constant capital, which can never be converted into revenue. The simplest observation of the process of production shows this clearly. The difficulty does not begin, until the process of production is studied as a whole. The fact has to be faced that the value of the entire portion of the product, which is consumed in the form of wages, profit and rent (immaterial whether the consumption is individual or productive), resolves itself under analysis wholly into a sum of values formed by wages plus profit plus rent, that is, into the total value of the three revenues, although the value of this portion of the product quite as well as that which does not pass over into the revenues contains a portion of value, equal to C, equal to the value of the constant capital contained in it, which on its very face cannot be limited by the value of the revenue. On the one hand we have the practically irrefutable fact, on the other hand the equally undeniable theoretical contradiction. This difficulty is most easily circumvented by the assertion that the value of commodities contains another portion of value, differing only seemingly, from the one existing in the form of revenue only from the point of view of the individual capitalist. The phrase that a thing is revenue for one man and capital for another saves all further thought. But then it remains an insoluble riddle, how the old capital is to be replaced, when the value of the entire product can be consumed as revenue; and how

wages and profits. In page 508 he says: ‘The value of a product, the value of productive service, the value of the cost of production, are all, then, similar values, whenever things are left to their natural course.’ Take a whole from a whole and nothing remains.” (Ricardo, *Principles,* Chapter XXII, p. 512, Note.) — By the way, we shall see later that Ricardo nowhere refuted the false analysis made by Smith of the price of commodities, its reduction to the sum of the values of the revenues. He does not take notice of it, and assumes it to be correct to such an extent that he “abstracts” from the constant portion of the value of commodities. He also falls back now and then into the same conception.

it is that the value of the product of each individual capital can be equal to the sum of the values of the three revenues plus C, the constant capital, whereas the sum of the values of the products of all capitals can be equal to the sum of the values of the three revenues plus zero. And the riddle must be solved by declaring that any analysis is incapable of finding out the simple elements of price, and must be satisfied with the faulty cycle and the progress into infinity. So that the thing which appears as constant capital may be resolved into wages, profit and rent, whereas the values of the commodities, in which wages, profit and rent are materialized, are determined in their turn by wages, profit and rent, and so forth to infinity.[147]

The entirely false dogma to the effect that the value of commodities resolves itself in the last analysis into wages plus profits plus rent expresses itself in the assertion that the consumer must ultimately pay for the total value of the total product, or that the money circulation between producers and consumers must ultimately be equal to the money circulation between the producers themselves (Tooke). All these assertions are as false as the axiom upon which they are founded.

The difficulties, which lead to this false and prima facie absurd analysis, are briefly the following:

1) The first difficulty is that the fundamental relationship of constant and variable capital, hence also the nature

---

[147] " In every society the price of every commodity finally resolves itself into some one or the other, or all of those three parts (viz. wages, profits, rent). . . . A fourth part, it may perhaps be thought, is necessary for replacing the stock of the farmer or for compensating the wear and tear of his laboring cattle, and other instruments of husbandry. But it must be considered that the price of any instrument of husbandry, such as a labouring horse, is itself made up of the same three parts: the rent of the land upon which he is reared, the labour of tending and rearing him, and the profits of the farmer, who advances both the rent of his land and the wages of his labour. Though the price of corn, therefore, may pay the price as well as the maintenance of the horse, the whole price still resolves itself either immediately or ultimately into the same three parts of rent, labour (meaning wages) and profit." (Adam Smith.) — We shall show later on, that Adam Smith himself felt the inconsistency and insufficiency of this subterfuge, for it is nothing but a subterfuge on his part to send us from Pontius to Pilate, while he nowhere indicates the real investment of capital, in the case of which the price of the product resolves itself ultimately into these three parts, without any remainder and any further progression.

of surplus-value, and with them the entire basis of the capitalist mode of production, are not understood. The value of each portion of any product of capital contains a certain portion of value equal to the constant capital, another portion of value equal to the variable capital (converted into wages for the laborer), and another portion of value equal to surplus-value (which later on becomes profit and rent). How is it possible that the laborer with his wages, the capitalist with his profit, the landlord with his rent, should be able to buy commodities, each one of which contains not only one of these elements, but all three of them, and how is it possible that the sum of the values of wages, profit and rent, that is, of the three sources of revenue together, should be able to buy the commodities passing over into the total consumption of the recipients of these incomes, since these commodities contain another portion of value, namely constant capital, outside of the other portions of value? How can they buy a value of four with a value of three? [148]

We have given our analysis in Volume II, Part III.

2) The second difficulty is that the way, in which labor, by adding a new value, preserves old value in a new form without producing this old value anew, is not understood.

3) The third difficulty is that the connections of the process of reproduction are not understood, as it presents itself, not from the point of view of individual capital, but from that of the total capital. The difficulty is to explain how it

---

[148] Proudhon, incapable of grasping this, exposes his incapableness in the formula: The laborer cannot buy back his own product, because the interest is contained in it, which is added to the purchase price. But how does Mr. Eugene Forcade teach him to know better? " If Proudhon's objection were true, it would strike not only the profits of capital, but would annihilate the possibility of all industry. If the laborer is compelled to pay 100 for each article for which he has received only 80, if his wages can buy back only the value which he has put into it, it would be as well to say that the laborer cannot buy back anything, that wages cannot pay for anything. In fact, there is always something more than the wages of the laborer contained in the purchase price, and always more than the profits of enterprise in the selling price, for instance, the price of the raw materials, which often goes to foreign countries. . . . Proudhon forgot about the continual increase of the national capital; he forgot that this increase refers to all laborers, the enterprising industrials as well as the hand laborers." (*Revue des deux Mondes*, 1848, tome, 24, p. 99.) Here we have the optimism of bourgeois thoughtlessness in the form of wisdom corresponding to it. First Mr. Forcade believes that the laborer could not live, if he did not receive a higher value than that which

is that the product, in which wages and surplus-value, in short the entire value produced by all the labor newly added during the current year, can be converted into money, can reproduce the constant part of its value and yet at the same time resolve itself into a value confined within the limits of the revenues; and how it is that the constant capital consumed in production can be replaced by the substance and value of new capital, although the total sum of the newly added labor is realized only in wages and surplus-value, and is fully represented by the sum of the values of both. It it here where the main difficulty lies, in the analysis of reproduction and of the proportions of its various component parts, both as concerns their material substance and the proportions of their value.

4) To these difficulties is added another one, which is intensified still more as soon as the various component parts of the surplus-value appear in the form of revenues independent of each other. This is the difficulty that the fixed marks of revenue and capital are interchanged and occupy different places, so that they seem to be merely relative determinations from the point of view of the individual capitalist and to disappear as soon as the total process of production is viewed as a whole. For instance, the revenue of the laborers and capitalists of Class I, which produces constant capital, replaces the value and the substance of the constant capital of the capitalists of Class II, which produces

---

he produces, whereas the capitalist mode of production, on the contrary, could not exist, if he received all the value which he really produces. In the second place he correctly generalizes the difficulty, which Proudhon expressed only under a more narrow point of view. The price of the commodities contains not only more than the wages, but also more than the profit, namely the constant portion of value. According to Proudhon's reasoning then, the capitalist could not buy back the commodities with his profit. And how does Forcade solve this riddle? By means of a meaningless phrase: The increase of capital. The continual increase of capital is supposed to manifest itself, among other things, also in the fact that the analysis of the price of commodities, which is impossible for the political economist in the case of a capital of 100, becomes superfluous in the case of a capital of 10,000. What would he say of a chemist, who, on being asked: How is it that the product of the soil contains more carbon than the soil? would answer: It comes from the continual increase of the product of the soil. The well-meaning good will to discover in the bourgeois world the best of all worlds takes the place, in vulgar economy, of any necessity to cultivate love of truth and scientific methods of research.

articles of consumption. One may, therefore, get around the difficulty by means of the conception that the thing which is revenue for one is capital for another. This promotes the idea that these functions have nothing to do with the actual peculiarities of the component parts of value in the commodities. Furthermore: Commodities which are ultimately intended for the purpose of forming the substantial elements in the expenditure of revenue, in other words, articles of consumption, pass through various stages during the year, such as woolen yarn, cloth. In the one stage they form a portion of the constant capital, in the other they are consumed individually, and thus pass wholly into the revenue. One may, therefore, imagine with Adam Smith that the constant capital is but seemingly an element of the value of commodities, which disappears in the total interrelation. Furthermore, a similar exchange takes place between variable capital and revenue. The laborer buys with his wages that portion of the commodities which form his revenue. In this way he creates at the same time for the capitalist the money form of the variable capital. Finally: One portion of the products, which form constant capital, is replaced in its natural form or by means of exchange by the producers of the constant capital themselves. The consumers have nothing to do with this process. When this is overlooked the impression is created that the revenue of the consumers replaces the entire product, even the constant portion of its value.

5) Aside from the confusion created by the transformation of the values into prices of production, another confusion is due to the transformation of surplus-value into different, separate, independent forms of revenue traced back to different elements of production, into profit and rent. It is forgotten that the values of commodities are the basis, and that the division of the values of commodities into separate portions, and the further development of these portions of value into forms of revenue, their transmutation into relations of the various owners of the different agencies in production to these parts of value, their distribution among these owners according to definite categories and titles, does not

alter anything in the determination of value or in its law. Neither is the law of value changed by the fact that the equalization of profit, that is, the distribution of the total value among the various capitals, and the obstacles, which private land to some extent puts in the way of this equalization (in absolute rent), makes the regulating average prices different from the individual values of the commodities. This again affects merely the addition of the surplus-value to the different prices of commodities, but does not abolish the surplus-value itself, nor the total value of commodities in its capacity as the source of these different constituents of value.

This is the confusion, which we shall consider in our next chapter, and which is necessarily connected with the illusion that the value arises out of its own component parts. First the various component parts of value receive independent forms in the revenues, and in their capacity as revenues they are referred back to the particular substantial elements of production as their alleged sources instead of to the values of commodities, which are their real source. They are actually referred back to those sources, not as components of value, but as revenues, as components of value falling to the share of definite classes of agents in production, the laborer, the capitalist and the landlord. But one might imagine that these parts of value, instead of arising out of the distribution of the value of commodities, rather form it by their composition, and this leads to that nice and faulty circle, which makes the value of commodities arise out of the sum of the values of wages, profit, rent, and the value of wages, profit and rent, in their turn, is to be determined by the value of commodities, etc.[149]

[149] " The circulating capital invested in materials, raw products and machinery is itself composed of merchandise, the necessary price of which is formed of the same elements; so that, viewing the total merchandise in a certain country, it would mean using the same thing twice to count this portion of the circulating capital among the elements of the necessary price." (Storch, *Cours d'Economie Politique,* II, page 140.) — By these elements of circulating capital Storch means the constant capital (the fixed capital is for him merely a different form of the circulating). " It is true that the wages of the laborer, the same as that portion of the profits of enterprise which stands for wages, provided we consider them as a part of the means of subsistence, also consist of merchandise bought at current

Considering reproduction in its normal condition, only a part of the newly added labor is employed for production and thus for the reproduction of the constant capital. This is precisely the portion which replaces the constant capital used up in the production of articles of consumption, of substantial parts of the revenue. This is balanced by the fact that this constant portion does not require any additional labor on the part of Class II. Looking upon the total process of reproduction as a whole, in which this equalising exchange between Classes I and II is included, this constant capital is not a product of newly added labor, although the product of this labor could not be created without that capital. This constant capital, looking upon it from the point of view of substance, is exposed to certain accidents and dangers in the process of reproduction. (Furthermore, considering it from the point of view of value, it may be depreciated through a change in the productive power of labor; but this refers only to the individual capitalist.) Accordingly a portion of the profit, of surplus-value and of the surplus-product, in which only newly added labor is represented, so far as its value is concerned, serves as an insurance fund. In this case it does not matter, whether

prices and comprise likewise wages, interest on capital ground rent and profit of enterprise. . . . But this observation merely proves that it is impossible to resolve the necessary price into its simplest elements." (Ibidem note.) — In his *Considerations sur la nature du revenu national* (Paris, 1824). Storch realizes in his controversy with Say to what absurdity the false analysis of the value of commodities leads, when it resolves value into mere revenues. He points out the folly of such results, not from the point of view of the individual capitalist, but from that of a nation, but he does not go a step further himself in his analysis of the " prix nécessaire," saying in his " Cours " that it is impossible to resolve it into its simplest elements and tracing it back into an endless progression. " It is evident that the value of the annual product is distributed partly among capital and partly among profits, and that each one of these parts of the value of the annual product buys regularly the products needed by a nation, as much for the purpose of preserving its capital as for the purpose of renewing its consumable fund (pages 134, 135). . . . Can a self-employing peasant's family live in its barns or its stables, eat its seed and forage, clothe itself with its laboring cattle, dispense with its agricultural implements? According to the thesis of Mr. Say all these questions would have to be answered in the affirmative (pages 135, 136) . . . If it is admitted that the revenue of a nation is equal to its gross product, that is, if no capital has to be deducted from it, then it must also be admitted that a nation can spend the entire value of its annual product unproductively without impairing its future income in the least (147). The products which constitute the capital of a nation cannot be consumed." (p. 150.)

this insurance fund is managed by separate insurance companies or not. This is the only part of the revenue which is neither consumed as such nor serves necessarily as a fund for accumulation. Whether it actually serves in the accumulation, or covers merely a shortage in reproduction, depends upon accident. This is also the only portion of the surplus-value and surplus-product, and thus of surplus-labor, which would continue to exist, outside of that portion which serves for accumulation and for the expansion of the process of reproduction, even after the abolition of the capitalist system. This, of course, is conditioned upon the premise that the portion regularly consumed by the direct producers does not remain limited to its present minimum. Outside of the surplus-labor for those, who on account of age can not yet or no longer take part in production, all surplus labor for non-workers would disappear. If we transport ourselves back to the beginnings of society, we find no produced means of production, hence no constant capital, the value of which could pass into the product, and which would have to be replaced in its natural form out of the product in reproduction on the same scale, and to a degree measured by its value. But nature there supplies immediately the means of subsistence, which do not have to be produced. For this reason nature gives to the savage having but few wants the time, not to use non-existing means of production in new production, but to transform, outside of the labor required for the appropriation of naturally existing means of production, other products of nature into means of production, bows, stone knives, boats, etc. This process among savages, considered merely from the side of its substance, corresponds to the reconversion of surplus-labor into new capital. In the process of accumulation, this conversion of the product of surplus labor into capital takes place continually; and the fact that all new capital arises out of profit, rent, or other forms of revenue, that is, out of surplus labor, leads to the mistaken idea that all value of commodities arises from some revenue. On the other hand, this reconversion of profit into capital rather shows on closer analysis, that the additional labor, which is always represented in the form of revenue, does not serve for the conservation, or reproduction, of the old capital, but for the creation of new surplus capital to the extent that it is not consumed as revenue.

The whole difficulty arises from the fact that all newly added labor, to the extent that the value created by it is not dissolved into wages, appears as profit, that is, as a value which does not cost the capitalist anything and therefore cannot make good some capital advanced by him. This value rather exists in the form of available additional wealth, or, from the point of view of the individual capitalist, in the form of his revenue. But this newly created value can just as well be consumed productively as individually, equally well as capital and as revenue. In view of its natural form, some of it must be productively consumed. It is, therefore, evident that the annually added labor creates capital as well as revenue; this becomes evident in the process of accumulation. That portion of the labor-power, which is employed in the creation of new capital (analagous to that portion of the working day of a savage employed, not for the appropriation of subsistence, but for the manufacture of tools by which to appropriate subsistence), becomes evident in the fact that the entire product of surplus labor presents itself at first in the shape of profit; this use of it has indeed nothing to do with this surplus-product itself, but refers merely to the private relation of the capitalist to the surplus-value pocketed by him. In fact, the surplus-value created by the capitalist is divided into revenue and capital, that is, into articles of consumption and additional means of production. But the old constant capital, which was handed over from last year (outside of the portion that was injured and to that extent destroyed, in short, the old constant capital that does not have to be reproduced, and so far as there is any break in the process of reproduction, the insurance covers that), so far as its value is concerned, is not reproduced by the newly added labor.

We see, furthermore, that a portion of the newly added

labor is continually absorbed in the reproduction and replacement of consumed constant capital, although this newly
added labor resolves itself altogether in revenues, in wages,
profit and rent. But it is always overlooked, 1) that one
portion of the value of this new labor is not a product of
this new labor, but previously existing and consumed constant capital; that the portion of the product, in which this
part of value presents itself, cannot be converted into revenue, but replaces the means of production of this constant
capital in their natural form. 2) It is overlooked that the
portion of value, in which this newly added labor is actually
represented, is not consumed as revenue in its natural form,
but replaces the constant capital in another sphere, where
it is moulded into a natural form, in which it may be consumed as revenue, but which in its turn is not wholly a product of newly added labor.

To the extent that reproduction takes place on the same
scale, every consumed element of the constant capital must
be replaced by a new natural specimen of the same kind,
if not in quantity and form, then at least in natural ef-
fectiveness. If the productive power of labor remains the
same, then this natural replacement implies the reproduction
of the same value, which the constant capital had in its old
form. But if the productive power of labor is increased,
so that the same substantial elements may be reproduced
with less labor, then a smaller portion of value of this product can completely replace the constant part in its natural
shape. The surplus may then be employed in the formation
of additional capital, or a larger portion of the product may
be given the form of articles of consumption, or the surplus
labor may be reduced. On the other hand, if the productive power of labor decreases, then a larger portion of the
product must be used for the replacement of the old capital;
the surplus product decreases.

The reconversion of profit, or of any form of surplus-
value, into capital shows — without considering the historic
ally defined economic form and looking upon it merely as
a simple formation of new means of production — that the

condition still continues, in which the laborer performs surplus labor for the purpose of producing means of production, outside of the labor by which he acquires his means of
subsistence. Transformation of profit into capital signifies
merely the employment of a portion of the surplus labor
in the formation of new, additional, means of production.
That this takes place in the shape of a conversion of profit
into capital, signifies merely that not the laborer, but the
capitalist has control of the surplus labor. That this surplus labor must first pass though a stage, in which it appears as revenue (whereas in the case of a savage it appears
as surplus labor aiming directly at the manufacture of means
of production), means simply that this labor, or its product, is appropriated by the non-laborer. But what is actually
converted into capital, is not the profit as such. Transformation of surplus-value into capital signifies merely that the
surplus-value and the surplus-product are not consumed individually as revenue of the capitalist. What is actually so
converted is the value, the materialized labor, that is, the
product in which this value directly presents itself, or for
which it is exchanged after having been converted into
money. Even when the profit is reconverted into capital,
it is not this definite form of surplus-value, not the profit,
which is the source of the new capital. The surplus-value
is merely changed from one form into another. But it is
not this change of form which gives it the character of capital. It is the commodity and its value, which now perform
the function of capital. But that the value of the commodity is not paid for — and only by this means does it
become surplus-value — is quite immaterial for the materialization of labor, for value itself.

The misunderstanding expresses itself in various forms.
For instance, it is said that the commodities, of which the
constant capital consists, also contain elements of wages,
profit and rent. Or, that the thing, which is revenue for
the one, is capital for some one else, and that these are but
subjective relations. Thus the yarn of the spinner contains
a portion of value representing profit for him. If the weaver

buys the yarn, he realizes the profit of the spinner, but for himself this yarn is merely a part of his constant capital.

Aside from the remarks made on this score concerning the relations between revenue and capital, we add the following observations: The value which passes with the yarn as a constituting element into the capital of the weaver, is the value of the yarn. In what manner the parts of this value have resolved themselves for the spinner into capital and revenue, or, in other words, into paid and unpaid labor, is immaterial for the determination of the value of the commodity itself (aside from modifications by the average profit). Back of this lurks the idea that the profit, or the surplus-value in general, is a surplus above the value of the commodity, which can be made only by raising the price, by mutual cheating, by making a gain through sale. When the price of production is paid, or the value of the commodity, this pays, naturally, also for those portions of the value of commodities, which present themselves to the seller in the shape of revenue. Of course, we are not speaking of monopoly prices here.

In the second place, it is quite correct to say that the component parts of a commodity which make up the constant capital, like any other value of commodities, may be reduced to parts of value, which resolve themselves for the producers and the owners of the means of production into wages, profit and rent. This is merely a capitalist form of expression for the fact that all value of commodities is but the measure of the socially necessary labor contained in the commodities. But we have already shown in Volume I, that this does not prevent a separation of the produced commodities of any capital into separate parts, of which the one represents exclusively the constant portion of capital, another the variable portion of capital, and a third one only surplus-value.

Storch expresses the opinion of many others, when he says: "The salable products, which make up the national revenue, must be considered in political economy in two ways. They must be considered in their relations to indi-

viduals as values and in their relations to the nation as goods.
For the revenue of a nation is not appreciated like that of
an individual, by its value, but by its utility or by the wants
which it can satisfy." (*Considerations sur le revenu national,* p. 19.)

In the first place, it is a false abstraction to regard a
nation, whose mode of production is based upon value and
otherwise capitalistically organized, as an aggregate body
working merely for the satisfaction of the national wants.

In the second place, after the abolition of the capitalist
mode of production, but with social production still in vogue,
the determination of value continues to prevail in such a way
that the regulation of the labor time and the distribution
of the social labor among the various groups of production,
also the keeping of accounts in connection with this, become
more essential than ever

CHAPTER L.

THE SEMBLANCE OF COMPETITION.

WE have shown, that the value of commodities, or the price
of production regulated by their total value, resolves itself
into:

1) One portion of value replacing constant capital, or
representing past labor, used up in the form of means of production in the making of the commodity. This, in brief,
is the value, or price, which these means of production carried into the process of production of the commodities. We
never speak of individual commodities in this case, but of
commodity-capital, that is, of that form, in which the product of capital during a certain period of time, say of one
year, presents itself, and of which the individual commodity
forms one element, which, moreover, so far as its value is
concerned, resolves itself into the same analogous constituents.

2) One portion of value representing variable capital,

which measures the income of the laborer and converts itself into wages for him. The laborer has produced these wages in this variable portion of value. This, briefly, is that portion of value, which represents the paid portion of the new labor added to the above constant portion in the production of commodities.

3) Surplus-Value, which is that portion of the value of the produced commodities, in which the unpaid, or surplus labor is incorporated. This last portion of the value in its turn assumes the independent forms, which are at the same time forms of revenue, namely the forms of profit on capital (interest on capital as such and profit of enterprise on capital in productive work) and ground-rent, which is claimed by the owner of the land participating in the process of production. The parts mentioned under 2) and 3), that is, that portion of value, which always assumes the revenue forms of wages (but only after having first gone through the form of variable capital), profit and rent, is distinguished from the constant portion mentioned under 1) by the fact that in it that entire portion of value is dissolved, in which the additional labor added to that constant part, to the means of production of the commodities, is materialized. Now, if we leave aside the constant portion, then it is correct to say that the value of a commodity, to the extent that it represents newly added labor, continually resolves itself into three parts, which form three forms of revenue, namely wages, profit and rent,[150] in which the respective

---

[150] In separating the value added to the constant portion of value into wages, profit and ground rent, it is a matter of course that these are portions of value. One may, indeed conceive them as existing in the direct product created by laborers and capitalists in some particular sphere of production, for instance, yarn produced in a spinnery. But in fact they do not materialize in this product any more or any less than in any other commodity, in any other part of the material wealth having the same value. And in practice wages are paid in money, that is, in the pure form of value; likewise interest and rent. For the capitalist, the transformation of his product into the pure expression of value is indeed very important; in the distribution itself its existence is already assumed. Whether these values are reconverted into the same product, out of whose production they arose, whether the laborer buys back a part of the product directly produced by himself or the product of some other labor of a different kind, has nothing to do with the matter itself. Mr. Rodbertus quite unnecessarily goes into a passion about this.

3K

magnitudes of value, that is the aliquot portions, which they constitute in the total value, are determined by various peculiar laws, which we have analysed previously. But on the other hand, it would be a mistake to say that the value of wages, the rate of profit, and the rate of rent form independent constituent elements of value, whose composition gives rise to the value of commodities, leaving aside the constant part; in other words, it would be a mistake to say that they are constituent elements of the value of commodities, or of the price of production.[151]

The difference is easily seen.

Take it that the value of the product of a capital of 500 is equal to $400 c + 100 v + 150 s = 650$; let the 150 s be divided into 75 profit + 75 rent. We will also assume, in order to forestall useless difficulties, that this is a capital of average composition, so that its price of production and its value coincide; this coincidence always takes place, whenever the product of such an individual capital may be considered as the product of some portion of the total capital corresponding to the same magnitude.

Here the wages, measured by the variable capital, form 20% of the advanced capital; the surplus-value, calculated on the total capital, forms 30%, namely 15% profit and 15% rent. The entire portion of value of the commodity representing the newly added labor is equal to $100 v + 150 s = 250$. Its magnitude does not depend upon its division into wages, profit and rent. We see by the proportion of these parts to each other that a labor-power, which is paid with 100 in money, say 100 pounds sterling, has supplied a quantity of labor represented by money to the amount of 250 pounds sterling. We see from this that the laborer performed one and a half times as much surplus labor as he did labor for himself. If the working day contained 10 hours, then he worked 4 hours for himself and 6

---

[151] " It will be sufficient to remark that the same general rule, which regulates the value of raw produce and manufactured commodities, is applicable also to the metals; their value depending not on the rate of profits, nor on the rate of wages, nor on the rent paid for mines, but on the total quantity of labor necessary to obtain the metal and to bring it to market." (Ricardo *Principles,* Chapter III, p. 77.)

hours for the capitalist. Therefore the labor of the laborers paid with 100 pounds sterling is expressed in money to the amount of 250 pounds sterling. Outside of this value of 250 pounds sterling there is nothing to divide between laborer and capitalist, between capitalist and landlord. It is the total value newly added to the value of 400, which is the value of the means of production. The value of 250 thus produced and determined by the quantity of labor materialized by it in the commodities forms the limit of the dividend, which the laborer, the capitalist and the landlord will be able to draw out of this value in the shape of the revenues, wages, profit and rent.

Take it that a capital of the same organic composition, that is, of the same proportion between the employed living labor-power and the constant capital set in motion by it, should be compelled to pay 150 pounds sterling instead of 100 pounds sterling for the same labor-power which sets in motion the constant capital of 400. And let us further assume that profit and rent should share the surplus-value in a different proportion. As we have assumed that the variable capital of 150 pounds sterling sets the same quantity of labor in motion as the variable capital of 100 did, the newly added value would be 250 as before, and the total value of the product would be 650, also as before. But the formula would then read: 400 c + 150 v + 100 s, and these 100 s would be divided, say, into 45 profit and 55 rent. The proportion, in which the newly produced total value would now be divided among wages, profit and rent, would now be very different. The magnitude of the advanced total capital would also be very different, although it would set only the same total quantity of labor in motion. The wages would amount to $27\frac{3}{11}\%$, the profit to $8\frac{2}{11}\%$, and the rent to 10% of the advanced capital. The total surplus-value would, therefore, amount to a little over 18%.

In consequence of the raise in wages the unpaid portion of the total labor would be changed and with it the surplus-value. If the working day contained 10 hours, the laborer would work 6 hours for himself and 4 hours for the capitalist. The proportion of profit and rent would also be changed, the reduced surplus-value would be divided in a different proportion between the capitalist and the landlord. Finally, since the value of the constant capital would have remained the same, while the value of the advanced variable capital would have risen, the reduced surplus-value would express itself in a still more reduced rate of gross profit, by which we mean here the proportion between the total surplus-value and the advanced total capital.

The change in the value of wages, in the rate of profit, and in the rate of rent, whatever might be the effect of the laws regulating the proportion of these parts, could move only within the limits set by the newly produced value of commodities amounting to 250. An exception could take place only, if rent should rest upon a monopoly price. This would not alter the law itself, but merely complicate its analysis. For if we consider only the product itself in this case, then merely the division of the surplus-value would be different. But if we consider its relative value as compared to other commodities, then we should find no other difference but that a portion of the surplus-value had been transferred from them to this particular commodity.

Let us sum up:

Value of Product	New Value	Rate of Surplus-Value	Rate of Gross-Profit
First Case : $400 c + 100 v + 150 s = 650$	250	150 %	30 %
Second Case : $400 c + 150 v + 100 s = 650$	250	66 1/3%	18 2/11%

In the first place, the surplus-value falls by one-third from its former figure, it falls from 150 to 100. The rate of profit falls by a little more than one-third, from 30% to 18%, because the reduced surplus-value must be calculated on an increased advance of total capital. But it does not fall in the same proportion as the rate of surplus-value. This last falls from $\frac{150}{100}$ to $\frac{100}{150}$, that is, from 150% to 66$\frac{2}{3}$%, whereas the rate of profit falls only from $\frac{150}{500}$ to $\frac{100}{550}$ or from 30% to 18$\frac{2}{11}$%. The rate of profit, then, falls proportionately more than the mass of surplus-value, but less than the rate of surplus-value. We find, furthermore, that the values as well as the masses of products remain the same, so long as the same quantity of labor is employed, although the advanced capital has increased by the augmentation of its variable portion. This increase of the advanced capital would indeed make itself felt for a capitalist who would start out in business. But looking upon reproduction as a whole, the augmentation of the variable capital means merely that a larger portion of the new value added by newly performed labor is converted into wages, and thus at first into variable capital instead of into surplus-value and surplus products. The value of the product thus remains the same, because it is bounded on the one hand by the value of the constant capital, 400, and on the other hand by the figure 250, in which the newly added labor is represented. Both of these values remain unaltered. The product would represent the same amount of use-value in the same quantity of exchange-value, to the extent that it would return into the constant capital, so that the same mass of elements of constant capital would retain the same value. The matter would be different, if the wages should rise, not because the laborer would receive a larger share of his own labor, but if he should receive a larger portion of his own labor, because the productivity of labor would have decreased. In this case, the total value, in which this same labor, paid and unpaid, would be incorporated, would remain the same. But the mass of products, in which this quantity of labor would be incorporated, would be the same, so that the price of each aliquot portion of this product would rise, because each portion would contain more labor. The increased wages of 150 would not represent any more labor than the wages of 100 did before; the reduced surplus-value of 100 would represent merely two-thirds of the product which it did previously, only 66⅔% of the mass of use-values, which were formerly represented by 100. In this case the constant capital would also become dearer to the extent that this product would go back into it. But this would not be the result of the increase in wages. This increase in wages would rather be a result of the increase in the price of commodities and a result of the diminished productivity of the same quantity of labor. Here the impression is given that the raise in wages made the product dearer; however, this raise is not the cause, but rather a result of a change in the value of the commodities, due to the decreased productivity of labor.

On the other hand, so long as all other circumstances remain the same, so long as the same quantity of employed labor is represented by 250, and the value of the means of production handled by it should then rise or fall, then the value of the same quantity of products would rise or fall by the same magnitude. 450 c + 100 v + 150 s make the value of the product equal to 700. But 350 c + 100 v + 150 s would make the value of the same quantity of products only equal to 600, as against a former 650. Hence, if the advanced capital should increase or decrease, while it sets the same quantity of labor in motion, the value of its product would rise or fall, other circumstances remaining the same, if the increase or decrease of the advanced capital is due to a change in the value of the constant portion of capital. On the other hand, the value of the product remains unchanged, if the increase or decrease of the advanced capital is caused by a change in the value of the variable portion of capital, provided that the productivity of labor remains the same. In the case of the constant capital, the increase or decrease of its value is not balanced by any opposite movement. But in the case of the variable capital, so long as the productivity of labor remains the same, an increase or decrease of its value is balanced by the opposite movement on the part of the surplus-value, so that the value of the variable capital plus the surplus-value, that is, the new value added by new labor to the means of production and newly incorporated in the product, remains the same.

But if the increase or decrease of the value of the variable capital is due to a rise or fall in the price of commodities, that is, to an increase or decrease of the productivity of the labor employed by this investment of capital, then the value of the product is affected. Only, the rise or fall of wages in this case is not a cause, but an effect.

On the other hand, if the constant capital in the above illustration should remain at 400 c, and if the change from

100 v $+$ 150 s to 150 v $+$ 100 s, that is, an increase of the variable capital, should be due to a decrease in the productivity of labor, not in this same particular line of industry, say in cotton spinning, but perhaps in agriculture, so that it would be a result of a rise in the price of foodstuffs, then the value of the product would remain unchanged. The value of 650 would still be represented by the same quantity of cotton yarn.

The foregoing leads furthermore to the following conclusions: If a decrease in the expenditure of constant capital is due to economies, etc., in such lines of production as supply agriculture with their products, then this, like a direct improvement in the productivity of the employed labor itself, may lead to a reduction of wages, because it would lead to a cheapening of the subsistence of the laborer, and this would imply an increase of the surplus-value; so that the rate of profit in this case would grow for two reasons, namely on the one hand, because the value of the constant capital would decrease, and on the other hand, because the surplus-value would increase. In our analysis of the conversion of surplus-value into profit we assumed that the wages would not fall, but remain constant, because there we had to investigate the fluctuations of the rate of profit, independent of the changes in the rate of surplus-value. Moreover, the laws which we developed in that case are general ones, and apply also to investments of capital, the products of which do not pass over into the consumption of the laborer, and in that case changes in the value of the product are without influence upon the wages.

We know, then, that the separation and distribution of the new value added by new labor annually to the means of production, or to the constant part of capital, among the various forms of revenue, namely wages, profit and rent, do not alter the limits of this value itself, do not alter the sum of value to be so distributed; neither can a change in the proportions of these different parts alter their sum, which

makes up this given magnitude of value. A given figure of
100 always remains the same, whether it is divided into 50
+ 50, or into 20 + 70 + 10, or into 40 + 30 + 30. That
portion of the value of the product, which is divided into
these revenues, is determined, like the constant portion of
the value of capital, by the value of commodities, that is, by the
quantity of the labor incorporated in them from case to case.
In the first place, then, the quantity of value of the commodities to be distributed among wages, profit and rent is given;
in other words, the absolute limit of the sum of the portions
of value of these commodities. In the second place, as concerns the individual categories themselves, their average and
regulating limits are likewise given. The wages form the
basis in this limitation. The wages are regulated on the one
side by a natural law; their minimum is determined by the
physical minimum required by the laborer for the conservation of his labor-power and for its reproduction; this means
a minimum quantity of commodities. The value of these
commodities is determined by the labor time required for
their reproduction; it is determined by that portion of the
new labor added to the means of production, or by that portion of each working day, which the laborer must have for
the production and reproduction of an equivalent for the
value of these necessary means of subsistence. For instance,
if his average daily food requirements have the value of six
hours of average labor, then he must work on an average
six hours per day for himself. The actual value of his labor-
power differs from this physical minimum; it differs according to climate and condition of social development; it depends not merely upon the physical, but also upon the historically developed social needs, which become second nature.
But in every country and at any given period this regulating
average wage is a given magnitude. The value of all other
revenues thus has its limit. It is always equal to the value,
in which the total working day (which coincides in the present case with the average working day, since it comprises the
total quantity of labor set in motion by the total social capital) is incorporated, minus that portion of this working day,

which is incorporated in wages. Its limit is therefore determined by the limit of that value, in which the unpaid labor is expressed, that is, by the quantity of this unpaid labor. While that portion of the working day, which is required by the laborer for the reproduction of the value of his wages, finds its ultimate limit in the physical minimum of wages, the other portion of the working day, in which surplus labor is incorporated, and with it that portion of value which stands for surplus-value, finds its limit in the physical maximum of the working day, that is, in the total quantity of daily labor time, during which the laborer can be active altogether and still preserve and reproduce his labor-power. As we are here concerned in the distribution of that value, which represents the total labor newly added per year, the working day may here be regarded as a constant magnitude, and is taken for granted as such, no matter how much or how little it may differ from its physical maximum. The absolute limit of that portion of value, which forms surplus-value, and which resolves itself into profit and ground-rent, is thus given. It is determined by the excess of the unpaid portion of the working day over its paid portion, which means by that portion of the value of the total product, in which this surplus labor is realized. If we call the surplus-value thus limited and calculated on the advanced total capital the profit, as I have done, then this profit, so far as its absolute magnitude is concerned, is equal to the surplus-value and, therefore, determined in its boundaries by the same laws as it. On the other hand, the level of the rate of profit is likewise a magnitude inclosed within certain limits by the value of commodities. This rate is the proportion of the total surplus-value to the total social capital advanced in production. If this capital is equal to 500 (say millions) and the surplus-value equal to 100, then 20% form the absolute limit of the rate of profit. The distribution of the social profit at this rate among the various capitals invested in the different spheres of production creates prices of production, which swerve from the values of commodities, and these prices of production are the real regulating average market prices. But this deviation of prices of production from values abolishes neither the determination of prices by values nor the lawful limits of profit. Instead of the value of a commodity being equal to the capital consumed in it plus the surplus-value contained in it, its price of production is then equal to the capital, k, consumed in it plus the surplus-value falling to its share as a result of the average rate of profit, for instance 20% of the capital advanced in its production, counting both the consumed and the merely employed capital. But this addition of 20% is itself determined by the surplus-value created by the total social capital, and by its proportion to the value of this capital; and for this reason it is 20% and not 10% or 100%. The transformation of the values into prices of production, then, does not abolish the limits of profit, but merely alters its distribution among the various particular capitals, which make up the total social capital, distributes it uniformly among them in the proportion in which they form parts of the value of this total capital. The market prices fall below or rise above these regulating prices of production, but these fluctuations balance each other. If one studies price lists during a certain long period, and if one subtracts the cases, in which the real value of commodities is altered by a change in the productivity of labor, and likewise the cases, in which the process of production has been previously disturbed by natural or social accidents, one will be surprised, in the first place, by the relatively narrow limits of the fluctuations, and, in the second place, by the regularity of their mutual compensation. The same domination of the regulating averages will be found here, which Quételet pointed out in the case of social phenomena. If the equalization of the values of commodities into prices of production does not meet any obstacles, then the rent resolves itself into differential rent, that is, it is limited to the equalization of the surplus-profits, which would be given to some of the capitalists by the regulating prices of production, but which are then appropriated by the landlords. Here, then, the rent has its definite limit of value in the fluctuations of the individual rates of profit,

which are caused by the regulation of the prices of production through the general rate of profit. If private ownership of land places obstacles in the way of the equalization
of the values of commodities into prices of production, and
appropriates absolute rent, then this absolute rent is limited
by the excess of the value of the products of the soil over
their prices of production, that is, by the excess of the surplus-value in them over the rate of profit assigned to the
capitals by the average rate of profit. This difference then
forms the limit of the rent, which is always but a certain portion of surplus-value produced and existing in the commodities.

Finally, if the equalization of the surplus-value into average profit meets with obstacles in the various spheres of production in the shape of artificial or natural monopolies, particularly of monopoly in land, so that a monopoly price
would be possible, which would rise above the price of production and above the value of the commodities affected by
such a monopoly, still the limits imposed by the value of
commodities would not be abolished thereby. The monopoly
price of certain commodities would merely transfer a portion of the profit of the other producers of commodities to
the commodities with a monopoly price. A local disturbance in the distribution of the surplus-value among the various spheres of production would take place indirectly, but
they would leave the boundaries of the surplus-value itself
unaltered. If a commodity with a monopoly price should
enter into the necessary consumption of the laborer, it would
increase the wages and thereby reduce the surplus-value, if
the laborer would receive the value of his labor-power, the
same as before. But such a commodity might also depress
wages below the value of labor-power, of course only to the
extent that wages would be higher than the physical minimum of subsistence. In this case the monopoly price would
be paid by a deduction from the real wages (that is, from
the quantity of use-values received by the laborer for the
same quantity of labor) and from the profit of the other capitalists. The limits, within which the monopoly price would

affect the normal regulation of the prices of commodities, would be accurately fixed and could be closely calculated.

Just as the division of the newly added value of commodities into necessary and surplus labor, wages and surplus-value, and its general division between revenues, finds its given and regulating limits, so the division of the surplus-value itself into profit and ground-rent finds its limit in the laws regulating the equalization of the rate of profit. In the division into interest and profits of enterprise the average profit itself forms the limit for both of them. It furnishes the given magnitude of value, which they may divide among themselves and which is the only one that they can so divide. The definite proportion of this division is here accidental, that is, it is determined exclusively by conditions of competition. Whereas in other cases the balancing of supply and demand implies the cessation of the deviation of market prices from their regulating average prices, that is, the cessation of the influence of competition, it is here the only determinant. But why? Because the same factor in production, the capital, has to divide its share of the surplus-value between two owners of the same factor in production. But the fact that no definite, lawful, limit for the division of the average profit is found, does not do away with its limit as a part of the value of commodities, any more than the fact that two partners in a certain business, being under the influence of different circumstances, divide their profit unequally, affects the limits of this profit in any way.

Hence, although that portion of the value of commodities, in which the value of the new labor added to the means of production is incorporated, is divided into different parts, which assume independent forms as revenues, this is no reason why wages, profit and ground-rent should be considered as constituting elements, whose addition, or sum, would be the source of the regulating price of commodities (natural price, prix nécessaire): it is no reason to think that not the value of commodities, after the subtraction of the constant portion of value, is the original unit separated into these three parts, but rather the price of each one of these three parts is independently determined, and that the price of commodities is then formed by an addition of these three independent magnitudes. In reality the value of commodities is the magnitude which exists first, and it comprises the sum of the total values of wages, profit and rent, whatever may be their relative magnitudes. In the wrong conception, wages, profit and rent are three independent magnitudes of value, whose total magnitude is supposed to produce the magnitude of the value of a commodity, to limit and to determine it.

In the first place it is evident that, if wages, profit and rent constitute the price of commodities, this would apply as much to the constant portion of the value of commodities as to the other portion, in which variable capital and surplus-value are incorporated. This constant portion may here be left entirely out of consideration, since the value of the commodities of which it is made up would likewise resolve itself into wages, profit and rent. We have already shown that this conception denies the existence of such a constant portion of value.

It is furthermore evident that all meaning of value is here eliminated. Only the conception of price remains, in the sense that a certain amount of money is paid to the owners of labor-power, capital and land. But what is money? Money is not a thing, but a definite form of value, hence it is again conditioned upon value. Let us say, then, that a definite amount of gold or silver is paid for those elements of production, or that they are equalled in our minds to this amount. But gold and silver (and the enlightened economist is proud of this understanding) are themselves commodities, like all others. The price of gold and silver is therefore likewise determined by wages, profit and rent. Hence we cannöt determine what wages, profit and rent are, by making them equal to a certain amount of gold or silver, for the value of this gold and silver, by which they are supposed to be estimated as equivalents, is precisely supposed to be determined by them, independently of gold and silver, that is, independently of the value of any commodity, for this value is supposed to be the product of those three. To say that the value of wages, profit and rent consist in their being equivalent to a certain quantity of gold and silver, would merely be the same as saying that they are equal to a certain quantity of wages, profit and rent.

Take wages first. For it is necessary to make labor the point of departure, even in this view of the matter. How, then, is the regulating price of wages determined, the price around which its market prices oscillate?

Let us reply that it is determined by the demand and supply of labor-power. But what sort of a demand is this? It is a demand made by capital. The demand for labor is therefore at the same time a supply of capital. In order to speak of a supply of capital, we should know above all what capital is. What is capital made of? If we select its simplest forms, it consists of money and commodities. But money is merely a form of commodities. Capital, then, consists of commodities. But the value of commodities, according to our assumption, is first determined by the price of the labor producing them, by wages. The existence of wages is here a prerequisite and is considered as a constituting element of the price of commodities. Now this price is to be determined by the proportion of the supplied labor to capital. The price of the capital itself is equal to the price of the commodities of which it is composed. The demand of capital for labor is equal to the supply of capital. And the supply of capital is equal to the supply of a quantity of commodities of a given price, and this price is regulated in the first place by the price of labor, and the price of labor in its turn is equal to that portion of the price of commodities, which makes up the variable capital, which is transferred to the laborer in exchange for his labor; and the price of the commodities, of which this variable capital is composed, is in its turn primarily determined by the price of labor; for it is determined by the prices of wages, profit and rent. In order to determine wages, we cannot, therefore, assume the previous existence of capital, for the value of the capital is itself determined in part by wages.

Besides, the dragging of competition into this problem does not help any. Competition makes the market prices of labor rise and fall. But suppose that the demand and supply of labor are balanced. What determines wages in that case? Competition. But we have just assumed that competition ceases to act as a determinant, that it abolishes its effects by the equilibrium of its two opposing forces. We are precisely trying to find the natural price of wages, that is, the price of labor not regulated by competition, but which, on the contrary, regulates it.

Nothing remains but to determine the necessary price of labor by the necessary subsistence of the laborer. But these articles of food are commodities, which have a price. The price of labor is therefore determined by the price of the necessary means of existence, and the price of the means of existence, like that of all other commodities, is determined primarily by the price of labor. Therefore the price of labor determined by the price of the means of existence is determined by the price of labor. The price of labor is determined by itself. In other words, we do not know by what the price of labor is determined. Labor in this case has any price at all, because it is considered as a commodity. In order, therefore, to speak of the price of labor, we must know what price itself means. But what price itself is, we do not learn in this way at all.

But let us assume, that the necessary price of labor had been determined in this agreeable manner. Then how is the average profit determined, the profit of every capital in normal conditions, which forms the second element of the price of commodities? The average profit must be determined by an average rate of profit; how is this rate determined? By the competition between the capitalists? But this competition itself is conditioned upon the existence of profit. It presupposes the existence of different rates of profit, and thus of different profits, either in the same, or in different spheres of production. Competition can influence the rate of profit only to the extent that it affects the prices of commodities. Competition can merely make the producers within the same sphere of production sell their commodities at the same prices, and make them sell their commodities in different spheres of production at prices which will give them the same profit, will give them the same proportional addition to the price of commodities, which has already been partially determined by wages. Hence competition cannot balance anything but inequalities in the rate of profit. In order to balance unequal rates of profit, the profit as an element in the price of commodities must already exist. Competition does not create it. It lowers or raises its level, but it does not create this level, which appears whenever the balance has been struck. And when we speak of a necessary rate of profit, we wish precisely to know the rate of profit which is independent of the movements of competition, and which rather regulates these movements. The average rate of profit appears, when the forces of the competing capitalists balance each other. Competition may bring about this balance, but cannot create the rate of profit which appears whenever this balance is found. As soon as the equilibrium is reached, why is the rate of profit 10, or 20, or 100% ? On account of competition ? No, on the contrary, competition has done away with the causes, which produced deviations from the rate of 10, or 20, or 100%. It has brought about a price of commodities, by which every capital yields the same profit in proportion to its magnitude. The magnitude of this profit itself is independent of it. It merely reduces all deviations to this magnitude. One man competes with another, and competition compels him to sell his commodities at the same price as the other. But why is this price 10 or 20 or 100% ?

Nothing remains under these circumstances but to declare that the rate of profit, and with it the profit itself arises in some unaccountable manner by a certain addition to the price of commodities, which to that extent was determined by the wages. The only thing which competition tells us is that this rate of profit must have a certain figure. But we knew that before, when we spoke of an average rate of profit and of a " necessary price " of profit.

It is quite unnecessary to thrash this absurd process over in the case of ground-rent. It is evident, even so, that it, logically pursued, makes profit and rent appear as additions made by unaccountable laws to the price of commodities, which is primarily determined by wages. In short, competition has to shoulder the duty of explaining all inexplicable ideas of the economists, whereas the economists should rather explain competition.

Now, if we leave aside the illusion of a profit and rent created by the circulation, that is of parts of price arising through sale — for circulation can never give what it did not first receive — the matter simply amounts to this:

Let the price of a commodity determined by wages be 100; let the rate of profit be 10% of the wages, and the rent 15% of the wages. Then the price of the commodity determined by wages, profit and rent is 125. These added 25 cannot come from the sale of this commodity. For all sellers sell to each other at 125 what has actually cost only 100 in wages, and the result is the same as though they had all sold at 100. The operation must rather be studied independently of the process of circulation.

If the three revenues share the commodity itself, which now costs 125 — and it does not alter the matter, if the capitalist should first sell at 125, then pay 100 to the laborer, 10 to himself, and 15 to the landlord — then the laborer receives $\frac{4}{5}$, equal to 100, of the value and of the product. The capitalist receives $\frac{2}{25}$ of the value and of the product, and the landlord $\frac{3}{25}$. When the capitalist sells at 125, instead of at 100, he merely gives to the laborer $\frac{4}{5}$ of the product, in which his labor is incorporated. This would be the same, if he had given 80 to the laborer and kept back 20, of which he would share 8 and the landlord 12. In this case he would have sold the commodity at its value, since in fact the additions to the price of the commodity are made independently of the value of the commodity, which is assumed to be determined here by the value of labor-power. This amounts in a roundabout way to saying that in this conception the term wages, here 100, is equal

3L

to the value of the product, that is, equal to that sum of money, in which the same definite quantity of labor is represented; but that this value again differs from the real wages and therefore leaves a surplus. Only, in the present case, this is obtained nominally by an addition to the price. Hence, if the wages were 110 instead of 100, the profit would have to be 11 and the ground-rent $16\frac{1}{2}$, so that the price of the commodity would be $137\frac{1}{2}$. This would leave the proportion unaltered. But as the division would always be obtained by a nominal addition of definite percentages to the wages, the price would rise and fall with the wages. The wages are here first assumed as equal to the value of the commodity, and then again separated from it. In fact, however, the matter amounts in a roundabout and meaningless way to this, that the value of the commodity is determined by the quantity of labor contained in it, whereas the value of wages is determined by the price of the necessities of life, and the surplus of value above the wages forms profit and rent.

The separation of the value of commodities, after the subtraction of the value of the means of production consumed in their creation, this separation of this given quantity of value determined by the quantity of labor incorporated in the produced commodities into three parts, namely into wages, profit and rent, which assume the shape of independent and mutually unrelated revenues, this same separation appears on the surface of capitalist production, and consequently in the minds of the agents bounded by it, in an inverted form.

Let the total value of a certain commodity be 300, of which 200 may be the value of the means of production, or elements of constant capital, consumed in its production. This leaves 100 as the amount of the new value added to this commodity in its process of production. This new value of 100 is all that is available for division among these three forms of revenue. Let us place the figure for wages at x, for profit at y, for ground-rent at z, then the sum of x + y + z will always be 100 in our present case. In the conception of the industrials, merchants and bankers, as in that of the vulgar economists, matters are supposed to pass in an entirely different way. According to them it is not the value of the commodity, which equals 100 after subtracting the value of the means of production consumed in it, nor is it this 100 which is divided into x, y and z. According to them it is rather the price of the commodity, which is composed of wages, profit and rent, whose figures of value are determined independently of the value of this commodity and independently of each other, so that x, y and z exist independently, each by itself and is so determined, while the sum of these magnitudes, which may be larger or smaller than 100, makes up the value of the commodity by adding these three different values together. This case of mistaken identity is necessary:

1) Because the component parts of value in the commodities face each other as independent revenues, which are referred back as such to three very dissimilar agencies in production, namely to labor, capital and land, and which then seem to arise out of these. The ownership of labor-power, of capital, of land, is the cause, which assigns these different parts of the value of commodities to these respective owners, and transforms these parts into revenue for them. But the value does not arise from a transformation of its parts into revenue, it must rather exist before it can be converted into revenue, before it can assume this form. The appearance of the reverse must fortify itself so much the more, as the determination of the relative magnitude of these three parts follows different laws, whose connection with and limitation by the value of commodities themselves does not show itself on the surface by any means.

2) We have seen that a general rise or fall of wages, by causing a movement in the opposite direction on the part of the average rate of profit, so long as other circumstances remain the same, changes the prices of production of the different commodities, raises some and lowers others, according to the average composition of the capital in the respective spheres of production. There is no doubt that at least in some spheres of production the experience is made, that the

average price of a commodity rises, because wages have risen, and falls, because wages have fallen. What is not " experienced " is the secret regulation of this change by the value of commodities, which is independent of wages. But if the rise of wages is local, if it takes place only in particular spheres of production in consequence of peculiar circumstances, then a corresponding nominal raise of prices may occur in the case of these commodities. The rise of the relative value of one kind of commodities as against others, which have been produced with an unchanged scale of wages, is then merely a reaction against the local disturbance of a uniform distribution of surplus-value among the various spheres of production, a means of leveling particular rates of profit into an average rate. The " experience," which is met in that case, is once more the determination of the price by the wages. In both these cases, the same experience shows that the wages determine the prices of commodities. What is not " experienced," is the hidden cause of this interrelation. Furthermore: The average price of labor, that is, the value of labor-power, is determined by the price of production of the necessary articles of subsistence. If the price of these falls, so does that of those. What is once more experienced here, is the existence of a connection between wages and the price of commodities. But the cause may seem to be an effect, and the effect a cause, as is also the case in the movements of market prices, where a rise of wages above its average corresponds to the rise of the market prices above the prices of production during periods of prosperity, and subsequent fall of wages below their average corresponds to a fall of market prices below the prices of production. Owing to the dependence of prices of production upon the values of commodities, the primary experience, aside from the oscillating movements of the market prices, should always be that the rate of profit falls whenever wages rise, and vice versa. But we have seen that the rate of profit may be determined by the movements of the value of constant capital, independently of the movements of wages; so that wages and the rate of profit, instead of moving in opposite directions, move in the same direction, and may rise or fall together. If the rate of surplus-value were directly identical with the rate of profit, then this could not happen. Even if wages should rise as a result of a rise in the prices of food-stuffs, the rate of profit may remain the same, or may even rise, owing to a greater intensity of labor or a prolongation of the working day. All these experiences corroborate the illusion created by the apparently independent and reversed form of the parts of value, as though either the wages alone, or wages and profit together determined the value of commodities. As soon as this seems to be the case with reference to wages, so that the price of labor and the value created by labor seem to coincide, the same applies as a matter of course to profit and rent. Their prices, that is, their expression in money, must then seem to be regulated independently of labor and of the value produced by it.

3) Let us assume that the values of commodities, or the apparently independent prices of production, coincide seemingly directly and continually with the market prices of commodities, instead of merely enforcing themselves as the regulating average prices by the continual balancing of the fluctuations of market prices. Let us assume, furthermore, that reproduction always takes place under the same unaltered conditions, so that the productivity of labor remains constant in all elements of capital. Finally, let us assume that that portion of the value of the produced commodities, which is formed in every sphere of production by the addition of a new quantity of labor, or by the addition of a newly produced value to the value of the means of production, is always divided according to the same unaltered proportion into wages, profit and rent, so that the actually paid wages, the actually realized profit, and the actual rent always directly coincides with the value of labor-power, with that portion of the total surplus-value which falls to the share of every active part of total capital by means of the average rate of profit, and with the limits, in which ground-rent is normally held upon this basis. In one word, let us assume that the division of the produced social values and the regulation of

the prices of production takes place on a capitalist basis, but that competition is abolished.

Under these assumptions, then, under which the value of commodities would be constant and would appear so, under which that part of the value of commodities which resolves itself into revenues would remain a constant magnitude and would always present itself as such, and under which, finally, this given and constant part of value would always be divided according to constant proportions into wages, profit and rent, even under these assumptions would the real movement necessarily appear in an inverted form: not as a division of a previously given quantity of value into three parts, which assume mutually independent forms of revenue, but on the contrary, as the formation of this quantity of value by the sum of the independent and selfdetermined elements of wages, profit and rent, of which it is composed. This illusion would necessarily arise, because in the actual movement of the individual capitals and of the commodities produced by them not the value of the commodities would seem to precede their division, but vice versa, the parts into which it is divided would seem to exist before the value of the commodities. In the first place we have seen that to every capitalist the cost price of his commodities appears as a given magnitude and continually presents itself as such in the actual price of production. But the cost price is equal to the value of the constant capital, the advanced means of production, plus the value of labor-power, which, however, presents itself to the agent in production in the irrational shape of a price of labor, so that the wages appear at the same time as a revenue for the laborer. The average price of labor is a given magnitude, because the value of labor-power, like that of any other commodity, is determined by the labor time required for its reproduction. But as concerns that portion of the value of commodities, which resolves itself into wages, it does not arise from the fact that it assumes this form of wages, nor from the fact that the capitalist advances to the laborer his share of his own product in the shape of wages, but from the fact that the laborer produces an equivalent for his wages, that is, that a portion of his daily or annual labor produces the value contained in the price of his labor-power. But the wages are stipulated by contract, before the value equivalent to them has been produced. As an element of price, whose magnitude is given before the commodity and its value have been produced, as a constituent part of the cost price, wages do not appear as a part which detaches itself in an independent form from the total value of the commodity, but rather as a given magnitude, which predetermines this value, a creator of price or value. A role similar to that of wages in the cost price of commodities is played by the average profit in their price of production, for the price of production is equal to the cost price plus the average profit on the advanced capital. This average profit figures practically, in the conception and in the calculation of the capitalist himself, as a regulating element, not merely to the extent that it determines the transfer of the capitals from one sphere of investment into another, but also in all sales and contracts, which embrace a process of reproduction extending over long epochs. But whenever it figures in this way, it is a previously existing magnitude, which is in fact independent of the value and surplus-value produced in any particular sphere of production, and still more independent of the value and surplus-value produced by any individual investment of capital in any sphere of production. It does not present itself as a result of a division of value, but rather as a magnitude independent of the value of the produced commodities, as existing from the start and determining the average price of the commodities, that is, as a creator of value. Indeed, the surplus-value, owing to its separation into various and mutually unrelated parts, appears in a still more concrete form as a prerequisite for the creation of the value of commodities. A part of the average profit, in the form of interest, faces the capitalist independently as an element preceding the production of commodities and of their value. Although the fluctuations of the amount of interest are considerable, yet at any specific moment it is a given magnitude for every capitalist, and it enters into the cost price of the commodities produced by any individual capitalist. So does also the ground-rent in the form of lease money fixed by contract in the case of the agricultural capitalist, and in the form of rent for business rooms in the case of other business men. These parts, into which surplus-value is divided, being given as elements of cost price for the individual capitalist, appear for this reason inversely as creators of surplus-value; they appear as creators of a portion of the price of commodities, just as wages appear as the creator of the other portion. The secret of the continual reappearance of these divided parts of commodity value in the role of prerequisites for the formation of value itself is simply this, that the capitalist mode of production, like any other, does not merely always reproduce the material product, but also the economic conditions, the definite economic forms of its creation. Its result, therefore, appears as continually as its prerequisites, as its prerequisites appear in the role of its results. And it is this continual reproduction of the same conditions, which the individual capital anticipates in a matter of fact way as an indubitable fact. So long as the capitalist mode of production persists as such, a portion of the newly added labor resolves itself continually into wages, another into profit (interest and profit of enterprise), and a third into rent. In the contracts between the owners of the various agencies of production this is always assumed, and this assumption is correct, no matter how much the relative proportions may fluctuate in individual cases. The definite shape, in which the parts of value face each other, is assumed as pre-existing, because it is continually reproduced, and it is continually reproduced, because it is continually taken for granted.

It is true, that both experience and the appearance of things demonstrate the fact that the market prices, whose influence seems to the capitalist to be indeed the whole thing in the determination of values, are by no means dependent upon these anticipations, so far as their amount is concerned. They are not governed by any contracts demanding a high or a low rent and interest. But the market prices are constant only in their changes, and their average for a certain long period results in the respective averages of wages, profit and rent as magnitudes dominating the constant ones, such as the market prices, in the last analysis.

On the other hand, it seems like a simple reflection, that if wages, profit and rent are creators of value for the reason that they seem to precede the production of value, and that they are taken for granted by the individual capitalist in his cost price and price of production, then the constant portion of value, whose value enters as a given quantity into the production of every commodity, is also a creator of value. But the constant portion of value is nothing but a quantity of commodities and, therefore, of values of commodities. Thus we should arrive at the absurd tautology that the value of commodities is the creator and cause of the value of commodities.

If the capitalist were interested in reflecting about this — and his reflections as a capitalist are dictated exclusively by his interests and his interested motives — his experience would show him, that the product, which he himself produces, passes over into other spheres of production as a constant part of capital, and that products of these other spheres of production pass over into his own product as constant parts of capital. Owing to the fact that the additional value of his own new production, from his point of view, seems to be formed by means of wages, profit and rent, the same appearance holds good also in the case of the constant portion consisting of products of other capitalists. And so the price of the constant portion of capital, and with it the total value of the commodities, reduces itself in the last resort, although in a somewhat unaccountable manner, to a sum of values resulting from the addition of the independent creators of value, wages, profit and rent, which are regulated by different laws and come from different sources.

4) Whether the commodities are sold, or not sold, at their values, whether their value is determined in one way or another, is quite immaterial for the individual capitalist. This determination of values is from the very outset a process

passing behind his back and controlled by conditions independent of himself, because it is not the values, but the divergent prices of production, which form the regulating average prices in every sphere of production. The determination of values as such, interests and influences the individual capitalist and the capital in each sphere of production only to the extent that the reduced or increased quantity of labor required in accordance with the rise or fall of the productive power of labor, enables him in one case to make an extra profit, and compels him in another to raise the price of his commodities, because an additional amount of wages, an additional amount of constant capital, and consequently some more interest, fall upon each individual part of the product, or upon the individual commodities. This determination of values interests him only to the extent that it raises or lowers the cost of production of commodities for himself, in other words, only to the extent that it places him in an exceptional position.

On the other hand, wages, interest and rent appear to him as regulating boundaries, not only of the price at which he can realize the profit of enterprise, that is, the profit falling to his share in his capacity as a producing capitalist, but also of the price at which he must be able to sell his commodities, if he is to keep his reproduction going at all. It is quite immaterial for him, whether he realises the value and surplus-value in his commodities by their sale, provided only that he gets the customary profit or enterprise or more than that, so long as he pockets this surplus over and above the individual cost price determined for him by wages, interest and rent. Aside from the constant portion of capital, wages, interest and rent appear to him, therefore, as the limiting, creating, determining elements of the price of commodities. For instance, if he can succeed in depressing wages below their normal level, below the value of labor-power, if he can obtain capital at a lower rate of interest, if he can pay less than the normal amount for rent, then he does not care, whether he sells his product below its value, or even below its price of production, so that he gives away without any equivalent a portion of the surplus-value contained in the commodities. This applies even to the constant portion of capital. For instance, if an industrial capitalist can buy his raw material below its price of production, then this protects him against loss, even if he sells it in his own finished product under its price of production. His profit of enterprise may remain the same, or may even increase, so long as the excess of the price of commodities over its elements remains the same or increases. But aside from the value of the means of production, which enter into his own production with a given price, it is precisely wages, interest and rent which enter into this production as limiting and regulating amounts of price. Consequently they appear to him as elements determining the price of commodities. The profit of enterprise, from his point of view, seems determined either by the excess of the market prices, dependent upon accidental conditions of competition, over the immanent value of commodities determined by those elements of price. Or, to the extent that this profit itself exerts a determining influence upon market prices, it seems itself dependent upon the competition between buyers and sellers.

In the competition, both of the individual capitalists among themselves and in the competition on the world market, it is the given and presupposed magnitudes of wages, interest and rent which enter into the calculation as constant and regulating magnitudes. They are constant, not in the sense of being unalterable magnitudes, but in the sense that they are given in any individual case and that they form the constant boundary for the continually fluctuating market prices. For instance, in the competition on the world market the question is exclusively as to whether the commodities can be sold at, or below, the existing world market prices with a profit, as to whether, with the existing wages, interest and rent a corresponding profit of enterprise can be realized. If the wages and the price of land are low in a certain country, while the interest on capital is high, because the capitalist mode of production has not been developed in it, whereas in some other country the wage and the price of land are nominally high, while the interest on capital is low, then the capitalist employs in the one country more labor and land, in the other relatively more capital. These factors enter as determining elements into the calculation by which the degree of possible competition between these two countries is estimated. Here, then, experience shows theoretically, and the interested calculation of the capitalist shows practically, that the prices of commodities are determined by wages, interest and rent, by the price of labor, of capital and of land, and that these elements of price are indeed the regulating factors of price.

Of course, this always leaves an element which is not assumed as pre-existing, but which rather results from the market price of commodities, namely the surplus above the cost price formed by the addition of these elements, namely of wages, interest and rent. This fourth element seems to be determined in every individual case by competition, and in the long average of cases by the average profit, which in its turn is regulated by this same competition, only at longer intervals.

5) On the basis of capitalist competition it becomes so much a matter of course to separate the value, in which the newly added labor is represented, into the forms of revenue known as wages, profit and ground-rent, that this method is applied (not to mention past stages of history, of which we gave illustrations under the head of ground-rent) even in cases, in which the conditions required for those forms of revenue are missing. In other words, everything is counted under these heads by analogy.

If an independent laborer — for instance, a small farmer, in whose case all three forms of revenue may be used — works for himself and sells his own product, he is, in the first place, considered as his own employer (capitalist), who employs himself as a laborer, and as his own landlord, who employs himself as his own tenant. To himself as a wage worker he pays his wages, to himself as a capitalist he turns over his profit, and to himself as a landlord he pays his rent. Assuming the capitalist mode of production and the conditions corresponding to it to be the general basis of society, this conception is correct, in so far as he does not owe it to his labor, but to his ownership of means of production — which have here assumed the general form of capital — that he is able to appropriate his own surplus labor. And furthermore, to the extent that he creates his own product in the shape of commodities, and thus depends upon its price (and even if he does not depend upon it, this price can be estimated), the quantity of surplus labor, which he can realize, does not depend upon its own size, but upon the general rate of profit; and in like manner any surplus above the amount of surplus-value allowed by the general rate of profit is not determined by the quantity of labor performed by himself, but can be appropriated by him only because he is the owner of the land. Because a form of production not corresponding to the capitalist mode of production may thus be brought in line with its forms of revenue — and to a certain extent not incorrectly — the illusion is strengthened so much the more that the capitalist conditions are the natural conditions of any mode of production.

On the other hand, if we reduce the wages to their general basis, namely to that portion of the product of the producer's own labor which passes over into the individual consumption of the laborer; if we relieve this portion of its capitalist limitations and extend it to that volume of consumption, which is permitted, on the one hand, by the existing productivity of society (that is the social productivity of his own individual labor in its capacity as a truly social one), and on the other hand, required by the full development of his individuality; if we reduce the surplus labor and the surplus product to that measure, which is required under the existing conditions of social production, on the one hand for the formation of an insurance and reserve fund, and on the other hand for the continuous expansion of reproduction to an extent dictated by social needs; finally, if we include in number one, necessary labor, and number two, surplus labor, that quantity of labor, which must always be performed by the ablebodied for the incapacitated or immature members of society, in other words, if we deprive both wages and surplus-value, both necessary and surplus labor, of their specifically capitalist character, then we have not these forms, but merely their foundations, which are common to all social modes of production.

Moreover, this manner of generalizing was also used in previous modes of production, for instance, in the feudal one. Conditions of production, which did not correspond to it at all, which stood entirely outside of it, were counted in as feudal relations. This was done, for instance, in England, in the case of tenures in common socage (as distinguished from tenures on knight's service), which comprised merely monetary obligations and were feudal in name only.

CHAPTER LI.

CONDITIONS OF DISTRIBUTION AND PRODUCTION.

THE new value added by the annual new labor — and thus also that portion of the annual product, in which this value is represented and may be drawn out of the total fund and separated from it — is divided into three parts, which assume three different forms of revenue. These forms indicate that one portion of this value belongs, or goes to, the owner of labor-power, another portion to the owner of capital, and a third portion to the owner of land. These, then are forms, or conditions, of distribution, for they express conditions, under which the newly produced total value is distributed among the owners of the different agencies of production.

To the ordinary mind these conditions of distribution appear as natural conditions, as conditions arising from the nature of all social production, from the laws of human production in general. While it cannot be denied that precapitalist societies show other modes of distribution, yet those modes are interpreted as undeveloped, imperfect, disguised, differently colored modes of these natural conditions of distribution, which have not reached their purest expression and their highest form.

The only correct thing in this conception is this: Assuming some form of social production to exist (for instance, that of the primitive Indian communes, or that of the more artificially developed communism of the Peruvians), a distinction can always be made between that portion of labor, which supplies products directly for the individual consumption of the producers and their families — aside from the part which is productively consumed — and that portion of labor, which produces surplus products, which always serve for the satisfaction of social needs, no matter what may be the mode of distribution of this surplus product, and whoever may perform the function of a representative of these social needs. The identity of the various modes of distribution amounts merely to this, that they are identical, if we leave out of consideration their differences and specific forms and keep in mind only their common features as distinguished from their differences.

A more advanced, more critical mind, however, admits the historically developed character of the condition of distribution,[152] but clings on the other hand so much more tenaciously to the unaltering character of the conditions of production arising from human nature and thus independent of all historical development.

On the other hand, the scientific analysis of the capitalist mode of production demonstrates that it is a peculiar mode of production, specifically defined by historical development; that it, like any other definite mode of production, is conditioned upon a certain stage of social productivity and upon the historically developed form of the forces of production. This historical prerequisite is itself the historical result and product of a preceding process, from which the new mode of production takes its departure as from its given foundation. The conditions of production corresponding to this specific, historically determined, mode of production have a specific,

[152] J. Stuart Mill: *Some Unsettled Questions in Political Economy,* London, 1884.

historical, passing character, and men enter into them as into their process of social life, the process by which they create their social life. The conditions of distribution are essentially identical with these conditions of production, being their reverse side, so that both conditions share the same historical and passing character.

In the study of conditions of distribution, the start is made from the alleged fact, that the annual product is distributed among wages, profit and rent. But if so expressed, it is a misstatement. The product is assigned on one side to capital, on the other to revenues. One of these revenues, wages, never assumes the form of a revenue, a revenue of the laborer, until it has first faced this laborer in the form of capital. The meeting of the produced requirement of labor and of the general products of labor as capital, in opposition to the direct producers, includes from the outset a definite social character of the material requirements of labor as compared to the laborers, and with it a definite relation, into which they enter in production itself with the owners of the means of production and among themselves. The transformation of these means of production into capital implies on their part the expropriation of the direct producers from the soil, and thus a definite form of property in land.

If one portion of the product were not transformed into capital, the other would not assume the form of wages, profit and rent.

On the other hand, just as the capitalist mode of production is conditioned upon this definite social form of the conditions of production, so it reproduces them continually. It produces not merely the material products, but reproduces continually the conditions of production, in which the others are produced, and with them the corresponding conditions of distribution.

It may indeed be said that capital (and the ownership of land implied by it) is itself conditioned upon a certain mode of distribution, namely the expropriation of the laborers from the means of production, the concentration of these conditions in the hands of a minority of individuals, the exclusive ownership of land by other individuals, in short, all those conditions, which have been described in the Part dealing with Primitive Accumulation (Volume I. Chapter XXVI). But this distribution differs considerably from the meaning of "conditions of distribution," provided we invest them with a historical character in opposition to conditions of production. By the first kind of distribution is meant the various titles to that portion of the product, which goes into individual consumption. By conditions of distribution, on the other hand, we mean the foundations of specific social functions performed within the conditions of production themselves by special agents in opposition to the direct producers. They imbue the conditions of production themselves and their representatives with a specific social quality. They determine the entire character and the entire movement of production.

Capitalist production is marked from the outset by two peculiar traits.

1) It produces its products as commodities. The fact that it produces commodities does not distinguish it from other modes of production. Its peculiar mark is that the prevailing and determining character of its products is that of being commodities. This implies, in the first place, that the laborer himself acts in the role of a seller of commodities, as a free wage worker, so that wage labor is the typical character of labor. In view of the foregoing analyses it is not necessary to demonstrate again, that the relation between wage labor and capital determines the entire character of the mode of production. The principal agents of this mode of production itself, the capitalist and the wage worker, are to that extent merely personifications of capital and wage labor. They are definite social characters, assigned to individuals by the process of social production. They are products of these definite social conditions of production.

The character, first of the product as a commodity, secondly of the commodity as a product of capital, implies all conditions of circulation, that is, a definite social process through which the products must pass and in which they as-

sume definite social forms. It also implies definite relations
of the agents in production, by which the formation of value
in the product and its reconversion, either into means of subsistence or into means of production, is determined. But
aside from this, the two above-named characters of the product as commodities, and of commodities as products of capital, dominate the entire determination of value and the regulation of the whole production by value. In this specific
form of value, labor appears on the one hand only as social
labor; on the other hand, the distribution of this social labor
and the mutual supplementing and circulation of matter in
the products, the subordination under the social activity and
the entrance into it, are left to the accidental and mutually
nullifying initiative of the individual capitalists. Since
these meet one another only as owners of commodities, and
every one seeks to sell his commodity as dearly as possible
(being apparently guided in the regulation of his production
by his own arbitrary will), the internal law enforces itself
merely by means of their competition, by their mutual pressure upon each other, by means of which the various deviations are balanced. Only as an internal law, and from the
point of view of the individual agents as a blind law, does the
law of value exert its influence here and maintain the social
equilibrium of production in the turmoil of its accidental
fluctuations.

Furthermore, the existence of commodities, and still more
of commodities as products of capital, implies the externali-
zation of the conditions of social production and the personification of the material foundations of production, which
characterize the entire capitalist mode of production.

2) The other specific mark of the capitalist mode of production is the production of surplus-value as the direct aim
and determining incentive of production. Capital produces
essentially capital, and does so only to the extent that it produces surplus-value. We have seen in our discussion of relative surplus-value, and in the discussion of the transformation of surplus-value into profit, that a mode of production
peculiar to the capitalist period is founded upon this. This

is a special form in the development of the productive powers of labor, in such a way that these powers appear as self-dependent powers of capital lording it over labor and standing in direct opposition to the laborer's own development. Production which has for its incentive value and surplus-value implies, as we have shown in the course of our analyses, the perpetually effective tendency to reduce the labor necessary for the production of a commodity, in other words, to reduce its value, below the prevailing social average. The effort to reduce the cost price to its minimum becomes the strongest lever for the raising of the social productivity of labor, which, however, appears under these conditions as a continual increase of the productive power of capital.

The authority assumed by the capitalist by his personification of capital in the direct process of production, the social function performed by him in his capacity as a manager and ruler of production, is essentially different from the authority exercised upon the basis of production by means of slaves, serfs, etc.

Upon the basis of capitalist production, the social character of their production impresses itself upon the mass of direct producers as a strictly regulating authority and as a social mechanism of the labor process graduated into a complete hierarchy. This authority is vested in its bearers only as a personification of the requirements of labor standing above the laborer. It is not vested in them in their capacity as political or theoretical rulers, in the way that it used to be under former modes of production. Among the bearers of this authority, on the other hand, the capitalists themselves, complete anarchy reigns, since they face each other only as owners of commodities, while the social interrelations of production manifest themselves to these capitalists only as an overwhelming natural law, which curbs their individual license.

It is only because labor is presumed as wage labor, and the means of production in the form of capital, only on account of this specific social form of these two essential agencies in production, that a part of the value (product) presents itself

as surplus-value and this surplus-value as profit (rent), as a
gain of the capitalists, as additional available wealth belonging to the capitalist. But only because they present themselves as his profit, do the additional means of production,
which are intended for the expansion of reproduction, and
which form a part of this profit, present themselves as new
additional capital, and only for this reason does the expansion
of the process of reproduction present itself as a process of capitalist accumulation.

Although the form of labor, as wage labor, determines the
shape of the entire process and the specific mode of production itself, it is not wage labor which determines value. In
the determination of value the question turns around social
labor time in general, about that quantity of labor, which
society in general has at its disposal, and the relative absorption of which by the various products determines, as it were,
their respective social weights. The definite form, in which
the social labor time enforces itself in the determination of
the value of commodities, is indeed connected with the wage
form of labor and with the corresponding form of the means
of production as capital, inasmuch as the production of commodities becomes the general form of production only upon
this basis.

Now let us consider the so-called conditions of distribution
themselves. Wages are conditioned upon wage labor, profit
upon capital. These definite forms of distribution have for
their prerequisites definite social characters on the part of the
conditions of production, and definite social relations of the
agents in production. The definite condition of distribution,
therefore, is merely the expression of the historically determined condition of production.

And now let us take profit. This definite form of surplus-
value is a prerequisite for the new creation of means of production by means of capitalist production. It is a relation
which dominates reproduction, although it seems to the individual capitalist as though he could consume his entire profit
as his revenue. But he meets barriers which hamper him
even in the form of insurance and reserve funds, laws of com-

petition, etc. These demonstrate to him by practice that profit is not a mere category in the distribution of the product for individual consumption. Furthermore, the entire process of capitalist production is regulated by the prices of products. But the regulating prices of production are in their turn regulated by the equalization of the rate of profit and by the distribution of capital among the various social spheres of production in correspondence with this equalization. Profit, then, appears here as the main factor, not of the distribution of products, but of their production itself, as a part in the distribution of capitals and of labor among the various spheres of production. The division of profit into profit of enterprise and interest appears as the distribution of the same revenue. But it arises primarily from the development of capital in its capacity as a self-expanding value, creating surplus-value, it arises from this definite social form of the prevailing process of production. It develops credit and credit institutions out of itself, and with them the shape of production. In interest, etc., the alleged forms of distribution enter as determining elements of production into the price.

Ground-rent might seem to be a mere form of distribution, because private land as such does not perform any, or at least no normal, function in the process of production itself. But the fact that, first, rent is limited to the excess above the average profit, and, secondly, that the landlord is depressed by the ruler and manager of the process of production and of the entire social life's process to the position of a mere holder of land for rent, a usurer in land and collector of rent, is a specific historical result of the capitalist mode of production. The fact that the earth received the form of private property is a historical requirement for this mode of production. The fact that private ownership of land assumes forms, which permit the capitalist mode of production in agriculture, is a product of the specific character of this mode of production. The income of the landlord may be called rent, even under other forms of society. But it differs essentially from the rent as it appears under the capitalist mode of production.

The so-called conditions of distribution, then, correspond to and arise from historically defined and specifically social forms of the process of production and of conditions, into which human beings enter in the process by which they reproduce their lives. The historical character of these conditions of distribution is the same as that of the conditions of production, one side of which they express. Capitalist distribution differs from those forms of distribution, which arise from other modes of production, and every mode of distribution disappears with the peculiar mode of production, from which it arose and to which it belongs.

The conception, which regards only the conditions of distribution historically, but not the conditions of production, is, on the one hand, merely an idea begotten by the incipient, but still handicapped, critique of bourgeois economy. On the other hand it rests upon a misconception, an identification of the process of social production with the simple labor process, such as might be performed by any abnormally situated human being without any social assistance. To the extent that the labor process is a simple process between man and nature, its simple elements remain the same in all social forms of development. But every definite historical form of this process develops more and more its material foundations and social forms. Whenever a certain maturity is reached, one definite social form is discarded and displaced by a higher one. The time for the coming of such a crisis is announced by the depth and breadth of the contradictions and antagonisms, which separate the conditions of distribution, and with them the definite historical form of the corresponding conditions of production, from the productive forces, the productivity, and development of their agencies. A conflict then arises between the material development of production and its social form.[153]

[153] See the work on *Competition and Co-operation* (1832?).

CHAPTER LII.

THE CLASSES.

THE owners of mere labor-power, the owners of capital, and the landlords, whose respective sources of income are wages, profit and ground-rent, in other words, wage laborers, capitalists and landlords, form the three great classes of modern society resting upon the capitalist mode of production.

In England, modern society is indisputably developed most highly and classically in its economic structure. Nevertheless the stratification of classes does not appear in its pure form, even there. Middle and transition stages obliterate even here all definite boundaries, although much less in the rural districts than in the cities. However, this is immaterial for our analysis. We have seen that the continual tendency and law of development of capitalist production is to separate the means of production more and more from labor, and to concentrate the scattered means of production more and more in large groups, thereby transforming labor into wage labor and the means of production into capital. In keeping with this tendency we have, on the other hand, the independent separation of private land from capital and labor,[154] or the transformation of all property in land into a form of landed property corresponding to the capitalist mode of production.

The first question to be answered is this: What constitutes a class? And this follows naturally from another question, namely: What constitutes wage laborers, capitalists and landlords into three great social classes?

[154] F. List remarks correctly: "Prevalence of self-management in the case of large estates proves only a lack of civilization, of means of communication, of home industries and rich cities. For this reason it is found everywhere in Russia, Poland, Hungary, Mecklenburg. Formerly it prevailed also in England. But with the rise of commerce and industry came their division into medium-sized farms and their occupancy by tenants." (*The Agrarian Constitution, the Petty Farm, and Emigration,* 1842, p. 10.)

At first glance it might seem that the identity of their revenues and their sources of revenue does that. They are three
great social groups, whose component elements, the individuals forming them, live on wages, profit and ground-rent, or
by the utilization of their labor-power, their capital, and their
private land.

However, from this point of view physicians and officials
would also form two classes, for they belong to the two distinct
social groups, and the revenues of their members flow from
the same common source. The same would also be true of
the infinite dissipation of interests and positions created by
the social division of labor among laborers, capitalists and
landlords. For instance, the landlords are divided into
owners of vineyards, farms, forests, mines, fisheries.

[Here the manuscript ends.]

END OF VOLUME III.

INDEX.

A

Abolition of Capitalism within the capitalist mode of production, 519.

Absolute and relative growth of surplus-value with a falling rate of profit, 253.

Absolute Ground Rent, arises when agricultural capital sets in motion more surplus-labor than an industrial capital of the same size, 882.

Absolute Rent, a surplus of value above the price of production, when agricultural products are sold at a monopoly price, 885.

Absolute Rent, the cause of the increased price of agricultural products, 886.

Absolute Rent, plays an important part in extractive industries, 897.

Absolute Rent, conditioned either upon the realized surplus above the price of production or upon a monopoly price exceeding the value of the product, 936.

Absolute Overproduction of capital, 299.

Abstinence, in the form of actual saving, falls upon the shoulders of those, who get the least reward under capitalism, 596.

Accident, its role in the determination of a general rate of interest, 427.

Actual Capital, its relation to money-capital, 559.

Additional Capital, its investment in agriculture influenced by stringency or prosperity, 895.

Additional Capital, a case where its doubling trebles production, 817.

Additional Capital, upon land, may bring forth additional surplus profit, but at a decreasing rate, 803.

Additional Capital, upon land, may bring forth larger quantities of product than original investments, 805.

Additional Capital, required for the withdrawal of the original capital from one soil and its transfer to another, may be invested with a falling, rising, or constant rate of rent per acre, 818.

Additional Capital, whose productivity is lower than that of the original capital invested in the worst soil, lowers the difference between the better and the worst soil, 852.

Adulteration, a means of raising the rate of profit, 100.

Advances on Bills, a regular practice of banks, 626.

Advantages resulting from release or tie-up of variable capital affect only capital already engaged, 138.

Agricultural labor, as a special occupation, a modern product, 742.

Agricultural Production, the price of production of its worst soil is always the regulating market price of production, 770.

Agricultural Products, may be sold as a whole below their value while industrial products are sold above their value, 887.

Agriculture, its capitalist form considered as a basis of the Marxian analysis of ground rent, 720.

Agriculture, its capitalist form implies the expropriation of the rural laborers from the land, 721.

Agriculture, its rational management prevented by capitalist production, 144.

American Firms, ruined by English overspeculation, 655.

Annual Product, its value equal to wages plus surplus-value, 971.

Appreciation of capital in value may be accompanied by a fall of the rate of profit, 134.

Auxiliary Capital used for circulation by the industrial capitalist creates no value or surplus-value, 343.

Average Rate of Interest, instruction how to find it, 426.

Average Profit defined, 186.

Average rate of profit appears as a mutual compensation of capitalists, 246.

Average Rate of Profit, causes which turn the law of its fall into a tendency, 272.

Average Profit depends on profits of individual AND on profits of social capital, 187.

Average Rate of Profit determined by two factors, 192.

Average Rate of Profit formed by the average of rates for each 100 of invested capitals during a specified time, 190.

Average Rate of Profit, how it comes about, 205.

Average Rate of Profit, its general formation, 183.

Average Rate of Profit leads to difference between mass and rate of surplus-value and of profit, 198.

Average Rate of Profit, theory of its law explained, 248.

Average Rate of Profit, warring tendencies which try to raise and to lower it, 273.

B

Balance of Trade, in time of crisis against every commercially developed nation, 578.

L

capital increases faster than the total capital, 76.

Profit, its rate varies through economies in constant capital or fluctuations in the price of raw materials, even if wages and rate of surplus-value remain unchanged, 125.

Profit, reality of its high rate demonstrated, 91.

Profit, that portion, which is not consumed as revenue is accumulated as money-capital only when it is not immediately able to find a place of investment, 595.

Profits in different spheres of production are not proportional to the magnitude of the different capitals invested in them, 177.

Profit, not necessarily legitimate surplus-value, but a result of cheating, etc., 963.

Profit of Enterprise, antagonistic to interest, 445.

Profit of Enterprise, its magnitude determined by the rate of interest, if gross profit is equal to net profit, 438.

Profit of Enterprise, not in opposition to wage laborer, but only to interest, 446.

Profits of Enterprise, a fruit of industrial function as distinguished from interest as a fruit of ownership of money-capital, 440.

Profits of Enterprise, no standard of measure for the rate of interest, 601.

Protection to laborers abolished by English laws, 108.

Proudhon did not understand the nature of capital, 408.

Proudhon, his conception of the role of money-capital, 406.

Proudhon, his conception of value does not reveal the origin of surplus-value, 407.

Provincial Banks, have their agents in the metropolis, 477.

Public Funds, their depreciation through fraudulent speculation, 491.

Q

Quandary of capitalists during crises, whether they should drop cash payments or production, 633.

R

Railroad Stocks, a means of fraudulent banking, 484.

Ramsay classes merchants' capital with productive capital by confounding it with the transportation capital, 329.

Rate of exchange, differs from Rate of Interest in form, 682.

Rate of Profit as a point of departure for historical inquiry into the transformation of surplus-value into profit, 56.

Rate of profit, calculated for one year and for several years, 266.

Rate of Profit calculated on the total capital invested, 55.

Rate of Profit falls, not because labor is less exploited, but because less labor is employed in proportion to the employed capital, 288.

Rate of Profit is particularly important for all new investments of capital, 304.

Rate of Profit, its fall and the overproduction of capital are caused by the same conditions, 296.

Rate of Profit, its fall cannot be explained by a rise in the rate of wages, except in particular cases, 281.

Raw Material, its good quality determines in part the rate of profit, 99.

Raw Materials, no control in their production, 142.

Relation between changes in the cost price of individual commodities and the average rate of profit, 202.

Relation between Magnitude of individual capitals and average rate of profit, 191.

Relative Decrease of variable capital and profit accompanied by an absolute increase of both, 261.

Relative Overpopulation, 256.

Relative Surplus-Population increases because productivity of labor increases, 260.

Release of capital defined, 132.

Renewal of due bills, kept secret, 625.

Rent, as a surplus above profit, its historical genesis, 931.

Rent, develops as money-rent only on the basis of a production of commodities, 747.

Rent, different heads under which it is analyzed, 843.

Rent, frequently absorbs not only the surplus product, but even a part of the necessary product of the tenant, 733.

Rent, from an absolute point of view, is a result of an increased investment of capital in the soil, regardless of whether productivity increases, falls, or remains constant, with rising, falling or constant prices, 827.

Rent, in the great majority of all possible cases it rises per acre and as a total, as a result of the investment of additional capital, 841.

Rent, its average per acre and per capital may fall while the total rental may increase, 778.

Rent, its general interrelations overlooked by economists, 781.

Rent, may be derived from a monopoly price of product or from a monopoly of land, 900.

Rent, may rise through a larger investment of capital without an increase of the rate of productivity, 802.

Rent, not considered by classic economy with reference to the quantity of land, but rather with reference to the product or to capital, 904.

Rent, sometimes higher for small estates than for large ones, 738.

Rent, which is a deduction from wages or from the average profit is not rent in the economic meaning of the term, 877.

Rent, with additional capital, increases absolutely upon all classes of soil, but

COSIMO is a specialty publisher of books and publications that inspire, inform, and engage readers. Our mission is to offer unique books to niche audiences around the world.

COSIMO BOOKS publishes books and publications for innovative authors, nonprofit organizations, and businesses. COSIMO BOOKS specializes in bringing books back into print, publishing new books quickly and effectively, and making these publications available to readers around the world.

COSIMO CLASSICS offers a collection of distinctive titles by the great authors and thinkers throughout the ages. At COSIMO CLASSICS timeless works find new life as affordable books, covering a variety of subjects including: Business, Economics, History, Personal Development, Philosophy, Religion & Spirituality, and much more!

COSIMO REPORTS publishes public reports that affect your world, from global trends to the economy, and from health to geopolitics.

FOR MORE INFORMATION CONTACT US AT
INFO@COSIMOBOOKS.COM

❋ if you are a book lover interested in our current catalog of books

❋ if you represent a bookstore, book club, or anyone else interested in special discounts for bulk purchases

❋ if you are an author who wants to get published

❋ if you represent an organization or business seeking to publish books and other publications for your members, donors, or customers.

COSIMO BOOKS ARE ALWAYS
AVAILABLE AT ONLINE BOOKSTORES

VISIT COSIMOBOOKS.COM
BE INSPIRED, BE INFORMED

LaVergne, TN USA
07 April 2010
78380LV00005B/137/A